Remaking Europe

Remaking Europe

The European Union and the Transition Economies

edited by
Jozef M. van Brabant

ROWMAN & LITTLEFIELD PUBLISHERS, INC.
Lanham • Boulder • New York • Oxford

To Miyuki with many thanks.
Have I at all furthered your europeanization?

ROWMAN & LITTLEFIELD PUBLISHERS, INC.

Published in the United States of America
by Rowman & Littlefield Publishers, Inc.
4720 Boston Way, Lanham, Maryland 20706
http://www.rowmanlittlefield.com

12 Hid's Copse Road
Cumnor Hill, Oxford OX2 9JJ, England

British Library Cataloguing in Publication Information Available

Library of Congress Cataloging-in-Publication Data
Remaking Europe : the European Union and the transition economies /
    edited by Jozef M. van Brabant.
        p. cm.
    Includes bibliographical references and index
    ISBN 0–8476–9323–6 (alk. paper). — ISBN 0–8476–9324–4 (pbk. :
alk. paper)
        1. European Union—Eurpoe, Eastern. 2. European Union—Europe,
Central. 3. Europe, Eastern—Economic conditions—1989– 4. Europe,
Central—Economic conditions. 5. Europe—Economic integration.
    I. Brabant, Jozef M. van.
HC240.25.E852R46   1999
337.4—dc21   99–15376
                                                                  CIP
Printed in the United States of America

♾™ The paper used in this publication meets the minimum requirements of American
National Standard for Information Sciences—Permanence of Paper for Printed Library
Materials, ANSI Z39.48–1992.

Contents

Tables

Acronyms

ACP	African, Caribbean, and Pacific
APA	Association Partnership Agreement
BFTA	Baltic Free Trade Agreement
CAP	common agricultural policy
CEFTA	Central European Free Trade Agreement
CFSP	Common Foreign and Security Policy
c.i.f.	cost, insurance, and freight
CIS	Commonwealth of Independent States
CMEA	Council for Mutual Economic Assistance
CN	Combined Nomenclature
CNB	Czech National Bank
Coreper	*Comité des Représentants Permanents*
€	euro as successor to the ecu
EA	Europe Agreement
EC	European Communities
ECB	European Central Bank
ECOFIN	Council of Economic and Finance Ministers
ECSC	European Coal and Steel Community
ecu	European currency unit
EEA	European Economic Area
EEC	European Economic Community
EFTA	European Free Trade Area
EMS	European Monetary System
EMU	Economic and Monetary Union
EPU	European Political Union
ERM	exchange-rate mechanism

EU	European Union
EU-11	charter members of the EU's monetary union
EU-4	Greece, Ireland, Portugal, and Spain
EU-12	EU membership until end 1994
EU-15	EU membership from early 1995
Euratom	European Atomic Energy Community
FDI	foreign direct investment
f.o.b.	free on board
FTA	free trade agreement
G-7	Group of Seven (Canada, France, Germany, Italy, Japan, the United Kingdom, and the United States)
G-24	Group of Twenty-four (the members of the OECD prior to the accession of Mexico)
GATT	General Agreement on Tariffs and Trade
GDP	gross domestic product
GDR	German Democratic Republic
GNP	gross national product
GSP	generalized system of preferences
IGC	Intergovernmental Conference
IIT	intra-industry trade
IMF	International Monetary Fund
LDC	least-developed country
MFN	most-favored nation
NATO	North Atlantic Treaty Organization
NBH	National Bank of Hungary
NBP	National Bank of Poland
NIE	newly industrializing economy
NTB	nontariff barrier
ODA	official development assistance
OECD	Organisation for Economic Co-operation and Development
OSCE	Organization for Security and Cooperation in Europe
PCA	Partnership and Cooperation Agreement
PHARE	*Pologne/Hongrie—assistance à la restructuration économique*
PPP	purchasing-power parity
R&D	research and development
REER	real effective exchange rate
RUV	relative unit value
SEA	Single European Act
SEM	single European market
SITC	standard international trade nomenclature
SME	small and medium-size enterprise
SOE	state-owned enterprise
TACIS	technical assistance to the CIS

TE-5	Czech Republic, Estonia, Hungary, Poland, and Slovenia
TE-10	Bulgaria, Latvia, Lithuania, Romania, Slovakia, plus TE-5
TEU	Treaty on European Union
TIIT	total intra-industry trade
TNC	transnational corporation
U.K.	United Kingdom
UNO	United Nations Organization
U.S.	United States of America
UVM	unit value of imports
UVX	unit value of exports
VIIT	vertical intra-industry trade
WEU	Western European Union
World Bank	International Bank for Reconstruction and Development
WTO	World Trade Organization

Preface

The gradual transformation of the erstwhile state-socialist economies of the eastern part of Europe into pluralistic democracies firmly anchored to market-based resource allocation was from the outset bound to be complicated and divisive—a very long-term policy task whose terminal point is not yet in sight. In some countries progress has been limited, possibly because of policy reversal or reluctance to engage the transformation agenda to the extent many observers in the early 1990s had fervently hoped. In others, disagreement continues to rage over moving forward even with the foundations of constructing markets and political democracy.

Bringing some of these countries under the umbrella of western European integration formats, the European Union (EU) in the first instance, has proved to be even more cumbersome. There are many diverse reasons for this state of affairs. The real economic, political, and social situation in the countries aspiring toward membership in western European institutions offers one broad set of issues. Another undoubtedly derives from the fact that the integrating economies have essentially opted for working toward a highly circumscribed unified market with rather complex rules and regulations on a diverse range of economic and related issues that bear on competition. But there are other reasons that prevent a smooth merger of east and west on the European continent.

Fusing parts of the east with the western integration processes from the very beginning had to overcome a triple hurdle: (1) the remaking of the eastern economies, polities, and societies; (2) reaching a platform for genuine competition in a highly regulated environment; and (3) keeping up with the moving target that the unifying market in the western part of Europe represents. Realistically submerging the eastern economies into western unification schemes could, therefore, have been nothing less than a highly involved exercise in political economy to be carefully nurtured over a protracted period of time.

In some contrast, policy makers of the transition economies have lodged claims on early and far-reaching membership, whereas policy makers of the western integration schemes have underlined in Janus fashion that these countries do indeed belong in the western concert of nations, but that this reality is not necessarily coterminous with the one that the transition economies desire to join. Misapprehensions, fears, and accusations of bad faith, and indeed worse slurs, have been rife almost from the moment the eastern countries sought to beef up their own security and well-being by aspiring toward, and indeed claiming the right to, membership in (western) European organizations. The decision to commence negotiations for accession with five eastern economies, as well as Cyprus, in March 1998 has not convincingly removed this mutual distrust, as the recent acrimony about western behavior in the accession negotiations and over the pre-accession assistance efforts has amply underlined.

Clarifying the core issues at stake in both east and west is, then, warranted for several reasons. Whereas the EU's further enlargement must necessarily remain a highly political decision, the latter does not solely depend on simply mustering sufficient political will. There are indeed many other determinants of whether such expansion can realistically be embarked upon. Similarly, the transition economies that aspire toward joining the EU must display a good deal of political will to engage themselves fully for this venture. They must also possess the technical competence to work constructively within the framework of the highly developed club that the EU represents. But also various commentators on both sides of the Atlantic, and then chiefly the Anglo-American cabal, have imputed motives to the EU that would seem to be far removed from the organization's reality or even ability. However much overlap there may be, it is best not to confound the EU's activities with the remaking of the continent, even though one cannot realistically proceed without the other. Laying bare the essential technical issues as they appear to economists is the purpose of this modest volume. I am not suggesting that economic matters should take precedence over other aspects, primarily in the political and security realms, of the relationship on the European continent. No, I maintain only that technical economic matters cannot, and should not, be given short shrift in pondering the remaking of the European continent.

In preparing this collection I have benefited over the years from numerous contacts with colleagues, friends, and acquaintances in Europe and the United States, including those upon whom I could prevail to contribute their thoughts in writing to this project. But many others have spared me a casual chat, phone call, e-mail message, or letter of encouragement or advice. I am grateful to all of them without, however, implicating any one in particular. Three of the collaborators here had earlier entrusted their thoughts to a collection of essays that I bundled for

Comparative Economic Studies (Vol. 40, No. 3). Some of the chapters here build upon those earlier contributions by expanding, revising, updating, and otherwise redirecting the inquiry to the issues prevailing in late 1998, looking primarily toward the future of the EU's eastward enlargement.

As with most of my work over the past two decades plus, this book was edited and my contributions to it written in my own time. The views reflected here are mine. They are not necessarily shared by my employer, the Secretariat of the United Nations Organization (UNO) in New York.

Finally, I am delighted to acknowledge the generosity and patience with which my spouse has tolerated, once again, my wandering off into yet another book-making adventure in spite of my earlier promises to the contrary. The challenge of clarifying the uniqueness of the transformations under way in the eastern part of Europe and what that entails for remaking the European economy, and indeed the continent in other respects as well, at a time of wildly varying menus advocated and ambitions coveted by many commentators on those issues, proved too alluring. My heartfelt gratitude for the forbearance and for so much more.

Chapter 1

Introduction

Jozef M. van Brabant

Much has been written about the uniqueness and portent of the so-called revolutions in the eastern part of Europe since 1989. In many ways, from the inception of the transitions in that part of the world, the cultural, economic, political, and social scenery on the European continent has been surprisingly convoluted. The opportunities for remaking the continent as a whole offered so adventitiously by the unprecedented scale of these ongoing (and further required) transformations in its eastern part had rarely been as promising since the medieval *res publica*. At the same time, resistance to seizing the unique chances that crystallized has been very pronounced. And efforts to build upon the certainties and measure of cohesion of (western) European integration in the economic but also in the political and social domains, while jumping the hurdles of history and politics, often have foundered. It is important to gain a solid grasp of the reasons behind these paradoxical responses to the forgone quasi-unique chances to seize the high ground.

Backdrop to the West's Thorny Embrace of the East

Unlike their counterparts in the former Soviet Union, once that federation began to fall apart, eastern Europe's new political leaders almost immediately aired that they cherished several aspirations. Two have remained uppermost: moving toward political pluralism and anchoring market-based resource allocation largely to privately held property rights within an 'open' environment. Those coveted objectives were in turn inspired by decisive rejection of the economics and politics, and indeed of many other aspects, of the communist past. Especially the more western of these economies sought to move away forcefully and irrevocably from the Soviet economic, political, and security stranglehold. In acting upon these precepts, their policy makers left no door ajar for redesigning a constructivist eastern partnership, not even in economic interchanges. At the same time, they aspired toward fusing nearly complete their economies, but arguably not their polities and societies, into the existing western European economic, political, and security structures, including foremost the European Union (EU), at the earliest opportunity. This has remained a first-order priority among the core items of the foreign-policy agenda of these countries.

Any keen observer of the relationship between the EU and the leadership of the transition economies (TEs), especially those most eager to accede to the EU, must have been struck on more than one occasion by grievous misapprehensions, on both the eastern and western sides. Although the TE leaders have more recently strengthened the depth and breadth of their understanding of the EU, all too frequently substantial erroneous precepts about the EU and what the organization could conceivably do for the TEs continue to prevail. At the very least, "the return to Europe" cherished by the TE leadership should not be confounded with "EU membership" (see, for example, Havel, 1996). The two simply *cannot* be congruent. Not only that, the leadership has exhibited only tepid understanding of what the EU is, and conceivably could be, all about, given realities on the European continent, however defined.

Moves toward democratization and market liberalization found ample support among western policy makers in general and western European politicians in particular, but the ambitions of the leadership of TEs of quick merger into the EU did not fall on fertile soil. Indeed the TEs could not have been ushered into the EU without major transformations. These were in the first instance required for the TEs themselves. But also the EU, and its heterogeneous membership, would have to undergo substantial mutations before such a marriage between the two parts of Europe could be successfully sealed. True, western policy makers saw several advantages potentially accruing from durable economic and political changes in the TEs. But they were rather reluctant to accelerate the melding of the two parts of Europe, certainly prior to advancing in a major way with, if perhaps not quite completing, wholesale economic, political, and social transformations in the TEs. Even if the political will to move decisively toward the remaking of Europe in this manner had been present, quick merger of the TEs into the EU could not have been engineered without changing the latter's fundamental nature. That said, building toward the given vision of a remade Europe does not solely depend on formally merging the TEs desiring western security into the EU. There are alternative, perhaps better suited and arguably more effective, ways of extending assistance to the TEs. And many of these alternatives to hastily engineering premature membership could have been conceived so as to accelerate the pace of the economic, legal, political, and social transformations required precisely to facilitate the TEs' accession to EU membership or other forms of partnerships at the earliest realistic opportunity. Membership would, of course, have been realistic only for those TEs that wished to join the EU and would fit there, as per the EU's club rules. For other TEs, those that cannot or do not wish to join the EU, the rapprochement would have aimed at solidifying the foundations for a full partnership relationship, if only because many of these economies are of strategic interest to the EU.

Although I do not focus on rendering assistance here, if only because I have done so elsewhere at some length (see Brabant, 1995, 1996a), it is important to distinguish between membership and rendering appropriate assistance, given the EU's sui generis integration variant. The EU is indeed a club with complex rules and regulations (but by no means limited to market access) to which aspiring members must be willing to subscribe in full and be able to live up to (almost) in full, after passing other admission tests many of whose criteria are not among the recorded rules of the game. Rather, they emerge from general declarations and the precepts embraced in earlier enlargements. In any case, permanent deviations from the ideal modi operandi are granted only in exceptional circumstances, usually to accommodate new integration initiatives and even then only on the understanding that the 'opt-out' will not be exercised permanently. Remaking Europe through the EU has always been a choice between full membership, with all the obligations and privileges that entails, or working with the EU and other 'European' countries outside the strict club rules. Given the prevailing constitutional provisions there can be no golden middle path, something like "partial membership," an eventuality entertained under various guises chiefly during the first half of the 1990s.

Even if the purposes and means of the EU by themselves had not hindered swift unification, an early merger of the TEs into the EU could have been detrimental to the economic reconstruction of the eastern part of Europe. Several plausible reasons can be invoked, considering the absence of stability in the TEs with their need to engineer a quick turnabout of external relations while managing many economic, political, and social pressures. In fact, even at this stage considerable doubts remain about the balance of gains and losses of EU membership in the short to medium run for the TEs themselves. Seen from within the perspective of completing the transition toward vibrant market economies with a solid democratic anchor (Bauer, 1998), application of the EU's club rules may not be the most desirable means to those ends. Also, premature eastward expansion might even have severely weakened, and perhaps undermined, the EU's very nature, given that its integration élan remains less than buoyant or inspiring. In fact, the EU's ongoing integration process has once again become rather shaky notwithstanding appearances to the contrary.

It is in part because of the poor understanding of these special features of the EU club that western Europe's reaction to the new leadership's aspiration "to return to Europe" was perplexing, certainly something of a surprise, to the east's leadership. Many reasons help to explain these parallel monologues that failed to converge to a genuine dialogue on other than surface issues. They range from sheer political naïveté among the more daring TE leaders to a fundamental lack of appreciation of and a blurred insight into how developed markets and societies in general, and highly regulated, complex markets like those of the EU grouping in particular, really function. This applies not only to the 'horizontal' aspects—the way the single European market (SEM) presently functions. It is impossible to comprehend how the EU operates without having a perspective on its genesis and further aspirations. Among the latter, the EU's *finalité politique*, or its ultimate constitutional shape, figures prominently. Where precisely this will settle, undoubtedly somewhere in-between intergovernmentalism and supranationalism, is yet to be determined. If policy makers were to advocate moving to the former, such an auspicious redirection would destroy the EU's original aspirations. Not only that, particularly intergovernmental approaches are potentially seriously encumbered by any substantial rise in the number of participants for each possesses by definition veto power over the decisions subject to intergovernmentalism. On the other hand, opting for greater federalism would probably undermine the EU as well for all too many of its members are opposed even to mild forms of supranationalism. Any sensible federalization of EU relations would seem to be out of reach within any conceivable future, and so the vacillation between the two governance formats will continue for years to come.

The Purpose of the Volume

The purpose of the eight chapters that follow is precisely to clarify the most important reasons behind the contrasts between the EU's reality and the TEs' disappointment. A careful dissection of these incongruities, with some discreet recommendations for remedying the perceived ills, should help in molding a more rounded picture of the at times rocky relationship between the two parts of Europe since 1989. Such an analytical approach to tackling the salient policy-making conundrums is arguably even more critical in assessing the obstacles ahead in charting constructive headway with accession negotiations. And it is crucial in order to identify concretely the advantages and drawbacks of moving into the EU that the TEs are likely to experience as time marches on.

In an effort to contribute toward achieving those endeavors, the chapters that follow have been inspired by three principal considerations. One is the historic opening of the EU toward the eastern part of Europe. This has presented a seminal opportunity to remake the continent economically, politically, and socially, as well as in several other societal dimensions. Europe in that sense is not, and cannot be, a 'grand illusion' (Judt, 1996). Since negotiations for accession of TEs started in late March 1998, this is an appropriate occasion to identify the most salient issues around the substance of the deliberations. These are here projected against the backdrop of the evolving relationship between the TEs and the EU, and the latter's longer-term ability to live up to its billed aspirations. Accession deliberations cannot possibly be confined to the narrow economics of custom-union formation, let alone its heuristic 'trade creation' and 'trade diversion' aspects, however important the tangible economic gains and losses may be in their own right. Rather, the core tasks confronting the negotiators are inextricably anchored to the history of 'Europe' in general and the difficulties encountered in knitting "an ever closer union," as stated so promisingly in the Maastricht Treaty (European Commission, 1992, p. 4), at all too many milestones of the postwar period.

The paramount issues at stake are inextricably intermingled with the future of 'Europe,' both east and west. And so a second set of issues arises from ushering new members into the EU at a time when the process of 'deepening' the integration movement is far from over. Indeed, enlargement can best be seen as a challenge that must somehow be reconciled with forging ahead with the EU's ultimate destiny, for which EU members have in recent years been encountering severe, truly fundamental and obdurate, obstacles. As events since the early 1990s have amply underlined, there is no guarantee whatsoever that the EU's achievements logged over more than four decades provide a sufficiently robust and broad platform from which 'Europe' can be remade in the image that the intellectual *and* political fathers of EU integration envisioned. At the very least, a suitable mix of deepening and widening steps needs to be thoroughly explored and agreed upon. The issues are multiple and complex. Those concerning deepening revolve around governing the integration process toward some ultimate constitutional arrangement yet to be fine-tuned. But they also have to heed the compass of integration across the various interstate and interregional exchanges in "an ever closer union" that is far from being a federation and as yet lacks even a moderately clear-cut constitution. But I realize that others in the field hold very different views on this matter. Some even claim that the EU's governance structures are fully in place, leaving a weak executive, a country-specific Council of Ministers, and a locally representative federalist state.[1] While that is certainly formally so, one can observe very little of that predictable governance in actual integration practices, however; hence the real problems of reconciling 'deepening' with 'widening.'

For aspiring newcomers to the EU this means two things. One is that the hurdles to be overcome in order for TEs to blend into a complex and contentious integration process in midstream, and still on the move however shakily, may be raised as progress toward accession is booked. But also less than smooth passage along the integration path, whose prospective steps are yet to be fully designed, encumbers the enlargement process. This would not be so in the event that stalemate in forging ahead toward a veritable constitutional arrangement, that is, a more profoundly embedded union, were to undermine the fundamentals of that very aspiration. One may well question whether joining such an eroding, when perhaps not yet altogether fragmented and debilitated, grouping might then remove most of its attractiveness and usefulness for strengthening the foundations of the transformations in the eastern part of Europe as well.

Finally, one needs to be aware of hurdles arising in joining the EU for newcomers even without there being serious current and foreseeable problems deriving from uneasy, cumbersome, and at times confounding 'deepening' efforts on the part of the existing membership. That is to say, even under propitious circumstances, with the political will and ability to expand on the part of EU leaders, the accession negotiations will have to overcome very daunting obstacles indeed. These high hurdles derive in the first place from the need to ensure, as part and parcel of the EU rules of the game, that widening will not encroach upon the delicate political-economy balance seemingly required to sustain momentum in adhering to and delivering on integration commitments. These obstacles stem from core features of the policies associated with moving gingerly toward quasi federalism, gradualness, smoothing, solidarity, and subsidiarity that have been determinant for most of the solutions around 'deepening' and 'widening' innovated at least since the completion of the EU's customs union in 1967. One might legitimately argue that those features of EU collaboration came into play even earlier in order to construct an effective customs union as the foundation of a veritable economic union, possibly to be expanded into a political and social union at some indeterminate future stage. It is one central thought running through the eight substantive chapters here that these guidelines have dominated policies with respect to the narrow calculus of visible budgetary costs and benefits of EU participation. TE accessions in the foreseeable future are likely to markedly affect this calculus and shift the resulting balance.

But considerations inspired by the same guiding principles are arguably even more important in configuring the political economy of the benefits and costs of widening other than those that directly impinge upon budgetary revenues and expenditures. These are not always calculable in euros (€) and cents. Yet political behavior on the part of the EU's leadership will be inspired by objective and subjective perceptions thereof. These derive in one way or another from the competitive strengths and weaknesses of new members as compared to those of the existing membership. But they are also propelled by the willingness, and indeed the ability in practice, of new members to abide constructively by the rules of the game of the SEM in place. The *acquis communautaire*, and increasingly also, it is widely hoped, the *acquis communautaire et politique*, imposes stringent institutional and behavioral constraints on participants. These entail for new-comers in particular substantial up-front costs to be defrayed well before the full benefits of participating in a large SEM—one that is hopefully transparent, open, predictable, stable, and to some degree equitable—will be within reach. The illusion of gaining access to very substantial budgetary transfers from Brussels that will play *the* critical role in modernizing the TEs (Inotai, 1997a, b; Kiss, 1997) is just that.

The upshot of this brief sketch of the environment for the accession negotiations is threefold. First, these deliberations will be *complex* as present EU members must ascertain the readiness—and ability in practice—of the TEs to abide fully by these obligations. Second, they will be *difficult* as the impatience of the aspiring members conflicts with a more deliberative search for a strategic preparation for accession, including importantly the continuing progress being booked by the applicants in readying themselves for the SEM. And, finally, these negotiations will be *protracted* as the dynamics of political sentiments and economic realities will generate asymmetries over time and across the present and aspiring EU members. This means that entry of even the best prepared TE is more likely to occur toward the second half of the first decade of the twenty-first century than around the turn of the millennium as several weighty political leaders in east and west alike had, until recently, been holding out for some time, largely for their own public relations or political purposes.

Need I stress that the analyses presented in this book are manifestly *not* meant to cast a pall over the ways in which the EU has been treating the TEs? Rather, all contributors have been guided primarily by a common perception: the need to clarify the complexity of accession negotiations even under the most favorable political circumstances, and to do so in a realistic and objective manner. An ambient political environment would surely smooth the negotiations. But it would not altogether remove the intrinsic three-dimensional character of those impending deliberations, as just indicated.

Conventions

For the sake of simplicity and readability, I have introduced several conventions for this volume. First of all, throughout the book EU designates the various formalized efforts launched to integrate western Europe after World War II, unless the context requires identification of the European Free Trade Association (EFTA) or the appropriate earlier names for the EU, such as the European Economic Community (EEC) or European Communities (EC). Similarly, the European Commission (or Commission) is the central institution in Brussels entrusted with safeguarding the SEM, although its official designations have changed since 1958 for reasons that will be clarified notably in chapter 2.

Second, much has been written about the *acquis communautaire et politique* or the rules of the EU club to which newcomers have to subscribe, and be able to abide, until they can help shape appropriate revisions once they will have obtained full membership. We refer to them as the *acquis* for short. Its compass is not, however, confined to the EU's body of formal laws developed since 1958. In addition to the EU's legal corpus, the *acquis* encompasses all the rules and regulations comprising the SEM and monetary integration. It also refers to the entire catalogue of the EU's legal and administrative instruments as well as the spirit within which common policies are being tackled through quasi-supranational endeavors but also through intergovernmental approaches, such as in the various acts endorsed by the European Council since it first came into existence.

Third, in what follows we often refer to the quasi-constitutional instruments that govern the EU. The reference is primarily to the Treaty on European Union (TEU), of course, as revised at and after the 1997 Amsterdam Council, with the Rome Treaty as the foundation antecedent. But the instruments also include the Single European Act (SEA) of 1986 and related legislation.

Fourth, the TEs of relevance in this discussion are the twenty-seven countries in the eastern part of Europe that were formerly, possibly in the context of a now defunct federation (as in Czechoslovakia, the Soviet Union, and Yugoslavia), ruled under a single polity dominated by the Communist Party or its variant (as in Yugoslavia) with their economy managed through some form of centralized administrative planning. Specifically, reference is to the former Soviet Union and the area that used to be known as Eastern Europe with a capital *E* but now without the German Democratic Republic (GDR); that is, Albania, Bulgaria, Czechoslovakia, Hungary, Poland, Romania, and Yugoslavia).

Most references in this volume are to the period since the transitions erupted. It is useful in that context to separate the eastern part of Europe into eastern Europe with a lower case *e* and the Commonwealth of Independent States (CIS). The former, then, presently encompasses fifteen countries: Albania, Bosnia and Herzegovina, Bulgaria, Croatia, the Czech Republic, Estonia, Hungary, Latvia, Lithuania, Macedonia, Poland, Romania, Slovakia, Slovenia, and rump Yugoslavia (or Serbia and Montenegro). The CIS consists of twelve countries: Armenia, Azerbaijan, Belarus, Georgia, Kazakhstan, Kyrgyzstan, Moldova, Russia, Tajikistan, Turkmenistan, Ukraine, and Uzbekistan. Note that the latter grouping has not always been synonymous with the formal membership of the CIS, but I ignore that here.

Ten TEs have a Europe Agreement (EA): Bulgaria, the Czech Republic, Estonia, Hungary, Latvia, Lithuania, Poland, Romania, Slovakia, and Slovenia; the latter's is yet to be ratified, however. This group is captured under the acronym TE-10. These TEs are presently involved in accession negotiations but in two groups. The fast-track TEs are the Czech Republic, Estonia, Hungary, Poland, and Slovenia. These are at times designated as TE-5. The other five are on a slower path, but formally involved in accession negotiations of one kind or another. Most of the discussions in the chapters that follow deal with those ten countries and they pay even more attention to the TE-5.

Fifth, referring accurately to the 'system' existing prior to the transition's inception is not an easy task. In this volume it is captured under the notion of state socialism. This shorthand is invoked in preference to what has been variously known as communism, socialism, real socialism, market socialism, reformed socialism, central planning, command economy, and so on to characterize the nature of the economic and political systems as they evolved in the eastern part of Europe until the early 1990s. I have justified my choice of real socialism in some detail elsewhere (Brabant, 1998a, p. 10).

Sixth, to avoid needless confusion or cumbersome specifications, I have adopted the symbol € to denote both the ecu (European currency unit) and the euro. Strictly speaking, the euro came into existence only in 1999. Before that shift, EU accounting was in ecu. For simplicity's sake, I use the same symbol because the euro was introduced in 1999 at par with the ecu.

Finally, much confusion exists in the literature, not to mention more cursory or political debates, about the meaning of EMU. While an investigator should be free to define his or her own acronyms, in this case one may legitimately revoke this academic freedom. EMU in official EU materials and policy deliberations stands for Economic and Monetary Union. Many observers either use EMU as a shorthand for monetary union or define EMU as standing for European Monetary Union. This is not a very useful practice. While the aim is to build up an EMU encompassing all EU members, for the foreseeable future there will be EU members subject to the rules of the *economic union*, but not, or only to a much weaker extent, to those of *monetary union*. In this volume, then, EMU is strictly reserved for its official designation, whereas all matters revolving around its second component—monetary union—will be treated under that heading.

A Road Map

The chapter by Jozef M. van Brabant that follows provides crucial elements of the backdrop for better coming to grips with the uneasy relationship between the EU and the TEs since 1989. Expectations on both sides differed widely and on all too many occasions they continue to run separate courses, thus hindering a more constructive rapprochement between the TEs and the EU. After a brief summary of the various strands that informed the EU's integration movement, key components of the economic, political, and social situation in the EU on the eve of the east's transitions are sketched. Then the essential ingredients of the two intergovernmental conferences (IGCs) organized in 1990-1991 are sketched. Although these IGCs were concurrent with the rapidly evolving 'political revolutions' in the eastern part of Europe, the dynamics of the two processes moved almost independently, save for the implications of German unification for both east and west. And the focus of the chapter is on these implications for understanding the uneasy relationship between the two parts of Europe since 1989.

Next, Marie Lavigne underlines that the future of the more western TEs is directly linked to the eastward enlargement of the EU, because the latter is expected to spur on growth of the TEs and enhance credibility of transformation strategies. Entry into the EU should therefore be accelerated, provided the TEs can meet conditions for membership. These come in various layers. The chapter first examines the conditions for accession as spelled out at recent European Councils and subsequently elaborated on in the recommendations issued by the European Commission. Because these official conditions for accession are fuzzy, the TEs will have to pass other tests in order for them to conform reasonably well to the profile of 'suitable,' possibly the 'ideal' and thus nonexisting, future EU members. Also the negotiation process itself may modify these conditions, if only because some candidates may obtain derogations and transitional arrangements upon entry.

The conditions for merging the TEs into the TE, as per the criteria enunciated at the Copenhagen Council in June 1993, include the capacity of the EU to accommodate another expansion. This may refer to a variety of hurdles. In the third substantive chapter, Jozef M. van Brabant focuses on the conundrum of 'widening' versus 'deepening' EU integration with particular reference to the IGC convened in 1996 as called for in the Maastricht Treaty. By the time that conclave was ceremoniously opened in March 1996, the implications of the transformations in TEs had become much clearer than they were at the outset; the EU had committed itself to engage prospectively in accession negotiations with the TEs, as well as Cyprus and Malta[2]; and the economic and political, but perhaps less the social, uncertainties in the core central European TEs had become less troublesome. However, the reasons that had led the negotiators in Maastricht to call for a "Review Conference" had by then also been expanded in various dimensions. Indeed the backdrop for setting the IGC's agenda had become overloaded with many other issues, some that could not have been foreseen in the early 1990s. The chapter details the backdrop to the IGC, the way the negotiations were conducted, the conclusion at Amsterdam with the follow-up in Luxemburg and Cardiff with a view to identifying the degree to which the perceived need for 'deepening' EU integration can now be more easily reconciled with the political obligation to accommodate some of the TEs under the EU's wings within a reasonable future.

The following four chapters discuss various aspects of convergence between TEs and the EU membership. Lucjan T. Orlowski devotes his elaborations to nominal convergence. He examines in detail the relationship between exchange-rate and monetary policies in TEs bent on entering the EU in the near term and eventually acceding to its monetary union. After detailing the present exchange-rate systems and monetary regimes in the central European TEs, he reviews prevailing targets of monetary policy and proposes some policy changes in response to the requirements eventually to be met in order to join the monetary union. He suggests that such a policy move should be a priority once the transformations are well along for the TEs to benefit from the policy credibility and commitment membership in the monetary union is likely to impart. Thereafter he examines whether the candidates are likely to have to resort to a final currency devaluation no more than two years prior to acceding to monetary union and the implications for policy making this may entail. He concludes with some suggestions for desirable adjustments in short- and long-term monetary policy.

Wladimir Andreff contends that, however important nominal convergence might be for accommodating the TEs under the EU's umbrella, which he opines to be inappropriate at this stage, real convergence deserves much greater attention in honing and assessing, certainly at this stage, the relationship between the EU and the candidates for accession. Real convergence can be variously defined, but in the end it should lead to moderating the gaps in productivity, income, wealth, and so on between the EU and aspiring members; one important side effect thereof would be lowering the budgetary transfers required by the EU programs in place. However, real convergence in that sense may well become feasible only by engineering convergence in the institutions of the market, though the latter is needed in its own right in order for the TEs to function constructively within the SEM. After measuring nominal and real economic convergence between the TEs and the EU, both in static and dynamic terms, the chapter draws from the current convergence dilemmas implications for reshaping transformation processes. The author stresses in particular the need to buttress growth recovery. Finally, he notes a few institutional aspects of convergence that are at the core of accession negotiations and touches upon some aspects of the EU's current approach toward negotiating accessions.

As one crucial instance of real convergence, Hubert Gabrisch and Klaus Werner devote their chapter to the relationship between trade liberalization and desirable structural adjustments in the liberalizing economy. Trade liberalization and entry of TEs into the EU should induce structural adjustments at the firm level so as to move trade and production profiles closer to the EU's patterns. This should manifest itself in more intra-industry trade (IIT) based on horizontal product differentiation. As recent experience has amply demonstrated, trade liberalization by itself does not suffice to bring about such structural transformation. The record of TEs to date tends to suggest the existence of persistent inter-industry trade and vertical product differentiation as outcomes of the trade liberalization. The minimalist role the managers of the transformations have tended to accord to government in designing policies to foster this microeconomic restructuring may have played a crucial role in this emerging pattern of industrial specialization. Restricted access to foreign capital, information asymmetries, and the persistent lack of well-functioning markets argue in favor of formulating industrial policies to strengthen the competitiveness of manufacturing firms rather than of the regional approach more typical of the EU. The EU's legal framework leaves room for designing such a subsidy policy provided it is adjudicated as compatible with the EU's competition policy.

Elaborating further on the problems of structural change for catching up by the TEs during their transformation, Paul J. J. Welfens devotes special attention to the role of trade, foreign direct investment (FDI), and institutional adjustments in both east and west to facilitate enlargement. For the TE-5, he musters a number of arguments favoring enlargement on economic grounds—modest gains for the EU but considerable ones for the TEs—provided long adjustment and phasing-in periods are negotiated. His analyses cast grave doubts, however, on the ambitions for the other five TEs with an EA, if only because the economic and political problems are far more daunting, giving rise to a potential for "imperial over-stretch" on the part of the EU. While appropriate constitutional reforms of the EU might address some of the problems he envisions for the sixth enlargement and beyond of the EU, he advocates looking at alternative options for building a constructive relationship between the EU and these TEs, including other than the privileged TE-10.

Because the EU has sought from its earliest history to accommodate nonmember countries through various preferential arrangements, Jozef M. van Brabant underlines in the penultimate chapter that EU expansion toward the eastern part of Europe is bound to affect the benefits that partners in these preferential arrangements can prospectively count on. The effects of entering TEs can be direct, as a result of the TE obtaining access to the EU's four freedoms—of movement of goods, services, people, and capital. Also indirect effects result from the way enlargement alters the calculus of benefits and costs for present EU members. The chapter examines these arrangements and the major shocks that may occur for their beneficiaries as a result of the EU's enlargement.

In the final chapter, Jozef M. van Brabant assembles present knowledge about what is likely to happen over the next twelve months or so as regards the process of negotiating for accession. Thereafter he conjectures about what *may* crystallize beyond that date as regards the further course of the accession negotiations, the potential for derogations to be accorded the TEs during a phasing-in transition after formal entry, which candidates are likely to enter first, and when this is likely to occur.

Notes

1. Robert P. Inman and Daniel L. Rubinfeld (1998) recently claimed that the EU already has a full-fledged constitution with a mature governance structure based on federalism anchored to subsidiarity but with a weak executive. Only the number of participants and the assignment of policy responsibilities to the various 'federal' institutions allegedly remain to be settled.

2. As detailed in chapter 4, Malta stayed its request for accession, following parliamentary elections, from October 1996 until the fall of 1998, again following parliamentary elections. It is currently not included among the candidates for accession and the Commission will have to prepare its special *avis* for Malta. In February 1999 the Commission (1999d) issued a favorable recommendation to the Council, which may be acted upon by mid-year.

Chapter 2

Transitions and Their Impacts on European Integration

Jozef M. van Brabant

The origin of the pro-integration sentiment in the western part of Europe, and the movement toward rebuilding the (western) European economy and, to a much lesser extent, its polity as well, spawned after World War II is multifaceted. One strand of impulses stemmed from a genuine desire to overcome deeply embedded obstacles to security and political coexistence, thus forestalling the recurrence of war and conflict, on the European continent. Of course, by dint of circumstance the EU's ability, and earlier the EFTA's as well, to contribute toward the implementation of these goals within its accessible remit was forcefully limited to the 'western' countries as the 'eastern' part of the continent was drawn into its own, rather peculiar and in retrospect ill-designed, integration movement in the context of the Council for Mutual Economic Assistance (CMEA) from 1949 until its demise in the early 1990s. But the postwar attempts to galvanize policy makers and the public at large also had well-founded economic motivations. The desire to enlarge the effective market size as a gateway for post-conflict reconstruction; for catch-up with the then more developed countries, largely the United States (U.S.); and as a source of sustainable growth and welfare, with adequate redistribution and socioeconomic security, should not be ignored. Finally, strengthening western Europe's capacity to withstand the challenges of state socialism, notably as a political-ideological pole of attraction, a source of social appeasement, and a seemingly promising avenue toward economic modernization undoubtedly furnished another set of preoccupations.

This is not the proper place to reassess the complete raison d'être of economic, political, and social integration in Europe (Brabant, 1995, pp. 78ff.). My more limited objective here can best be captured by clarifying the chapter's central proposition: the seminal changes in the eastern part of Europe since 1989 have changed dramatically the willingness and purview of integration ambitions in the EU context and will continue to do so for decades to come. Some can only be welcomed. Other mutations encumber several of the dynamic integration processes that were earlier considered, however. In particular, the marked diminution of the state-socialist threat has by no means altogether compromised, let alone sweepingly removed, the rationale behind European integration. That has many cultural, economic, environmental, health, political, social, strategic, and other transnational dimensions.

To anchor this multiple perspective more robustly, I first point to the underlying goals of European integration. Then I briefly restate the situation in the EU on the eve of the east's transitions, especially as regards the broader economic, political, and social ambience with respect to integrating into the EU, at least de facto. Next I examine the outcome of the two IGCs initiated in 1990 and concluded in 1991 in Maastricht, of which at least one received its major impetus from the eastern turmoil. To grasp the potential importance of these IGCs, however, a brief note on the role of IGCs in the EU's governance structure is first required. Thereafter I sketch the backdrop to essential elements of the Maastricht Treaty, formally known as the TEU, and the IGC called for 1996 (henceforth IGC96). Before concluding, I detail some of the expectations aired during the run-up to this IGC, primarily as seen from the perspective of engaging constructively in yet another enlargement.

The EU's Integration Ambitions

Revisionist commentators have recently attributed the origin of postwar western European integration overwhelmingly to the cold war for which the EU in its various earlier incarnations allegedly provided a defensive strategy against the challenge of the division of Europe and the threats of state socialism (Calleo, 1997; Feldstein, 1997; Judt, 1996; Newhouse, 1997; Reinicke, 1992). Any such rationalization is historically and politically myopic. At the very least, it ignores the economic rationale for propping up postwar reconstruction and seeking to catch up with the United States as the most advanced economy. That economic dimension encompassed essential ingredients for reaching sustainable growth and underpinning the welfare state on the 'old' continent. It also views the political and social ambitions of postwar EU integration all too much through the lens of, principally, the security challenges earlier posed by the state-socialist east. That the latter played a role is beyond dispute. But EU integration has focused on other objectives as well for which sui generis impulses other than the cold war prevailed. These, I submit, have since the early 1990s become even more salient than they were earlier in the EU's evolution.

Recall first of all that endeavors to seek common ground in Europe reach back at least a century, and arguably much longer than that (Swann, 1972, pp. 13ff.). History is littered with federalist blueprints, policy proposals, and negotiated arrangements designed to foster greater European unity. Only the traumatic experiences of the two world wars in this century with their calamitous aftermath provided without a doubt the paramount impetus to (western) European integration. This new attention to gradually uniting Europe had also been inspired, after World War I, by the implausible viability, largely in isolation, of a number of new states created on the eastern fringes of 'Europe' in the war's wake and the failure of Wilsonian 'self-determination.' At the very least, efforts to reinstate a more multilateral environment in spite of rampant nationalism must be fully reflected in any coherent attempt to explain the motivations underlying the drive toward EU integration (Hobsbawm, 1992).

Particularly the utter carnage, destructiveness, savagery, and inhumanity of World War II pleaded for launching serious policy efforts at the highest level to overcome the age-old divisiveness on the continent, if only in an attempt to rescue its nation states (Milward, 1992), and lay the foundations for lasting peace in Europe. At the same time, joining forces would buttress efforts to recover from the economic exhaustion affecting most of Europe in the second half of the 1940s and to counter the perceived threats of state socialism issuing from the eastern part of the continent. Not in the least, it also enabled the erstwhile 'great powers' of Europe to contemplate, with some plausibility, alternative modes of recovering some shreds of their erstwhile central position in global affairs, now within an increasingly bifurcated world. Recapturing some center-stage role in world affairs would have been futile if countries had attempted to regain their past grandeur on their own strength or to polish up part of their tarnished image and reputation in isolation.

Regardless of the logic arguing for intensifying European economic cooperation, it was notably the U.S. stance on global economic organization in general and on European affairs in particular during and after World War II that imparted a qualitatively novel impetus to pursuing European integration. The United States recognized early on that a revival of economic as well as military, political, and strategic cooperation among the Europeans was essential to overcome the worst legacies of "[t]he 'European civil war' of 1914 to 1945, that second and still bloodier Thirty Years' War" (Garton Ash, 1998, p. 54). At the same time, only in this manner could it hope to realize its interests in reorganizing the world at a cost that its electorate and policy makers would be willing to support and able to mobilize, given fundamental constraints on sharing its wealth, for cementing the foundations of a solid and durable European economic recovery. The eruption of the cold war only strengthened the U.S. resolve to forge tighter economic and other ties on the continent.

In order to deal seriously with the many intricate questions arising in connection with the prospective expansion of effective cooperation on the part of the EU to the benefit of the east of Europe, I deem it essential to keep these multiple strands of the EU's origins in mind. Perhaps one pointed example may help to clarify why I am so adamant on this point.

In addition to the reference to the cold war as the main trigger for western European integration, some commentators have recently placed great stress on the need for the EU to focus prospectively nearly all of its resources and attention on enlargement toward the eastern part of Europe rather than on safeguarding the SEM and moving forward with other integration ambitions, many of which inevitably will reach even into the most sensitive political and social realms of national sovereignty. As an exemplar of this strand of thinking I pick Timothy Garton Ash's (1998) recent elaboration on the subject for critique; but I could have easily selected a dozen or so alternative evaluations of EU priorities mainly in the Anglo-American literature on foreign affairs in general and western European integration in particular adducing essentially the same argument.

Garton Ash emphasizes the need to consolidate Europe's liberal order and spread it across the continent, although the eastern borders are left undefined. This he considers a most welcome foil for policy makers to the ongoing stress on reaching a workable monetary union and forging ahead with forms of political and social union for which the continent is unprepared at this stage, and which he probably considers inappropriate in any case. Together with other recent commentators (Feldstein, 1997; Newhouse, 1997) he firmly believes that the relentless and single-minded stress on reaching monetary union, as well as on forging ahead with political and social union, will almost certainly destroy the EU from within. Martin Feldstein (1997) has even predicted that the outcome of monetary union may well be unvarnished civil wars among the present EU membership in not too distant a future! Even if this prediction is held to be fanciful (Frieden, 1998), one cannot escape the view that there is a good deal of skepticism about EMU and beyond among American observers in particular (Karczmar, 1998).

By my reckoning Garton Ash's views rest on several fallacies of which three deserve to be mentioned here. First of all, he confounds the 'state' of EU integration with the ongoing long-term integration 'process.' As I shall underline later in this chapter, building EU integration as envisaged in the prevailing quasi-constitutional documents—its famously muddled *finalité politique*—is far from a done exercise. Without further 'deepening' integration in the EU, as I explain below, there would be little point in pursuing 'widening' unless the EU's ambitions and evolving goals were to be compressed to fostering intergovernmentalism, mainly in economic matters if perhaps not restricted to canonical free-trade ambitions. Second, he intermingles the EU's aspirations (including as concerns monetary union) with building a liberal order. Except perhaps in its broadest contours of aiming at liberalizing goods and factor markets within the SEM and of forestalling military conflict on the continent, the EU's purpose has not really been about spreading the liberal order. Indeed, the SEM is a highly circumscribed market with several policies, such as the common agricultural policy (CAP), that can only cynically be captured as a bona fide part of the liberal order. Finally, Garton Ash does not seem to shrink from taking the EU's immanent purposes as synonymous with the goal of monetary union in 1999. The monetary union means much more than a simple French-German bargain and is not a goal in itself but hinges essentially on the proposition that competition within the single market, however illiberally circumscribed, must be anchored, to the greatest extent possible, to genuine productivity differences.

In any case, several reasons other than the cold war and the associated Soviet threat as negative and U.S. interests as positive external integrators (Garton Ash, 1998, p. 54) can thus be invoked as background to postwar EU integration. But a much similar rationale can also be deduced by alternative means: if the EU's architects had primarily been motivated by the postwar division of Europe and the cold war, would there still be a case for integrating some of the TEs into the EU, at least within its present setup and with its still-prevailing longer-term ambitions? Not only has the EU not become superfluous since 1989, in spite of strong centripetal forces observed in the aftermath of German unification, its integration efforts are now arguably more relevant than ever before, including in order to pull the TEs into the global economy. After all, the EU was established for the purpose of serving *all* European countries imbued with democracy and committed to a market-economy framework. That task, as stated so eloquently in the EU's quasi-constitutional instruments (European Commission, 1992, p. 4), remains to be accomplished. In light of the tremendous societal changes in the eastern part of Europe, reaching that goal can now realistically be envisioned. Whereas many long-standing political and economic conflicts among the (western) European countries have been overcome through postwar cooperation, a good many tasks of smoothing cooperation among the EU governments remain to be addressed, if only because EU integration presents a sui generis case. Indeed, it cannot be reduced to just another attempt at forging a rather simple free-trade or customs area, or even an economic union.

In any case, soon after war's end, the countries of the western part of Europe began to carve out some common path toward economic and political unity, largely under U.S. prodding. Rather than harping too much on economic issues, particularly as narrow as they are often posed in the context of debates on trade creation and trade diversion in a world that is otherwise presumed to be multilaterally integrated, if ridden with varying instances of tariff and other protection, I would suggest two propositions. One is that considerations around other than strictly economic gains and losses have always provided the major impetus to European integration as far as policy makers are concerned; business leaders have pushed this agenda along largely for their own economic interests, of course. Also, though some of the noneconomic concerns have waned somewhat over the years, one overriding objective remains the irrevocable prevention by any peaceful means of repeating the history of western Europe in general or reenacting any of the great conflicts on that continent in the twentieth century in particular. This continues to provide a paramount litmus test for moving ahead with building a more homogeneous, prosperous, and fairer Europe for all, in spite of the all too apparent hindrances arising from the need to yield ever more on, and increasingly in more sensitive areas of, sovereign prerogatives of the nation state. The recent calamity in the Balkans, and the absence of a fair settlement of the lingering disputes there, has, in fact, strengthened the case for forging tighter cooperation on the continent through integration.

Dreams of eventually reaching a more integrated continent-wide Europe, largely with federalist structures, should not be marred by controversies over federalism and subsidiarity. On their merits, such aspirations are misplaced, however much one may cherish citizen involvement in high-level political decision making (Brabant, 1995, pp. 480-88; Scott, Peterson, and Millar, 1994). That (western) European integration has tended toward success beyond the initial dreams of its most enthusiastic architects is now part of history. Yet, that reality too forms an essential component of the story to be retained intact when contemplating what could conceivably be mustered to the benefit of the eastern part of Europe in the context of smoothing the TEs' entry into the EU integration movement. For some TEs, that would eventually amount to membership, once they can meet in full the conditions for such a status. For others, it would mean setting forth a robust framework for a reasonably equal partnership relationship to take root. Designing such a magnanimous and perspicacious strategy with all the care that the momentous remaking of Europe deserves has an important bearing as well on the timely updating of the EU's governance structures. As such, it constitutes an essential ingredient in fashioning Europe's present and prospective role in global economic management.

In short, just as the cold war was but one determinant of western European integration, the seismic events in the eastern part of the continent since the late 1980s have coalesced into one of the major challenges to, but by no stretch of the imagination the sole assignment for, western and eastern political leaders alike. Important as the TE mutations have undoubtedly been, and will continue to be for decades to come, they provide by far not the only, and in many respects arguably not even the most salient, hurdle facing western Europe's leadership in forging ahead with economic, political, and social integration without debilitating altogether the identity and sovereignty of the member states. Nevertheless, the entire gamut of concerns afflicting the TE leadership has challenged in more than one respect the original and prevailing justifications for EU integration. Their impacts on endeavors to 'deepen' this integration process deserve to be examined from multiple angles. Given the main purpose of this volume, I propose to do so here chiefly from the perspective of the eventual full accession of selected TEs to the EU.

Even when seen against this confined backdrop, some of the evident challenges strengthen the case for accelerating the pace at which Europe's societies are being melded while propping up the movement toward liberal democracies anchored to vibrant market economies in the eastern part of the continent.[1] They reinforce them largely because integration enhances security on the continent in its multiple dimensions and enlarges the effective scope of Europe's factor and product markets. Others threaten to weaken even the comparatively modest results attained during some four decades of deliberative cooperation ventures; some more earnest and revealing than others, of course. This is especially so given the priority of 'deepening' integration. That should not be sidetracked by the details and real obstacles encountered during 'widening' exercises. At the very least, the latter should never be allowed to hollow out the fundamental hopes cherished in the Rome Treaty: building a more cohesive, unified, stronger, prosperous, and reasonably equitable European polity in the full sense of that term.

These points, I trust, suffice to underline the central proposition of this book: the seminal changes in the eastern part of Europe have altered dramatically the willingness and purview of the EU's integration ambitions and will continue to do so for decades to come; but they have by no means altogether compromised, let alone displaced, much of the rationale behind European integration. That has many dimensions in cultural, economic, environmental, health, political, social, strategic, and other transnational affairs. Some of these unprecedented transformations can only be welcomed. Other mutations encumber several of the envisioned dynamic integration processes, however.

The Overall Climate for EU Integration in the 1980s

In addition to the fundamental motivations that led up to the EEC's establishment in 1958, the specific impetus to spurring on EU integration has ebbed and surged, at times in unpredictable ways, over the EU's history. On the eve of the transitions in the eastern part of Europe, EU integration endeavors had reached another major juncture. In the mid-1980s western Europe emerged from a protracted period of deep-seated europessimism. Recall that this had been engendered by slow growth since the early 1970s; the seeming inability of policy makers to agree on engaging EU integration beyond the customs union, and severe governance problems as membership expanded and members' interests became ever more diverse. In contrast to this decade of stasis, the second half of the 1980s in western Europe constituted a renaissance of sorts. Not only was eurosclerosis being rapidly remedied, growth revived while inflation, unemployment, and exchange-rate variability were markedly compressed. Even the most stalwart EU members had in record time become increasingly more disposed toward making another start with the construction of a genuine economic union, as called for somewhat vaguely by the Rome Treaty. It is important to recall the backdrop to the europessimism as well as to the sudden revival of the EU's fortunes by the mid-1980s and how this eurobuoyancy suddenly collapsed.

The pessimism about economic growth at a time of inflation with negative-to-low growth and rising unemployment from the mid-1970s until a decade later essentially rested on the belief that western Europe's economic and social structures were overly rigid. EU members should therefore have targeted protracted adjustments of their socioeconomic foundations. But orderly structural adjustments could not even be contemplated in earnest without engaging lengthy and divisive debates in order to elicit a minimal consensus. These broad features cast a pall over integration endeavors for well over a decade (Brabant, 1995, pp. 175ff.), during which attempts to move beyond building the customs union had failed. Indeed, efforts to move toward EMU date from the first aborted attempt to hammer out an understanding in 1962 about what to target by way of guiding integration beyond a functioning customs union. This set the tone for two decades of repeated failures to allow EMU arrangements to take root. Second, even the achievements of the customs union came under severe strains when the Bretton Woods system of fixed exchange rates began to collapse and finally disintegrated in the early 1970s. That at the very least invalidated some of the basic assumptions regarding the transparency, stability, reliability, and predictability of the postwar international economic 'order' on which moving forward with EU integration, including even the more mundane aspects of the CAP, had been predicated.

Undoubtedly the most important proximate factor bringing the EU integration pace to a virtual standstill in the early 1970s resulted from the several external shocks in the real sphere: the run-up in raw material prices in 1972, the sharp upward movement of energy prices in late 1973, the interruption in previously secure oil deliveries in 1973, the difficulties encountered in adjusting the real economies to the new relative world prices, the seeming termination of the postwar golden age of inexorable expansion (Marglin and Schor, 1990), the inflation imparted by the dollar regime as a result of the reckless financing of the Vietnam War, and the decision taken to enlarge EU membership in 1973 before arrangements for 'deepening' integration beyond the customs union could be agreed upon. Recall that the customs union had been completed much more smoothly than anticipated when the Treaty of Rome was signed in 1957. That stemmed in part precisely from the favorable external environment: stability in international economic relations and substantial growth over a protracted period of time with rapid trade liberalization in developed countries measurably facilitated the enactment of incisive structural adjustments. When in the early 1970s several major shocks to the global economic system were sustained in rapid succession, the tide turned precipitously against maintaining buoyancy in economic performance, thus undermining the perceived postwar certainties.

Some of the external disturbances had initially been interpreted as purely temporary. Especially western European policy makers thought it advisable to borrow their way out of the rising external and internal constraints. The latter were in no small measure being exacerbated by the liabilities of the welfare state, such as it had been elaborated mainly during the prosperous 1960s in part to cushion the impact of trade liberalization on labor (Rodrik, 1997). With the benefit of hindsight that 'policy maneuver' quickly proved to have been quite erroneous as it gave rise to a protracted period of stagflation. By then, however, the damage to economic structures—nationally, regionally, and globally—had been wreaked. Policy makers had become weary about Keynesian-type demand-management policies through fiscal means. By the late 1970s, under onslaught of the new economic-policy conservatism in major industrial countries, combating inflation and maintaining monetary stability became top policy priorities almost to the exclusion of any other available policy option throughout developed countries, and soon in many developing countries as well. This was reinforced by the stance taken by major multilateral financial organizations.

But setbacks to the idea of integrating Europe resulted also from other features, among which the crisis in governance originally brought into the open as a result of the Gaullist intransigence of the mid-1960s (Brabant, 1995, pp. 183-86) was perhaps the most deleterious. Not only that, when the first enlargement occurred in 1973, governing EU processes with more than six members without adjusting the rules and institutions originally designed for six, became more daunting as embedded unanimity constraints became far more formidable. Major shifts in governance criteria and institutions were called for. But they could hardly be designed on purely rational grounds. By their very political nature they required compromises among the members. Working those out too needed time, thus delaying progress with deepening integration as core members sought relief in the first widening exercise of the then EC.

Finally, it was felt that the buoyancy of the European economy left much to be desired, quite apart from external events and the debilitating impacts of the welfare state. Indeed Europe had for years failed to embrace policies to decisively adjust its seminal economic structures in the global economy. Investment sentiment in most countries remained weak as stagflation and europessimism were feeding upon one another, thus exacerbating eurosclerosis. As a result, productivity gains in western Europe trailed well behind those attained elsewhere, notably by Japan and the United States. They remained also far too tepid in comparison with what was desired to engineer the necessary changes in economic structures in order to regain in some sense full employment with strong growth. That would be obtained only by accessing the type of economies of scale and scope reaped by Europe's major competitors and the challenges emerging from the newly industrializing economies (NIEs), notably those of east and southeast Asia.

In spite of the successful elimination of internal tariffs, erection of the common external tariff ahead of schedule, and agreement on the CAP, movement toward a common commercial policy, and indeed some modest progress with cooperation in monetary affairs, by the early 1980s the EU still lacked significant foundational elements of a genuine common market. But the tide shifted markedly by the mid-1980s. Under the determined leadership of Jacques Delors as President of the Commission, although his predecessors in collaboration with the Commission staff had done formidable legwork to enable him to forge ahead in a singular manner and the environment for EU action had become much more congenial, the members were persuaded to change decision-making rules as well as to set the stage for "completing the single market" by the end of 1992. Forging a genuine single market was expected to provide a strong buttress for research and development (R&D) and the exploitation of economies of scale and scope for most, if perhaps not all, EU members.

This determination was so strong that no other challenge to and opportunity for propelling integration was to be entertained prior to completing the SEM, at any rate, its legal and administrative foundations. Requests for new accessions by, among others, EFTA members, which soon arose, were simply sidetracked in order not to jeopardize the march toward a genuine SEM. Other potential derailments were brought to the surface with German unification. This involved a de facto expansion of the EU almost without preparation or transitory accession process, and without the members other than Germany having had any say in this constitutional matter. Yet the manner in which unification was in the end engineered brought marked shifts in the EU's obligations and adverse exposure to the consequences of the German euphoria. And the EU was singularly unprepared to provide an adequate response to the internal as well as the external dimensions of the challenges and opportunities presented by or emanating from the fibrillations of the Soviet Empire.

The view is widespread that, as constituted by the debates of 1989-1991, the EU has become no longer adequately equipped to deal with the changes occurring on the European continent (Ludlow and Ersbøll, 1996, pp. 2ff.). Indeed one crucial factor is that for a long time members have felt that there are too many EU matters that cannot be adequately dealt with—'governed' in the broad sense of that term—in the institutional framework originally created in 1958 for the six founders. This became noticeably tighter soon after the Maastricht Treaty was agreed upon and the fourth enlargement undermined the fragility of the makeshift decision-making arrangements put in place in the mid-1980s. Given the already painfully felt governance obstacles in an EU with fifteen members, any further enlargement would exacerbate them into insuperable hindrances to operating the EU with reasonable efficiency and expediency, let alone in deepening the integration adventure.

Moreover, institutional and core elements of decision-making mechanisms had been deliberately set aside in the negotiations of the two IGCs held in 1990-1991 in order to facilitate the process of reaching a firm commitment on political union, at least in principle, though many leaders have cherished quite divergent interpretations of what precisely that should entail. This expedient had been resorted to in view of the seminal transformations under way in the eastern part of Europe, particularly German unification in 1990 and the implosion of the Soviet Union. Recall that of the two IGCs held in 1990 at least one was convened in direct response to the rapidly moving events in the eastern part of Europe, especially German unification. But the deliberations at both meetings were without a doubt influenced by the swiftly unfolding string of 'crises' in the eastern part of the continent.

Furthermore, in spite of an unexpectedly buoyant economic and political climate for integration enjoyed in the second half of the 1980s, major issues regarding governance of the EU, its component institutions, and its multiple integration ambitions had become an irritant in more than one respect. These concerns about hindrances to effective integration were bound to be aggravated by any further enlargement of the EU or any attempt to forge ahead with the EU's ultimate constitutional makeup. It is in this context that convening an IGC may be quite appropriate in preparing for high-level decisions with potentially ominous, at any rate irreversible, implications for national sovereignty.

The Role of the IGC in the EU's Governance

I cannot, of course, conduct here a rounded exegesis of governance and decision making in the EU. Even so, without a few key pointers to the latter, and notably to the decisions reached at the recent IGCs, it would be all but impossible to place the evolving relationship between the EU and the TEs since 1989 and its prospects for decades to come into an appropriate perspective. The EU's main governance structures have varied somewhat over time (Brabant, 1995, 1996a), but details of how integration moved along in the past should not detain us here.

There are essentially four core decision-making levels in the EU: the European Council (sometimes only one of the several possible Councils of Ministers[2]), the European Parliament, the European Commission, and the European Court of Justice. Some of these governance organs have had overlapping responsibilities. And members are not always in agreement on the substance of some of the ostensibly delegated responsibilities.

The European Parliament, elected in EU-wide elections, and the European Council (including the regular Council of Ministers), constituted by the Heads of Government and State (or responsible ministers in the appropriate Council of Ministers) of the members, are the so-called bicephalous legislative organs. Their powers are not neatly separated as the so-called codecision rule subjects decisions made in one organ to scrutiny in at least one other organ. Needless to say, the federalist idea aiming at endowing the European Parliament with powers similar to those incumbent on a veritable parliament, say, one in the western European mold, even with appropriate subsidiarity recognized for the member states and their respective administrative and political setups, has not so far been carried out. Even as a distant aim it is hotly contested by nearly all of the larger members and indeed by some of the smaller ones as well.

The European Council plays a unique role in EU decision making, although it is a relative newcomer in the EU's institutional development. It was first convened in 1974 by the then French President Valéry Giscard d'Estaing with a view to reactivating western European integration, following the setbacks incurred in the preceding decade in many areas of EU cooperation other than completing the customs union in 1967, by bringing together key decision makers of all member states at the intergovernmental level. For our purposes it is important to be aware of the paramount role of the Council's decisions in the governance of the EU. The European Council is the highest deliberative-executive body of the EU. The amalgam should be borne in mind too for, unlike a national government, as noted, the EU's governance is ensured through overlapping responsibilities.

By virtue of the fact that the Council is made up of the Heads of State or Government of the member states, assisted at least by their respective ministers of foreign affairs and the President of the Commission, it has on several occasions played a paramount role in setting the EU's integration strategy and determining common positions with regard to EU affairs. Frequently the issues resolved at the Council reach well beyond those that could properly be allocated to the domains of security and foreign affairs (European Commission, 1995, p. 2). It meets at least twice a year under the chairmanship of the Head of State or Government of the member that holds the Presidency of the Council, which itself rotates every six months (European Commission, 1993, p. 25). As such, it is a special emanation of the Council of Ministers, an organ that was formally created as one of the EEC's governance pillars by the Treaty of Rome. To avoid confusion in what follows, reference to a Council meeting at a particular city means a meeting of the European Council; otherwise Council refers to the Council of Ministers in charge of one particular area (such as finance or foreign affairs).

Another level of decision making is vested in the European Commission. Formally this is now known as the Commission of the European Communities even though, with the TEU, the EC was transformed into the EU. Briefly this somewhat arcane nomenclature derives from the fact that the Commission is responsible for what previously was assigned to the level of the three Communities (EEC, Euratom or the European Atomic Energy Community, and the European Coal and Steel Community or ECSC). Since the negotiations around the Maastricht Treaty, these matters have become known as 'pillar 1,' as I explain below. All other EU integration concerns belong to the TEU's two other pillars and remain governed through intergovernmentalism, with the Commission at best acting as secretariat, neither the initiator of legislation nor entrusted with its surveillance. The Commission does not, of course, decide autonomously. Its activities are closely dovetailed with those of the European Council and/or the sectoral or topical Council of Ministers. Together they form the EU's executive arm, albeit in a rather fluid relationship. The Commission consists of twenty commissioners (so far, one from each small country and two from the five big members) nominated by the member states. However, together with the President of the Commission, since the TEU was ratified, that cabinet needs to be approved in its entirety by the European Parliament.

The final decision-making organ of the EU is the European Court of Justice. As its name suggests, this organ is responsible for adjudicating conflicts in implementing the EU's laws and directives between the Commission as guardian of the SEM and the member states.

There are in addition various institutions that are involved in assisting one or more of the decision-making organs in technical matters. But they do not have substantive decision-making responsibility. They encompass the Court of Auditors, the European Investment Bank, the Economic and Social Committee, the Committee of the Regions, the European Ombudsman, and the European Monetary Institute (European Commission, 1998d), which was transformed into the European Central Bank (ECB) in July 1998.

As already indicated, the prerogatives of these various organs are by no means clear-cut because of the continuing conflict between two barely reconcilable precepts. On the one hand, national policy makers have more and more come to jealously guard national sovereignty, even as coveted in economic affairs. On the other hand, genuine integration, even of only the economic realm, requires delegating some national authority, hence yielding on national sovereignty, to 'supranational' governance organs. Particularly since the disenchantment with the Maastricht Treaty set in almost before the signature ink was dry, as explained below, key policy makers have been insistent on strengthening the importance of the European Council. This has been somewhat at the expense of the Council of Ministers and indeed the erstwhile Mandarin-like role of Coreper; but definitely more so at that of the European Commission even in areas of common policy—by and large the core contours of economic, but not monetary, union—on which national decision makers had earlier agreed to yield to higher authority. The Council has thus far at best sought to streamline its relationship with the European Parliament, with perhaps a more focused mechanism of decision making. It has also sought out a narrower place for lawmaking by the European Court of Justice.

At its inception, the Commission, including of the EEC but also of the two other communities, was expected to propose legislation in an activist manner, something that reached a high degree of intensity under the several Delors administrations. In other words, especially after the creation of the EC, the Commission was, as a matter of principle, expected to prepare proposals to be legislated by the Council and/or the Parliament. More and more often in recent years, however, that original role of the Commission has been incrementally usurped by the rising powers of initiative arrogated by the European Council and the direct representatives of the members, thus relegating the Commission to a less activist mode. This has often been justified under the heading of "codecision making," which requires involvement of more than one of the EU's real governance organs.

Apart from designing appropriate institutions and dividing the tasks at hand, the real problems of governing a regional organization such as the EU, which is neither intergovernmental nor strictly supranational, are acutely complex and rise rapidly with the expansion of membership without changing the unanimity rule. This all the more so since the EU's makeup in 1957 was essentially conceived for the six founder members under rather different and difficult circumstances in which the small were very apprehensive indeed about the intentions of the large and the latter among themselves, especially France and Germany, had to overcome deeply seated suspicions and antagonisms. These governance issues run through the history of the EU, and I return to them in more detail in chapter 4.

Where does the IGC enter into this institutional framework? This is not so easily laid out in view of two of its features: it occurs infrequently and its agenda is as a rule set in an ad hoc manner. The latter stems largely from the fact that an IGC can be called by the membership whenever a consensus deems it useful to proceed in this manner in order to advance with one or more of the cited objectives; as a rule most, if not all, are simultaneously at stake. Usually it is resorted to under pressure of circumstances, when burning broader policy and organizational issues cannot adequately be dealt with in the above-cited regular EU governance organs, such as the Council of Ministers or the European Council.

Let me address these two features in sequence. As indicated, an IGC is a fairly rare event in the EU. The most recent one, which opened in March 1996 and closed in June 1997 (see chapter 4), was only the sixth during the EU's existence—at the time of writing, over forty-eight years if its history is dated from the negotiations of the Paris Treaty that led to the ECSC's establishment in 1952. At the same time it is instructive to bear in mind that this was the fourth IGC in eleven years, after an hiatus of nearly three decades. That 'blank space' stemmed not so much from the smooth functioning of the EU than from the fact that the organization had been encountering severe constitutional problems, especially those revolving around the goals and means of EU integration after the completion of the customs union, as explained in the preceding section. That so many IGCs were convened within little more than a decade is indicative of the acceleration during that period of top-level deliberations about core integration matters (Brabant, 1996a, pp. 55ff.). Up until the launching of the preparations for IGC96 it was also symptomatic of the convergence, however gingerly, of views on more and more issues with real implications for keeping national sovereignty intact.

As intimated earlier, an IGC does not really fit into the quasi-constitutional decision-making structure around which the EU's governance is assured. But it could be treated as an ad hoc branch-off of the Council of Ministers for Foreign Affairs under whose auspices an IGC is as a rule convened, albeit at the direct behest of the European Council in recent decades (see below). An IGC as such therefore does not normally develop the specific content of integration policies. Rather it carves out essential components of the legal and institutional frameworks and of the procedures by which policy agreements are reached among the members by forging a broad consensus on paramount issues affecting their integration format. As such an IGC's agenda as a rule revolves around intragroup policies, institutions, cooperation mechanisms, governance issues, stances with respect to nonmember countries, and the potential widening of the membership.

Note, however, that recognizing the importance of the IGC in advancing the cause of integration in the EU does not imply endorsement of the position of some commentators (notably Moravcsik, 1993) to the effect that the successive IGCs have really reached seminal intergovernmental bargains, each of which set the agenda for an intervening period of consolidation. This is, of course, true in a purely procedural and semantic sense. After all, how else could intergovernmental negotiations, which are the very raisons d'être of the IGC, proceed with advancing the cause of EU integration than via bargains? However, the intricacies of the bargains struck at these infrequent IGCs are quite distinct from the way in which the legislative agenda in the EU has been propelled over the years as a result of the interactions among the Council of Ministers, the European Commission, and the European Parliament in particular (Garrett and Tsebelis, 1996).

It should be borne in mind that although an IGC is as a rule opened and concluded in full diplomatic summitry mode, the operative deliberations take place elsewhere and in different fora. Once the IGC is formally opened by the Heads of State and Government meeting in a special Council, the actual negotiations are entrusted to the Council of Ministers of Foreign Affairs and their Representatives. The Council actually negotiates about items on the agenda and how best to settle them. But it does so only after the relevant topics have been thoroughly examined and prepared by frequent, often weekly, meetings among the Ministers' Representatives. These can be either the country's ambassador in Brussels or someone of (deputy or junior) ministerial rank. The President of the European Commission also attends these deliberations. Once consensus, including on matters unresolved at the IGC itself, is reached at a European Council subsequent to the end of the IGC's deliberations, which then formally terminates the IGC in question, the members submit the texts hammered out to their respective parliaments for ratification in accordance with the national constitutions.

It is instructive to recall briefly that, without exception, all of the earlier IGCs marked crucial advances in laying the foundations of EU integration. The first, which began in May 1950, led to the Treaty of Paris signed in April 1951, followed by the establishment of the ECSC in early 1952. The second, which began in Messina in April 1955, led eventually to the Treaties of Rome, signed in March 1957, and the creation of the EEC and Euratom in January 1958. The third, which was started in September 1985, revolved around institutional reform, after a protracted period of stagnation in the building of Europe. As it culminated in the SEA in 1986 and the decision to create the SEM by the end of 1992 this move provided a welcome foil to the europessimism of the preceding decade. The fourth on EMU and the fifth on European Political Union (EPU), both initiated in 1990 and concluded in December 1991, were seminal in the preparation and conclusion of the TEU.

In more than one respect, the key institutional and governance topics addressed at IGCs derive from the gradualist approach to integration enshrined in the Treaty of Rome and in later quasi-constitutional acts. Prior to the relaunching of EU deliberations in the mid-1980s, the Treaty of Rome set specific goals only for the formation of a customs union according to a precise schedule. The ambitions of moving toward economic union and a unified market, and indeed toward some form of political and social union, were stated as firm intentions. But progress with implementing endeavors to realize those goals could be achieved only through subsequent negotiations at the highest policy-making level. That has proved to be a much more involved task than was apparently configured in the run-up to the Rome Treaty (Brabant, 1995, pp. 122-26, 176-86). From this two overriding characteristics of the EU's governance can be inferred. They can be encapsulated under the notions of 'gradualism' and 'distributional solidarity.' Gradualism means that new measures are as a rule introduced over a fairly protracted period of time. This holds not only for 'deepening' but also for 'widening' inasmuch as new members are ushered into the EU subject to their meeting all prevailing rules and regulations over some mutually agreed period of time, which can stretch out over a decade or even more. This gradualism forms an important ingredient of ensuring solidarity and some measure of distributional equity: any major policy measure has to spread its benefits and costs both over time and across the membership, at least those directly affected by them.

The Seminal IGCs of 1990-1991 and the Need for IGC96

Partly as a result of the buoyant optimism about EU integration aroused during the late 1980s, two IGCs were convened simultaneously in late 1990 and successfully concluded in Maastricht in late 1991. One focused on EMU with monetary union as the logical sequel to—indeed twin component of—the SEM. As such it was closely associated with the third IGC held in the mid-1980s (Brabant, 1996a, pp. 102ff.); but it would be historically quite inaccurate, as indicated in the beginning of the chapter, to view this IGC as having been convened solely as a tradeoff for political union, as some contend (Feldstein, 1997; Frieden, 1998). There is an immanence in working toward monetary union that has little to do with politics, but quite a lot with the transparency of fair competition among highly intertwined economies. Recall in this connection the essence of the EU's approach to economic integration, if not invariably adhered to in practice: ensuring fair competition based on genuine productivity differentials within a large single market. That cannot tolerate discriminatory exchange-rate movements for it would grant specific advantages to one country at the express expense of other EU members, especially given the very large share (between three-fifths and three-fourths) of trade that EU members transact among themselves. Hence the need in a nutshell for a common currency and monetary policy with more than a shared approach to fiscal affairs as well.

Recall furthermore that although the SEM was to have been completed at the end of 1992, major implementation tasks, and in some cases even drafting legislation on the thorniest issues, such as on fiscal and financial-service matters, have remained on the EU's policy agenda. There was hence a mutual reinforcement of *economic* and *monetary* union. Precisely that goal the IGC on EMU sought to accomplish by working out the rather technical details concerning the creation of the ECB and a common European currency subject to a highly concerted monetary policy, in the view of both insiders (see Pöhl, 1995) and the more academic assessment of the IGC on EMU (see Gros and Thygesen, 1992).

The interest of high-level policy makers in moving beyond the issues of economic union, which had dominated much of the agenda in the 1980s, also followed from the unexpected success achieved with the implementation of the SEM program, in spite of several unmet expectations. That in turn had been facilitated by, and in part gave rise to, the unanticipated and sharp economic upswing during the same phase with a noticeable decline in the high levels of unemployment that had emerged in part as a result of the particular policy response to the two oil shocks. But there was also a substantial increase in productivity growth and lowering of the pace of inflation, although there was no return to the scenario of high growth with minimal inflation and unemployment of the so-called golden age (Marglin and Schor, 1990). All this was quite remarkable, certainly in comparison to what these countries had been able to achieve over the preceding decade.

The discussions of the feasibility of monetary union by 1990 had advanced to the stage where it became a political project because of the success of the SEM but also because of the thorough preparations, at both the technocratic and bureaucratic levels, in the earlier part of the 1980s. The time had come for taking prompt decisions on grave matters of national sovereignty by the political leadership. Of course, politics has never been far from EU matters, and so when the other 'topic' of concern arose under impact of German unification and, to a lesser extent, the early turbulence in the rest of the eastern part of Europe, the debates on monetary union became inextricably interlinked with those on moving forward with political union. It would be cynical, however, to confound deliberately the EMU process, including monetary integration, with a French-German tradeoff (Garton Ash, 1998, pp. 57-58). True, the latter bargain may well have been instrumental in getting the two IGCs under way (Story and Walter, 1997, pp. 67ff.). However, the desire for monetary union antedates the French-German priorities of around 1990 (Frieden, 1998). Not only that, prior to German unification so much momentum militating for action on the monetary-union front had built up that the process itself, and hence what it hopes to accomplish and the reason why European leaders condone its rigidity and stringency, simply cannot be adequately, or even fairly, portrayed in the French-German tit-for-tat image.

In any case, the other IGC was devoted to moving forward with political union, but it did not take a clear stance on the fundamental constitutional issues surrounding the EU's so-called *finalité politique*. EPU has therefore remained a longer-term process of concertation of the national political wills in contrast to the architecture for EMU, notably monetary union, that was agreed upon. Nonetheless both meetings, but especially the second, in retrospect marked without a doubt paramount milestones on the way to the drafting and subsequent endorsement of the Maastricht Treaty. Debates on EPU, and the slight shift in emphasis on the expediency of EMU, were in good measure enhanced by the extraordinary rounds of diplomatic activity in the EU conducted in 1990-1991 in particular on account of the unease felt by a number of European economic and political leaders over the possible consequences, in the first place, of German unification, but also apprehensions about the then still very wobbly socioeconomic and political changes transforming the face of the eastern part of Europe more generally. Clearly, something had to be done to cope with these challenges if EU integration were to move forward at anything like a predictable and steady pace.

German unification had placed the 'German question,' the hub of most of the east-west conflicts during the postwar period, in a completely new light (Fritsch-Bournazel, 1992). To allay the fears on the part of some western European leaders about the future strategic interests of a unified Germany, anchoring the new Germany irrevocably deeper into the European framework became an urgent priority of European policy. A firm commitment toward political integration, aiming at gradually transcending the well-rehearsed intergovernmentalism, thus moving beyond monetary integration and the single market, so it was thought, would irreversibly tie Germany to 'Europe.' It would thus stave off any weakening of Germany's interest in and commitment to (western) European integration. Furthermore, the tumultuous developments in the eastern part of Europe with the near demise of state socialism as a political and economic system, the replacement of central planning with market-based resource allocation, and the rapid unraveling of the economic and political ties among the former state-socialist economies dramatically modified the traditional east-west conflict and opened up new prospects—economic and political—for European unification (European Commission, 1995, p. 4). But it also ushered new conflicts into the open.

Discussions about monetary union, as noted, were, of course, also informed by the impetus given to political union, and there may have been a tradeoff between the two, at least as far as the decision to move ahead for the fourth occasion,[3] but this time concretely, as far as monetary union is concerned. But it is simply wrong to claim EPU to have been sought by Germany to prevent its worst historical sins of hegemony from being repeated, in exchange for monetary union on which

French policy makers may have been very keen and Germany at the time (as opposed to the days of Helmut Schmidt as Chancellor) rather lukewarm (Feldstein, 1997; Garton Ash, 1998).

Whatever the original motivation, by late 1990 it was thought wise to proceed rapidly toward monetary union, even without policy makers having reached a broad understanding about the proximate shape of EPU or the kind of strategy to be pursued to reach it in a realistically feasible manner. Hence the hurried endorsement of the Maastricht Treaty and the call for holding a Review Conference in 1996—yet another IGC. That was slated to address numerous issues deriving from the inconclusive debates of 1990-1991 but not those associated with EMU. Those matters had been settled in the TEU with a precise deadline with further decisions being marked for future European Councils. Recall also that the Review Conference was not called to address the CAP, budget matters, or any kind of enlargement (see chapter 4).

The backdrop, therefore, of the Maastricht Treaty itself is quite convoluted. Only if that is firmly understood does it become clear why the then twelve members decided to schedule a Review Conference in 1996 as part and parcel of the negotiated Maastricht Treaty, however unusual at first sight it might be: a treaty that created a procedure for its own revision with a definite timetable to be met just two years after it came into effect (on 1 November 1993). The basic reason, as mentioned above, was that Europe as a whole, and especially the then EC members, were at the center of wide-ranging and radical changes, indeed in the grip of a vortex of seminal transformations throughout the continent.

Salient Aspects of the TEU

Although the Maastricht process does not really amount to a major shift in the EU's integration strategy, some differences between the Rome and the Maastricht paths deserve to be highlighted (Woyke, 1993, pp. 371-75). Some observers have read the 'ideal' of EPU into the TEU. Whereas intentions of some member states eventually to strive for such a status are reflected there, the language actually used makes no commitment whatsoever even with respect to the shape of such an EPU, let alone unambiguously to federalism. Some commentators (see Woyke, 1993, pp. 373-74) have precisely read this into the TEU, relying chiefly on the declaration of "an ever closer union," but that assertion can cover very different readings indeed. Not only that, the TEU contains unambiguous statements to the effect that it marks a new phase in the process of constructing an ever closer union (European Commission, 1992, p. 23). For my taste, then, the continuing importance of confederalism and intergovernmentalism, rather than supranationalism, hovers over virtually all the parts of the treaty. A commitment to a robust constitution remains to be negotiated, however (Herman, 1996).

Whatever its aims for the future may be, as matters now stand the EU diverges from the EC or EEC in a number of respects. For one thing, it obtained three so-called 'pillars.' The reason for this terminology has remained quite obscure (Boulouis, 1992, p. 8). However, only one can be equated with the three Communities that constitute the EC, as modified by the SEA and the SEM process, and indeed the negotiations of the Maastricht Treaty. There will presumably continue to be impacts emanating from the further implementation of the tasks and aspirations of the TEU and elaborations of concerted rules in the future, notably in the case of agreed opt-out options (Ehlermann, 1996).

Part and parcel of that pillar 1 is the *acquis*, with the accent clearly on the *communautaire*, rather than the *politique*, component, as reached prior to the endorsement of the TEU as well as the process leading to monetary union by 1999 at the latest. This specifically encompasses also the common policies (in agriculture, commerce, transportation, cohesion, and the single market), including the four freedoms (Tosi, 1997a, p. 9). However, governance of all other matters, including those dealing with foreign and security policy; juridical and home affairs; and components of the social chapter, which only in 1997, following protracted debates, became part of pillar 1, remains at the intergovernmental level. The Maastricht Treaty also calls for extending the competence of the Commission to issues concerning the environment, education, consumer protection, health policies, and all-European networks (including in communication and transportation). But most of these are slated to be subject to the strict 'subsidiarity rule,' a subject on which political decisions regarding operationalization of the concept are still to be taken, even at this stage.

As noted, pillar 1 is distinct from other matters, at least in principle. For these other components of European economic, political, and social integration do not form part of the supranational agenda, with neither the Commission's active involvement nor the possibility of adjudication in the European Court of Justice at stake until they are transferred to pillar 1 or pillars 2 and 3 emerge from the strict intergovernmental governance applicable at this stage. Crucial details of these two 'other' pillars are not even set forth in the Maastricht Treaty or its successors. It will remain up to the European Council—in many respects, the EU's preeminent intergovernmental arbiter—to settle basic questions unanimously, and this extends to some areas that were previously within the competence of the Commission (Toth, 1992, p. 1105). The execution of the tasks thus entrusted to the 'community' will then be taken up in the Council of Ministers, where a 'qualified majority' (of some 71 percent) reigns.

Indeed, pillar 2 rests on eventually elaborating common stances in external and security policy through the established intergovernmental machinery. Incidentally, this has ironically formed an integral part of the way in which the so-called supranationalism in the EU had previously proceeded! The agenda for the near term includes the process around the Conference on, and now Organization for, Security and Cooperation in Europe (OSCE), disarmament and arms control, containing the spread of nuclear weapons, and economic aspects of security ꭓꞁd defense policies. This component has been inspired by three events. First, the end of the cold war had paradoxically imparted greater uncertainty into Europe, including doubts about U.S. commitments to the North Atlantic Treaty Organization (NATO) and Europe. Second, key European policy makers perceived a strong need to reinforce Europe's position in global affairs and hence to take greater care of its own defense needs. Finally, the unexpected confrontations occurring on the European continent—especially the civil wars in the former Yugoslavia and the challenges emanating from economically, politically, and socially unstable countries on Europe's eastern fringes—had been posing a vexing problem for 'Europe,' regardless of the measures that could have been and were taken.

Finally, juridical and home affairs constitute pillar 3. These include cooperation among national police forces, combating drugs, stances and policies with respect to immigrants into the EU and to extending asylum to political refugees, migration, terrorism, and other issues.

Even though there is widespread disagreement in the literature, let alone in EU debates, one might well take issue with the inclusion of the social chapter in pillar 1. One could indeed argue that it might be more appropriate to treat social matters separately in the sense that the issues to be tackled may eventually require a more coherent common social policy[4] (Dinan, 1994, p. 22) reaching well beyond the interstices of economic and social affairs. In that sense, the entire range of social-agenda issues affecting EU integration debates can only awkwardly be accommodated under any of the present pillar headings. Just like the original motivation for monetary integration, a single market cannot function appropriately if the various constituent members adhere to widely diverging approaches to social security, unemployment, welfare provisions, working time, leaves, and so on since these may confer benefits on economic agents of some members that have nothing to do with genuine productivity gains. These matters are intrinsically different from those that form the subject of the three established pillars. But in time many of the issues at stake promise to come closer perhaps to those of pillar 1, where several are now formally located.

In addition to those old and new 'common' policy approaches, the TEU contains other provisions, some of which are worth recalling here. Perhaps the first and foremost is a commitment to streamline the efficiency of the EU's institutions by bolstering governance capabilities through a proper institutional infrastructure with adequate decision-making powers. One element thereof is the explicit recognition of the rather fuzzy concept of 'subsidiarity' in steering the EU and majority decision making on a number of integration matters that do not merit the label 'of vital importance' to the EU. Another element is strengthening codetermination on the part of the European Parliament, albeit in a limited range of topics. Examples of its newly acquired powers include rights, after three trials, to veto new EU law drafts, to confirm the EU's Commission and its President, and to have the term of office of the Commission and its President coincide with the Parliament's electoral cycle (Wallace, 1994).

Another of the special provisions is the agreement in principle to work toward balanced development within the EU, hence the need to streamline structural funds and regional policies with a view to better targeting the real 'cohesion' nodes. In addition, a commitment was made to work toward a common, truly European citizenship, which is important in fostering free movement of persons within the EU and to obtain the active and passive right to vote in 'other countries'—for now only in municipal elections. Furthermore, it was agreed, albeit rather vaguely, to strengthen social policies so as to foster a greater degree of harmonization than had earlier been the case, and in particular to elaborate on the social charter endorsed in 1989 (Abraham, 1994; Addison and Siebert, 1993; Pelkmans and Egenhofer, 1993). Finally, it opened the EU to enlargement negotiations with the EFTA candidates, as other claimants were adjudicated not yet to be ready, the moment the Commission succeeded in streamlining its budget situation for the coming seven years—the essence of the so-called Delors II proposals (Franzmeyer, 1993, p. 359)—which was accomplished at the Edinburgh Council in December 1992. Recall that this fixed the upper limit of the EU's common budget for the period through 1999 at 1.27 percent of the group's combined gross national product (GNP). It also reached agreement, after protracted haggling in the unavoidable political tug-of-war, on the broad composition of revenues and outlays, especially for CAP and structural funds (see Thomas, 1994) applicable for the period through 1999.

Disagreements about the TEU

Although the TEU had been prepared with some care, buoyed by the concerns about the momentous changes taking place on the European continent and the SEM's apparent success, by the time it was to have been solemnly endorsed at the Maastricht Council in December 1991, which closed the two IGCs, squabbling had begun among the key players, with Great Britain in the lead. After assuaging Britain's concerns about the declared intentions for social policy in the EU's context by offering it an 'opt-out,' smooth sailing seemed to be at hand. But the Danish voter threw a spanner in the works of ratification. Knock-on effects bolstered opposition by the broader European electorate, concerned over the nation and the individual in a wider, more organized Europe; and groups that felt they would be disadvantaged by the Maastricht Treaty, such as the French farmer, even though the CAP was not part of the new provisions.[5] But there were many other interest groups lobbying actively against the TEU, as I discuss in some detail below, for reasons that find their origin in particular in the political economy of EU-type integration.

And so, ratification of the Maastricht Treaty ran into unexpected obstacles, beginning with the Danish rejection in June 1992 and ending with its weak endorsement by several other members, notably France, Germany, and the United Kingdom (U.K.). That Danish vote was subsequently reversed but only after important treaty concessions had been introduced as regards participation in monetary union. Ambivalence toward the Maastricht process began to complicate moving ahead with other EU endeavors. This was further compounded by the fact that around ratification time western Europe was descending into its deepest and most protracted economic recession of the postwar period. It turned out to be convenient to blame many elements of the syndrome of recession on EU integration in general and the Maastricht Treaty in particular, even though, as already pointed out, the connection was remote at best. Western Europe's earlier approach to remaking the European continent had clearly become inadequate in order to proceed with constructive deepening and widening.

By then, of course, the debacle of German unification and of the way in which the huge transfers from west to east were being financed, with their adverse repercussions on currency and money markets throughout the EU and beyond, had become clearer. The economic recession in Europe intensified, entailing a rapid rise in unemployment to levels not seen in the postwar period. A wave of anti-foreigner sentiment, including political movements, swept through segments of France and Germany in particular, and soured part of the 'pro-Europe mood' of the late 1980s. EU-related policy constraints found in the Maastricht Treaty stipulations provided a convenient scapegoat for attributing causes to a variety of national ills and constraints arising from international obligations, including those then under negotiation in the context of the Uruguay Round. This affected in particular liberalization of trade in agriculture for which major adjustments in the CAP were required quite apart from the fact that CAP reform was, and remains, needed in order to stave off EU bankruptcy.

Whereas policy makers had been in the forefront of the debates on accelerating European unification in the preceding years, they now felt compelled to hone their domestic electoral attractiveness. They opted for this avenue even if at the cost of backtracking on earlier commitments to Europe and indeed by adopting rather fuzzy stances in matters of vital concern to the process of further unification that they had been instrumental in nursing along. The inevitable delay in preparing the imminent IGC96, in overloading the matters tabled for that meeting, in procrastinating with the elaboration of a transparent negotiation agenda supported by national policy makers, and in obfuscating national policy stances more generally stemmed only in part from this reversal in popular mood, as I detail in chapter 4.

There was little doubt in 1991-1992 that the public at large, even its educated layers, was badly informed about the thrusts of the Maastricht Treaty, the intentions that may have been propping up the visible veneer, and the further course of European unification. The allegedly pernicious intentions embedded in the Treaty soon portrayed in the media and bandied around by a variety of sectoral interest groups were fundamentally wrong in fact and seriously misguided in spirit. Unfortunately, little was done by the European institutions themselves to clarify the issues at stake for the broader public. The Commission had stood aside for much of the negotiations and aspirations of Maastricht, in marked contrast to the activist manner in which it had flexed its muscle in the preparations of the SEA and SEM. Perhaps because of the bruises sustained in the process, the Commission apparently did not feel inspired or compelled to take to heart the opportunity of the TEU, and the then rising electoral and popular concerns about regional integration, in order to strengthen the *acquis*.

In addition, many objections were raised to the supposedly autocratic manner in which EU affairs touching more and more upon the lives of the common citizen were being decided without consulting the electorate and their direct representatives, although it was often conveniently forgotten that little by way of EU strategy and actions can be applied, as distinct from germinate, without obtaining prior approval from the European Council or the appropriate ministerial Council. Hence the emergence of the debate on the so-called 'democratic deficit' in Europe and how it could best be remedied, particularly in moving toward the crucial IGC96.

Especially the deep and protracted recession of the early 1990s, and in particular the rapidly rising levels of unemployment and popular disenchantment about government in general and integration in particular, gave rise to another round of concerns about the wisdom of EU integration. The debates around ratifying the TEU soon became captive of sectional interests, especially in their attacks on the welfare state. True, the latter's domestic financial-support base and economic rationale had become unsustainable, thus creating awkward electoral conditions. Though that arose primarily for domestic policy reasons, it proved convenient to blame the TEU, EMU commitments, and the EU's deepening process more generally for tightening constraints on welfare provisions. It also became difficult to dispel the widespread belief that the processes enshrined in the Maastricht Treaty in general and EMU in particular were responsible for a whole range of domestic political ills in members (such as constraints on pension funds, stark levels of unemployment, or modifications in CAP) that had no bearing whatsoever on the integration process, including on the scheduled transition to monetary integration.

Furthermore, the earlier approach toward EPU proved ineffective for several reasons: the political and economic changes in eastern Europe, including German reunification; the unraveling of the European Monetary System (EMS) in 1992-1993 followed by the 'retreat' of some members to the earlier 'core' of monetary cooperation but with a redesigned exchange-rate mechanism (ERM); and the governance issues around the redistribution of votes and revision in majority-voting procedures that complicated the negotiations over the fourth enlargement with Austria, Finland, Norway (where the electorate subsequently rejected the deal), and Sweden. In and of itself this fourth enlargement added several important topics to the IGC96's agenda (European Commission, 1995, pp. 13-15), making a successful outcome so much more difficult to achieve, yet at the same time so much more crucial for Europe's future, as I underline in chapter 4.

On top of all this, evolving economic, political, and social events since the TEU's endorsement in late 1991 interfered with getting the Treaty ratified in anything like an orderly manner. They also made it more cumbersome to mobilize support for working toward feasible solutions for the many obstacles to 'deepening' that had been left dangling in order to get the TEU rapidly agreed upon in the first place, as examined in detail in chapter 4. Four important circumstances deserve to be cited. First, the foreign-exchange crises of 1992 and 1993 profoundly shook beliefs and undermined confidence in the process of moving gradually toward monetary union. Second, the severe recession was accompanied by substantial unemployment whose magnitude even during the subsequent upturn did not appreciably decline either in relative or absolute numbers. As a result, opposition to subordinating national priorities, notably on unemployment and social-welfare provisions, to regional objectives rose substantially in many countries. Third, the wave of disappointments led to a new kind of europessimism coupled with concerns about democracy, efficiency, subsidiarity, transparency, and accountability in the workings of the EU institutions and the comportment of policy makers and eurocrats alike. Finally, expectations regarding the swift completion of the 'turnaround' in the eastern part of Europe with vibrant market-based economies anchored to pluralistic political institutions were being frustrated, heightening anxieties and complicating the process of rapprochement with the TEs. This attitude continues to encumber the projected fifth enlargement of the EU in some important instances. It also impedes the elaboration of a coherent strategic vision of the relationship between the EU and all of the TEs (Brabant, 1996b).

Conclusions

I have attempted to sketch the broader context for integration as basic backdrop for grasping many aspects of the manner in which TE policy makers sought to galvanize support for their rapprochement with the EU and the way in which western European policy makers dealt with this overture in some fashion, almost from the moment the ice in Hungary and Poland rapidly crumbled in mid-1989. These contours certainly set the remit for negotiations on concrete agreements between the EU and TEs. They are also important in innovating ways and means of assisting these countries while safeguarding the EU's interests as an evolving union with several member states having special 'interests' in ongoing TE events. And they remain paramount in spurring on the EU to formulate its own vision of the remaking of Europe for which it would inevitably, even if only implicitly, be held responsible. Particularly the latter remains a major policy task even after nearly a decade of EU involvement throughout the TEs.

The topics touched upon in this chapter, I trust, help to clarify, even if only in broad brush strokes, the complexities of moving forward with EU integration in general while engineering another enlargement, this time toward the eastern part of Europe, in particular. Facile approaches to castigating EU leaders for not having seized the opportunity of the 'eastern' opening almost from the transitions' inception are simply misplaced. True, the EU can be blamed for many errors and shortcomings in its approaches to dealing with the TEs' unprecedented *problématique*. It could, however, never have sustained its own momentum and preserved the core of its reasons for being, as these emanated from the Rome and Maastricht Treaties, and are now enshrined in the Amsterdam Treaty, while accelerating in a hasty manner premature TE accessions.

Early accession would most likely have had a positive political resonance in the eastern part of Europe, if only because it would have honored the call for the "return to Europe" voiced so stridently by top-level policy makers. However, in terms of the economic and many political advantages of EU membership, such an ill-advised fifth enlargement at an early stage would in all likelihood have been detrimental to the TEs' interests. Indeed, it might have set back the transformation process in more than one respect, relegating the eastern part of Europe to its historical status of 'borderland' of the more or less vibrant western European economies. Such an outcome would amount to an unprecedented tragedy. It should therefore be assiduously avoided. While matters have changed in many respects since 1989, targeting widening without carefully heeding the needs for deepening is bound to yield results that differ in many respects from the parameters that should ideally be respected in remaking Europe. The many issues that arise in trying to blend deepening with widening are the subject of chapter 4.

Notes

This chapter presents a much expanded and updated version of the first part of Brabant, 1998c.

1. But I categorically reject the views of those who want to earmark all available integration energies at the political level to eastward enlargement or to buttressing more generally the export of western Europe's liberal order to the TEs (as in Garton Ash, 1998).

2. A Council of Ministers can be constituted for deliberations about a wide range of transnational topics, such as economic and financial, social, foreign, transportation, agriculture, and environmental affairs. Their meetings are prepared by Coreper (*Comité des Représentants Permanents*), which for many years was arguable the most powerful institution in Brussels.

3. Earlier efforts occurred around 1962, 1970, and 1979.

4. Prior to the Amsterdam Treaty, some treated the social agenda as part and parcel of pillar 3, that is, juridical and home affairs. Now with the full integration of the social agenda in the revised Amsterdam Treaty (see chapter 4), some consider it more appropriate

to include it with pillar 1, inasmuch as they deem the social agenda essentially to be a vehicle to avoid distorting market competition by adhering to different social precepts in treating labor in particular. Some of the ambitions of the social agenda reach far beyond this restricted arena, however. I therefore argue for making it eventually into a separate pillar.

5. As distinct from the then ongoing Uruguay Round negotiations and the concurrent Ray MacSharry CAP reform undertakings. It is unfortunate that the Uruguay Round could not be concluded, as originally foreseen, by the end of December 1990 precisely because of strong disagreements in the international community in general, and the EU in particular, on how best to further liberalize trade in agricultural products and services. The MacSharry reform was a prelude to concluding the Round in 1993. But both sets of issues weighed heavily on the endorsement of the TEU, as described.

Chapter 3

Conditions for EU Entry—The TEs

Marie Lavigne

From among the ten TEs that are considered to have the best chance to enter the EU in the foreseeable future, five "fast-track" countries (the TE-5) actually started formal accession negotiations at the end of March 1998. This in itself is an achievement. Indeed, though initially the EU was not at all enthusiastic about committing itself to embarking upon yet another enlargement, it recognized very early on the inevitability of the process, and moved to define a pre-accession strategy in several steps.

The European Council held in Copenhagen (June 1993) decided that TEs with an EA could request accession in a credible manner. Its success would depend on the candidate meeting several conditions, but no timetable at all was then entertained. The Copenhagen conditions, though very general, still remain the only comprehensive statement by the EU on the criteria for admitting applicants to the negotiation table. The Essen Council of December 1994 made a decisive step forward by calling for the elaboration of a pre-accession strategy. The strategy was to focus on the preparation for integration of the relevant TEs first and foremost into the EU's internal market, which was seen as "the key element in the strategy to narrow the gap" between the applicants and the EU. For the first time, the then six TEs with an EA (Bulgaria, the Czech Republic, Hungary, Poland, Romania, and Slovakia), even though not all had been ratified, were invited to observe official EU deliberations.

Following the Council's decisions, the Commission was invited to draft a White Paper[1] (European Commission, 1995b) on preparing the TEs with an EA for integration into the SEM. This was approved at the Cannes Council in June 1995. In addition, the Essen Council decided to launch a "multilateral structured dialogue," which would bring together all of the associates with all EU members to discuss some specific matters of common interest. However, this did not at all signal that the pre-accession process would be conducted collectively. Indeed, the EU has always harbored an implicit preference for case-by-case negotiations over a protracted period of time, and the meetings in the framework of the structured dialogue have remained formal.

In 1995, the main concerns of the EU members were twofold: (1) the agenda of the impending IGC96 meant to reform the EU institutions, as called for in the Maastricht Treaty; and (2) the timetable of the introduction of a single currency and moving toward monetary union (see chapter 2). These issues were the subject of several European Councils, pushing the concerns about enlargement in the background. At the Madrid Council (December 1995), the start of IGC96 was set for March 1996. It was then decided that the negotiations with the applicants (including at the time Cyprus and Malta) would begin at least six months after "successfully finalizing" the IGC. By that time seven TEs had officially applied for membership (the Czech Republic, Estonia, Hungary, Latvia, Poland, Romania, and Slovakia) while the three other TEs with an EA (Bulgaria, Lithuania, and Slovenia) were preparing their applications. In July 1997, despite the fact that the IGC had been concluded at the Amsterdam Council Summit in June without having "successfully finalized" even the institutional requirements for further enlargement (see chapter 4), the European Commission suggested to open negotiations in the beginning of 1998 with the TE-5 as well as Cyprus with a view to their eventual entry into the EU, sometime at the beginning of the new century. While there was broad agreement on the three Visegrád countries (Czech Republic, Hungary, and Poland, with Slovakia having been left out because it did not meet some political criteria), many observers felt that Estonia and Slovenia had been selected in spite of the fact that the Commission acknowledged the need for these countries to make headway with many major economic reforms.

One may well question why the Commission, and later the Council, endorsed only five TEs for fast-track accession negotiations. The other five TE applicants share the same ultimate aims, they apply the same policy instruments with greater or lesser consistency, and will be accepted for full-fledged negotiations as soon as their reform policies exhibit better results. There is much resentment among these five countries about their having been relegated to a "second circle." There is also a widespread feeling that the TE-5 have been privileged because the EU in its present format, due to IGC96's de facto failure, is not manageable with more than twenty members.

The structure of the chapter is as follows. After a discussion of the conditions to be met by the applicants, I turn to the so-called "Maastricht convergence criteria" if only because of the controversy surrounding them for they are not criteria for EU membership. The next section deals with the pressure exerted on the applicant countries in order to promote more cooperation among them, with a discussion of the past and future of the Central European Free Trade Agreement (CEFTA). Thereafter I examine how the European Commission checks the degree of implementation of the conditions and how the negotiation process may lead to some derogations from the *acquis* (see chapter 1). Finally, I gauge how close the applicants are to what may be defined as the 'ideal' new member from the incumbents' point of view.

The Formal Conditions for Accession

The basic conditions for accession follow not only from the Treaty of Rome, the SEA promulgated in 1986, and the Maastricht and Amsterdam Treaties, but also from the EU's other legal acts and the practices followed in earlier enlargements. The European Councils at Copenhagen and Essen restated the formal conditions for admission into the EU as follows: (1) any European country may apply for accession (art. 237 of the Treaty of Rome); (2) the applicant must be a stable pluralist democracy, which requires at least the existence of independent political parties and periodic elections, and be committed to the rule of law, to the respect for human rights, and to the protection of minorities; (3) the applicant must have a functioning market economy; (4) it must have the capacity to cope with competitive pressures and market forces within the EU, especially the circumscribed SEM; and (5) it must endorse the objective of economic, monetary, and political union and be able to assume the obligations of membership, in particular the stipulations of the *acquis*.

These conditions are so broad that they may be considered as met by and large and, at the same time, as unattainable in full for many years to come. It is impossible to spell out precise criteria for assessing compliance with the political conditions, such as "respect for human rights" or "protection of minorities." In fact, explicit reference to political conditionality is a novelty in EU practice for it has never before been a specific matter of concern in any of the four earlier enlargements, though of course the political context was present in the accessions of Greece, Portugal, and Spain. But in all these cases the end of a dictatorial regime was considered as irreversible, and the legacies of such a regime as subject to eradication in a short time span. This kind of political conditionality was first made explicit in 1993, when the EAs for Bulgaria and Romania were concluded. Unlike the earlier EAs, the latter two, and soon thereafter the renegotiated ones for the Czech Republic and Slovakia, following the breakup of Czechoslovakia, incorporated a clause explicitly mentioning "respect for democratic principles and human rights, and the principles of the market economy" (Laursen and Riishøj,

1996). Needless to say, especially the Czech Republic was at the time very apprehensive about signing off on such 'onerous stipulations,' as invoked for Bulgaria and Romania, but it reluctantly accepted the formula at the time just the same (Nyssen, 1996).

The condition linked to "the existence of a functioning market economy" cannot be assessed in measurable terms. It is subject to subjective judgment, involving potentially the whole range of the transformation process. All countries under review are true market economies as far as the liberalization of prices and trade is concerned, including currency convertibility for current transactions and in many cases for capital transactions. A functioning market economy also implies, according to the EU Commission (European Commission, 1997h, Vol. 1), that there is a consensus over the principles of economic policy and that macroeconomic stabilization has by and large been achieved.

But "the market environment" has to date not been fully achieved in any TE applicant. Privatization remains incomplete and the rules for corporate governance are not clearly established. The two-tier banking system is in place but the indebtedness of state-owned enterprises (SOEs) is not yet under control, and will not be until bankruptcy procedures are effectively applied on a large scale. The tax system has moved closer to the western format with the introduction of the value-added and of a standard income tax. But the comprehensive reform of the fiscal system is yet to be completed, in particular so as to introduce more clarity in the subsidy procedures and to strengthen revenue mobilization. Capital markets are indeed operating and have been booming, but their base remains shallow, and dramatic collapses have happened, as in Poland in the beginning of 1994 and in the Czech Republic in the spring of 1997, even well before the several shocks of the Asian and Russian crises in 1997-1998.

The capacity to cope with the EU's competitive pressures and market forces is, again, a very unclear concept. Everything that might enhance competitiveness comes, in principle, under this heading. This may include measures or situations otherwise contrary to other requirements for accession, such as low environmental standards or inadequate safety and health protection in the workplace. The TEs' main economic strength at this stage is low labor costs, although these have gradually been rising due to wage drift, including because of the real appreciation of the national currencies (see chapter 5). One might assume that this particular condition implies that competitiveness should not be enhanced, for example, through competitive devaluations. It has also been stressed that the ability to cope with market forces requires that the candidate possess a rather broad industrial base, and that a concentration of activities and exports in a small number of sectors, especially sensitive ones, as is the case for TEs, may make it more difficult to fulfill this requirement (Daviddi and Ilzkovitz, 1997). This condition may also require that sufficient progress toward privatization and demonopolization has been achieved.

The EU Commission has not really clarified the meaning of "coping with competitive pressures and market forces" (European Commission, 1997h, Vol. 1). It recommends taking into consideration several factors, such as "the existence of a functioning market economy" (which would suggest that above-cited condition 3 encompasses condition 4!), the availability of infrastructural capacities (in transport, telecommunications, and R&D), the role of the state in promoting competition, the degree of trade integration with incumbent EU members (measured through the volume and the composition of trade), and the share of small and medium-size enterprises (SMEs) in industrial activities. Curiously enough, in the discussion of this third condition the Commission mentions the fact that wages are still much lower than the average EU level, which is precisely a factor allowing the TEs to sustain "competitive pressures" within the EU!

The present enlargement process is in many ways more demanding than any of the earlier ones, which suggests that it is not "just another accession" (Eatwell et al., 1997). Daviddi and Ilzkovitz (1997, p. 21) stress, for example, that the new members will not be allowed to opt out of monetary union or the social chapter, which is now integral to the EU's constitutional acts—the social agenda forms a separate chapter of the Amsterdam Treaty. Political conditions were not so explicit in previous accessions, even for Greece, Portugal, and Spain. There is a danger that the whole process may turn "into a one-sided dictate that the applicants are obliged to accept" (Ellman, 1997, p. 2).

Even the TE-5 have to do better in fields specified by the Commission in July 1997, as expressed in the Commission's "opinion" (its so-called *avis*) on the applications made public in the annexes of its *Agenda 2000* (European Commission, 1997h, Vol. 2; *Financial Times*, 17 July 1997). The Czech Republic has been asked to improve corporate governance and to reform its banking and financial sectors; it should also do better on human rights as far as its policy vis-à-vis the Roma minority is concerned. Poland should fight corruption and go further with its structural reform, particularly in banking and in agriculture. Hungary has to book progress with reforming social security and to improve the treatment of the Roma. Slovenia has to complete enterprise restructuring, transform the financial sector, and fight corruption. Before the decision of the Commission was made, Slovenia had to change its constitution so as to permit foreigners to own real estate (*Financial Times*, 16 July 1997). Estonia has to improve its treatment of the Russian minority and to make progress with administrative reform.

The TEs scheduled for the second round of negotiations are understandably bitter. Slovakia has been 'sanctioned' basically for shortcomings on the political conditions, a situation substantially altered following the overturn of Mečiár's rule in September 1998. Bulgaria and Romania have been urged to move further along the reform path precisely at a time when their new governments were embarking on radical reform measures endorsed by the International Monetary Fund (IMF). Latvia and Lithuania feel discriminated against, and gain the sympathy of their Nordic partners on that score. These developments strengthen the conclusions of

Georges Mink and Gérard Wild (1996, p. 9) that there is "a kind of meritocratic logic in the integration mechanism," which "increases the role of emotional, psychosociological parameters in the very process of the negotiations."

To sum up, the applicants may have the impression that it is perfectly possible to decide first who is going to be admitted, and in what order, and second to grade the countries accordingly. Recent studies tend to confirm this subjective assessment. Researchers from a French state-owned bank have conducted a multivariate analysis of selected data so as to "objectivate" the Commission's selection, which leads them to conclude "that the Commission choice was appropriate in objective terms," especially as far as the potential ability to achieve viable integration (and not just the present capacity) of each of the applicants was concerned. The cited study reaches a second conclusion: the potential ability to integrate may become self-fulfilling "for both the accepted and the rejected countries: the accepted countries may find it easier to obtain financing, while the rejected[2] countries may face a restriction in their access to finance and a widening of their gap with the accepted countries" (CDC, 1998). While the first conclusion may be challenged on account of the well-known weaknesses of factor analysis itself, the second is unfortunately quite relevant: the selection itself increases the opportunities and means of the selected countries, and decreases the opportunities of those left out, irrespective of the initial amounts of assistance provided in the pre-accession strategy to all applicants.

Convergence Criteria: Do They Matter?

The so-called Maastricht convergence criteria for admission to monetary union come under this heading. Contrary to the widespread view in both east and west, these are definitely not conditions for accession, but for reaching the stage at which EU members may enter monetary union (see art. 109j of the Maastricht Treaty). As a result it is irrelevant when some TEs, but especially the Czech Republic and Slovenia, claim that they already meet several convergence criteria better than some EU members, even if this statement were factually correct. Though inflation has stabilized but at a level well above that observed in the EU, the budget deficit, though not always below the 3 percent hurdle, is indeed much lower in the Czech Republic and in Slovenia than on average in the EU (in 1997). The criterion related to the share of public debt in gross domestic product (GDP) also seems met. But though the purely statistical criteria of nominal convergence may have been satisfied, real convergence in the sense of the appropriate functioning of monetary, financial, budgetary, and exchange-rate mechanisms (see chapter 6), is far from complete at this stage (OFCE, 1996, pp. 19, 146). Not only that, it is in fact impossible to assess the extent of compliance of the TEs with the convergence criteria since the TEs' statistical procedures are by far not yet harmonized with EU practices, if appropriate measures of the nominal variables for convergence exist at all.

The latter is not a trivial matter. Consider, for example, the fact that in many TEs statistics on public debt are not consistent with those required by the EU for assessing the Maastricht criteria. Not only that, the consolidation of the debt of SOEs and banks is not yet over, and its impact on public debt is as yet unclear. Also on budget deficits matters are not clear: should privatization revenues really be included in budget revenues? Moreover, in several TEs the government budget is not the consolidated one (that is, of central, regional, and local governments as well as social security expenditures). Also in countries where privatization is not advanced many SOEs continue to provide social benefits that may eventually encumber the government budget. Furthermore, since capital markets in TEs are inchoate at best, which interest rates could best be used? In other words, even though the Maastricht convergence criteria may not be very relevant to the TEs, improving on eventually being considered in that light definitely is one of the implicit criteria.

Countries acceding to the EU from 1999 on, after the inauguration of monetary union, will be treated under a different, derogatory regime (art. 109k of the Maastricht Treaty). In principle, all EU incumbents are expected to join monetary union sooner or later, even those that did not qualify, such as Greece, or for their own reasons chose not to join early on (Denmark, Sweden, and the United Kingdom). These so-called "pre-ins" in EU parlance will be joined by the TE-5 as soon as the latter are admitted into the EU. The "pre-ins," according to decisions reached at the Dublin (December 1996) and Amsterdam (June 1997) Councils, will be included, if they so choose, in ERM II. This entails fixed but adjustable exchange rates with a central parity to the euro and a more or less wide fluctuation band of up to 15 percent on either side of parity.

The ERM II regime is very attractive. The "pre-ins" will be able to choose whether they want to enter ERM II, and in this case accept coordination and surveillance of their monetary policy by the ECB, or stay out of it, at least for some time, and retain more flexibility. But they will be expected to adopt the *acquis* of the euro zone regarding their monetary policy and will have to treat their exchange-rate policy as a matter of common interest. Not only that, they will eventually be held to the cited convergence measures. In particular, they should avoid excessive fluctuations of their exchange rate, such as sudden devaluations. The question thus arises whether they will be allowed to resort to a last and large devaluation just before joining ERM II (see chapter 5).

While staying out of ERM II may offer a 'free rider' option with some advantages, inasmuch as it allows the nonparticipant to benefit from the constraints that membership in the EU's monetary union or in ERM II otherwise imposes on its partners, participation in ERM II can also exert positive effects. It might bolster policy credibility for participants, smaller risk premia in their international borrowing, and make FDI in these countries more attractive. In any case, the TEs will soon engage in euro-denominated transactions, even before becoming "pre-ins," if only because of the volume of their trade with the euro zone; the management of investment and debt portfolios; and the use of the euro by global companies with subsidiaries in TEs (European Commission, 1998h, pp. 17-18, 29, 135).

Even prior to joining the EU, from the moment the euro replaces the national currencies in the members of the monetary union, the TEs will have to make choices regarding their exchange-rate regime. Those whose currency is pegged explicitly or implicitly to the German mark, which applies to most TEs, will have to replace this anchor, and logically might want to shift to the euro. Exchange-rate regimes will have to be modified for countries with a floating rate (Romania) or for countries with pre-announced crawling pegs (Hungary and Poland) when they join ERM II. The choice of the right exchange rate will then depend upon expectations regarding the prospective equilibrium exchange rate, and its evolution, of the euro against other major currencies (see chapter 5).

More generally, the economic policy of the candidates for accession is likely to be constrained by the prospects of eventual entry into the EU's monetary union. Indeed, the requirements of this membership are in line with the stringent macroeconomic policies either imposed by the IMF or self-imposed in most TEs. The 1995 White Paper unambiguously states: "sound macroeconomic policies are essential to the success of the reform and of the pre-accession strategy [...] The immediate requirement is to adjust the sequence and pace of legislative approximation in each associated country so that it reinforces economic reform" (European Commission, 1995b, Vol. 1, p. 5).

Thus, though the convergence criteria or their underlying policies are not pre-accession conditions, the legislative framework that is crucial for implementing such policies has to be heeded. More important is that these criteria belong to a monetarist philosophy more or less enthusiastically endorsed by the TE governments and built into the stabilization programs in force. As already stated, in *Agenda 2000* the European Commission insists upon macroeconomic stabilization as a component of a functioning market economy (European Commission, 1997h, Vol. 1). In the various *avis* on the situation of the applicants, the Commission always mentions the state of affairs as regards inflation, budget balance, or the external account, not as explicit conditions tied to a quantitative benchmark, but as a part of the general picture (European Commission, 1997h, Vol. 2). In other words, such "nonconditions" may be quite compelling in the negotiations.

The Pressure for Regional Cooperation

While one may consider the Maastricht nominal-convergence criteria as implicit or perhaps eventually applicable, it is not so easy to assess the attitudes of the EU toward cooperation among the associated countries themselves. At the transition's inception, the demise of the CMEA was hailed as a positive departure from the previous regime of international economic relations tying Eastern Europe to the Soviet Union. At the transition's inception, the TEs felt that the European Commission was pressing them to constitute some regional grouping as a way of delaying any discussion about future EU membership. Later, once the principle of membership was acknowledged, bolstering regional cooperation was seen as an implicit condition to any move toward more concrete steps on the way to accession negotiations. The moves toward greater cooperation developed in two directions. The first one was the constitution and strengthening of the so-called Visegrád group. The second direction was taken following the Essen Council meeting (1994) in the wake of the Pact for Stability.[3]

The Visegrád agreement was signed in February 1991 among Czechoslovakia, Hungary, and Poland. The Final Declaration recommended free movement of capital and labor to be promoted by the development of market-based economic cooperation and cooperation in infrastructure development, as well as in ecology. But no explicit mechanism or regulations were adopted to ensure that the goal be met. Following the signing of the first EAs in December 1991, which established a free-trade area between each central European country and the then EC, the Visegrád group negotiated the CEFTA, which envisaged the creation of a free-trade area, in December 1992. In September 1995 CEFTA members (by then four on account of the dissolution of Czechoslovakia) decided that new members could join provided they were members of the General Agreement on Tariffs and Trade (GATT), and more recently of the World Trade Organization (WTO), and had signed an EA with the EU (Richter, 1997). Slovenia was admitted in 1996, Romania in 1997, and Bulgaria in July 1998[4]; the Baltic states and Ukraine have expressed an interest in joining CEFTA even though they are not yet in WTO[5] and Ukraine is unlikely to obtain an EA any time soon.

While the share of the CEFTA trade of its members has slightly increased since 1993, it remains very small as compared to the share of its members' trade with the west (Hrnčíř, 1997, p. 97). In 1997, the share of intraregional trade in total trade of the CEFTA members had dropped back to its 1994 level, at 14 and 10.5 percent for exports and imports, respectively (UNECE, 1997c, p. 52). Few observers recommend strengthening CEFTA with a view to reviving mutual trade, and those who do favor a customs union among the CEFTA members argue that such a move may reduce the delays in the process of accession to the EU (UNECE, 1996); in other words, the 'implicit condition' crops up again.

What is the future of CEFTA once integration of the TE-5 into the EU will have been achieved? Few studies have been devoted to the issue. Matejka (1998) shows how the selection of the five 'fast-track' countries will cut CEFTA in two parts as Bulgaria, Romania, and Slovakia are left out. Slovakia will in addition be affected by the ending of its customs union with the Czech Republic. The CEFTA members once admitted to the EU will have to renounce the agreement and conduct relations with their former partners on the basis of the EA concluded between the EU and each non-EU member. This new status will, inter alia, jeopardize some of the exports from Bulgaria, Romania, and Slovakia to the TE-5, especially for agricultural goods and other sensitive products. The same outcome is expected in the case of the Baltic Free Trade Agreement (BFTA), which was signed in September 1993, for the relations between Estonia, which belongs to the TE-5, and its two Baltic neighbors, Latvia and Lithuania.

True, in discussing the impact of enlargement on the EU policies the European Commission has stated in *Agenda 2000* that when the applicant has special arrangements with third countries at the time of accession, the required adjustments should not harm these third countries (European Commission, 1997h, Vol. 2), and thus some accommodation can be reckoned with (see chapter 9). Also, the EU should take into account the needs of the latter when adjusting its remaining quantitative restrictions once new members have joined. All these provisions are, however, expressed in very vague terms. Thus the process of regional cooperation that has been encouraged by the EU in central and eastern Europe in the beginning of the 1990s seems severely impaired by the selective enlargement process.

CEFTA has not so far been able to achieve coordination among its members. But this will in the end be realized through the accession process itself. The European Commission is requiring all TEs in the pre-accession process to adopt similar regulations in the framework of the *acquis*, and similar policies in fighting corruption and crime, protecting the environment, building a sustainable social safety net, and improving corporate governance.

The EU has also sought to promote regional cooperation in noneconomic fields on its own initiative. The Essen European Council launched the Pact for Stability in 1994 (initially a French idea) to deal with border problems and difficulties linked with the status of minorities. A few agreements followed, namely, between Hungary and Slovakia and between Hungary and Romania. In March 1995, the Pact for Stability was handed over to the OSCE. In this field the aim of the EU was less to prepare the applicant countries to work together than to settle existing disputes among future members prior to accession.

Verifying Compliance with Accession Conditions

Measuring the degree of compliance with the accession conditions has been a very time consuming and bureaucratic process. What is first and foremost required from the applicants is that they take over all the *acquis* by the time of accession, and most have already taken steps to comply with major portions thereof. The 1995 White Paper does not affect the contractual relationship between the EU and TEs based on the EA. Nevertheless, though formally advisory, this document makes it clear that a great number of elements of the *acquis* need to be complied with early on, while others can be deferred to later stages, and lists first-order measures (stage I) and second-order ones (stage II). The list of the internal market *acquis,* though not exhaustive, is quite discouraging in its mere volume. The Annex to the White Paper detailing these measures comprises no less than 428 pages divided into twenty-three chapters. A crucial component of the White Paper is institution building. Not only does it require a legal framework but also internal political credibility: "The law must not only exist but it must also be applied and—above all—be expected to be applied" (European Commission, 1995b, Annex, p. 51). In addition, the *acquis* itself is bound to evolve in the years to come. As a result, the candidates are not just facing a fixed set of rules but a moving target as the scope and content of the rules undergo as yet unpredictable changes (Fayolle, 1996b, p. 22).

How many of the detailed European rules on the internal market do TEs have to implement for accession to be allowed to proceed? Given that these measures range from the tar content of cigarettes, animal welfare, or hot boilers, to such broad areas as the free movement of capital or the competition policy, what kind of weight should one attach to each?

In May 1996, the Commission submitted to the applicants a lengthy questionnaire, divided into twenty-three chapters (like the White Paper Annex), which had to be returned before the end of July 1996. All TEs complained about the short deadline, the frequent absurdity or irrelevancy of the questions, and the immense scope of the task, which implied that the minimum length of the completed exercise amounted to about 2,000 pages (Inotai, 1996, p. 80) and for many TEs a multiple thereof. Not only that, this process was followed "with new questions, answers and clarifications" (Inotai, 1997c, p. 204). Utilizing these replies as basis, the Commission formulated its *avis* on each application, including its recommendations. These were presented in July 1997 along with *Agenda 2000,* which contains, in addition to proposals for enlargement, estimates of the impact of enlargement on the reform of the CAP and on the structural funds, and recommendations on the level and structure of the EU's budget for the period 2000-2006.

Each of the ten *avis* is built around the Copenhagen criteria: political criteria, general economic criteria, ability to take on the obligations of membership, and administrative capacity to implement the *acquis.* In conclusion, the Commission recommends opening the negotiations as soon as possible or postponing them until the country has completed the requested changes. Slovakia is an interesting case: the Commission states that Slovakia almost satisfies the economic criteria and has taken important steps to implement the *acquis,* but is very deficient on the political criteria. Hence one may infer that once these deficiencies are suppressed, which should happen soon following the change of government in September 1998, Slovakia should qualify for fast opening of accession negotiations, once the next European Council issues the go-ahead on the basis of the Commission's annual review of the situation in the slow-track TEs.[6]

The Commission's proposals for enlargement were endorsed at the Luxembourg Council (December 1997). On 24 March 1998, the Commission approved the Association Partnership Agreement (APA) for each of the candidates (Figaro, 1998). These are a type of logbook for each applicant recording the areas requiring change. According to the decisions reached at the Essen Council, the PHARE assistance program[7] is now devoted to "help the associated countries to absorb the *acquis*" and to "complete market reforms and the medium-term restructuring of their economies and societies so as to create the conditions required for future membership" (Mayhew, 1998, p. 171). From the preliminary budgetary estimates for the period 2000 to 2006 (European Commission, 1997h, Vol. 1), it is already clear that the countries included in the first round of negotiations are to receive a larger share of the pre-accession financial assistance than the other five countries.

Bilateral negotiations for accession with the TE-5, following the ceremonial meetings of 30 and 31 March, were initiated in April 1998. The first stage, which is devoted to verifying compliance with the accession criteria, particularly with the *acquis* (what is called the screening phase), was initially scheduled for completion by end 1998. But that deadline is likely to be extended by at least six months, as has been first stated for Poland in June 1998 when the Commission decided to deprive Poland from €34 million earmarked for fourteen specific projects to be financed by PHARE funds (*Le Monde*, 16 June 1998). By the end of September 1998 only a third of the screening process was completed, and while the applicants wanted the negotiations to proceed on the chapters already screened (including telecommunications, industrial and audiovisual policies, and education and training), several EU members were pressing the Commission to delay the opening of formal negotiations in November until the screening was completed (*Financial Times*, 30 September 1998).

Will the prospective members of the EU request exemptions and be likely to obtain such derogations? In principle, there cannot be any exception from observing the *acquis* in practice. However, from earlier enlargements it is clear that "no country has ever been able to apply all the rules on the date of entry into the Union" (Nicolaides, 1998, p. 8). Spain got special assistance and a delay for adapting its steel industry. Austria, Finland, and Sweden obtained a consent whereby the EU adjusted its environmental, health, and safety standards to their own more stringent standards. In the past, most derogations were temporary, but the transition period itself was variously stretched out. The applicant may also ask for safeguard clauses instead of derogations, which means that the requested exemptions will be granted only if the need arises.

One potential problem at this stage is that the EU is conducting six parallel negotiations with the TE-5 and Cyprus, and faces the prospect of inaugurating up to six more if the other TEs were to be considered 'ripe' for accession negotiations in the annual assessments and Malta's reactivation request acted upon. As a result, the EU negotiators may be reluctant to accord concessions to one applicant for another might later request similar treatment (Nicolaides, 1998, p. 12). Already before the inception of the negotiations, Poland, which is the biggest applicant in a number of respects, asked for several waivers from the *acquis* in such areas as environmental protection, foreign investment in specific sectors, and sale of land in rural and border areas to EU citizens (*Financial Times*, 9 March 1998). Other TEs have tabled or expressed their intention to request various derogations. But the EU might be rather tough in granting derogations or exemptions, and might subject them to a longer "transition period" between accession and actual entry into force of all the provisions of the Amsterdam Treaty.

The experience so far with organizing the enlargement negotiations suggests that the EU remains reluctant, though resigned, to another expansion. The main problem is the EU's limited capacity to absorb new members (see chapter 4). Unlike the three new members admitted in January 1995 (Austria, Finland, and Sweden), the new applicants are poorer (in terms of the EU's average GDP) countries. Not only that, their current export potential may damage EU economies, in particular when it comes to agriculture and supporting the CAP and structural funds.

On the Actual and Desirable Profile of New EU Members

Given the above realities, one may well inquire into the 'desirable profile' of an applicant and how this compares with the 'actual profile.' The answer partly lies in the conditions discussed above: the EU wants countries that resemble the incumbent ones, that is, normal democracies and market economies that accept all the commitments already binding for the incumbents and conduct their macroeconomic policies without disturbing or damaging existing members. But a more complete answer can be formulated only by moving well beyond the official or implicit conditions for accession discussed earlier.

Among the implicit and tacit considerations that shape this desirable profile of a future new member, at least proximity, relative prosperity, a disciplined labor force, and a degree of competitive strength that will not harm EU interests matter.

Geography

One could endlessly discuss the borders of Europe. I assume that Europe's eastern borders stretch to encompass the ten TEs with a EA and pinpoint some of the special characteristics of this new European map.

Eastward expansion of the EU is logical by any geographical criterion. As IMF economists have put it: "How far is eastern Europe from Brussels?" (Fischer, Sahay, and Végh, 1998). The question is to be understood literally as well as figuratively. The TE-5 are closer to Brussels in distance than some EU members, distance being measured by the mileage from the capital of each country to Brussels. Indeed, "most are closer than Helsinki and Lisbon, and all are closer than Athens" (Fischer, Sahay, and Végh, 1998, p. 1).

Geography matters. This holds even more for geopolitics. When looking at a map and not just measuring physical distances, one sees that the eastward movement to the TEs now engaged in fast-track negotiations encompasses countries with a common border with the EU. The three Baltic countries should all have been included if only because that stretch of the territory's eastern border can be considered as the continuation of Poland's eastern frontier toward Finland. However, the hole between Estonia and Poland, shocking as this may be for the other Baltic countries, is much smaller than the gap between Germany and Greece in 1981. Estonia's entry, as was earlier the case for Greece, will be symbolic. For Greece it signaled the southeast limit to Europe, and hence it did not matter whether the selected country was exactly at the level expected from an applicant; likewise for delineating the northeast limit of Europe in the case of Estonia. The gap in the northeast will not be difficult to close in the coming years, once accession negotiations will start with the other five TEs. In the southeast, however, a gap will remain once Bulgaria, Romania, and Slovakia will be ushered onto the accession path, for five countries: Albania, Bosnia and Herzegovina, Croatia, Macedonia, and rump Yugoslavia. None has an EA and only one, Croatia, exhibits desirable macroeconomic achievements comparable to those attained to date by the TE-5; but its political vocation in the late 1990s has resembled Slovakia's, until September 1998 in the EU's eyes, that is. As long as many of these countries remain embroiled in civil unrest or armed conflict their 'European future' remains in doubt.

GDP Level and Growth Potential

There is no predetermined floor level for GDP per capita in order to accede to the EU. Ideally, the most suitable candidates are small rich countries, such as the three admitted in 1995. Being small, they do not destabilize the balance of votes in the governance organs (see chapter 2). Being richer than average, they do not claim large contributions from the EU. Even so, Austria obtained special funding for its Burgenland and Finland and Sweden for their arctic regions. These matters are quite different for nearly all TE applicants. They are much poorer than the incumbents. Though most are small countries, Poland is a large one as well as a poor country. Their potential voting rights will almost certainly disturb the existing balance of power in EU institutions.

The TE-5 display definite similarities (see table 3.1). True, their GNP per capita assessed at purchasing-power parity (PPP) ranges from $4,400 to over $10,000, with a weighted (according to population) average of $6,500. Even that is only 38 percent of the EU's average. It amounts to about half of the present four 'poor' EU members (Greece, Ireland, Portugal, and Spain). It is about 30 percent of the geographically closest (Austria) country's GNP per capita (Baldwin, Francois, and Portes, 1997, p. 130). Poland as the largest in size by population has the lowest GNP per capita after Estonia. But it is richer than any TE outside this group.

Table 3.1: Basic data of TE-5 and EU, 1995

Population (million)	GNP per capita (in $ PPP[a])	Share in value added			Exp./GDP (percent)
		agriculture	industry	services	
Czech Rep.	10.3	9770	6	39	55	50
Estonia	1.6	4220	8	28	64	78
Hungary	10.3	6410	8	33	59	35
Poland	38.6	5400	6	39	54	25
Slovenia	2.0	10594	3	38	59	59
TE-5[b]	**n.a.**	**6400**	**6**	**37**	**57**	**n.a.**
Greece	10.5	11710	16	31	53	29
Ireland	3.6	15680	8	34	66	67
Portugal	9.9	12670	6	36	58	33
Spain	39.2	14520	3	36	61	24
EU-4[b]	**n.a.**	**13740**	**6**	**35**	**59**	**n.a.**
Austria	8.1	21250	2	34	63	39
EU-15[b]	**n.a.**	**16200**	**4**	**31**	**65**	**n.a.**

Notes:
[a] Purchasing-power parity.
[b] Population-weighted average.
Sources: EBRD, 1997; Hrnčíř, 1997; UNECE, 1998; World Bank, 1997.

This is not the first time that the EU will admit new poorer members, however. In the past, it has done so very gradually, one or two countries at a time, with protracted time intervals between each round. Unlike the past, however, entry of the TE-5, let alone of other TEs, will have a massive impact unprecedented in the EU's history. The TE-5 have been recovering from the severe drop in output experienced since 1989-1991. But that applies also to the two Baltic countries not selected for the first round as well as Slovakia. Among the TE-10 only Bulgaria and Romania are still struggling with the consequences of the severe crisis.

The cost of the accession to the EU incumbents depends on the rate at which the TEs are catching up. Under present conditions, access to the bulk of structural funds depends on the share of countries or regions with a GDP per capita under 75 percent of the average EU level (see chapter 8). The estimates for catching up range from at least twenty years to several decades or more. The study by Fischer, Sahay, and Végh (1998) starts from the assumption, usual in the Bretton Woods institutions, that successful transition based on stabilization-*cum*-liberalization entails faster growth than in the slow-reforming countries. Once structural transformation is completed long-term growth may be forecast using models applicable to typical market economies—the models referred to in the study are neoclassical and endogenous-growth models with such variables as the investment rate, population growth rate, the share of government consumption in GDP, and magnitudes pertaining to human capital. With all caveats the authors estimate that the TE-5 and Slovakia will reach the average GDP per capita level of the three low-income EU countries (Greece, Portugal, and Spain) in fifteen to twenty-four years, while the other TEs will need up to thirty-four years, assuming average annual growth rates of 2 percent in the EU and 5 percent for the TEs. Let us just state that while in 1995 the rate of growth of the GDP in the TE-5 reached 5.8 percent, it dropped under 5 percent in 1996 and 1997, and most probably in 1998 as well (Rosati et al., 1998).

One may also question the very meaning of "catching-up." Quantitative estimates focus on the number of years needed to reach a given GDP per capita. This is relevant to one major concern of the EU incumbent—the size of structural funds needed for the applicants. But these estimates do not tell anything about other features of the applicants' economies. Will the tensions on the labor market be reduced? Will the competitiveness of these countries be enhanced by a higher rate of growth? Will growth entail changes in industrial structure? Standard models do not offer answers to these questions.

Labor Force

A condition that is not included in any list but is very much on the minds of EU policy makers is that the unemployed in TEs should not take advantage of the accession process to migrate to the west. By far the bulk of the provisions in EAs apply to trade in goods, workers being considered only under exceptional conditions. As L. Alan Winters (1992, p. 23) rightly observed, "little as the [EU] desires [goods from Czechoslovakia, Hungary, and Poland], it desires their workers even less." True, both parties granted each other national treatment in terms of establishment rights. However, exceptions were possible for up to ten years. Manpower movements are considered as a matter of national legislation. Hence the principle of nondiscrimination only applied to the workers already legally employed in the EU. No new facilities were granted, and the legal rules were defined exclusively by each member state. In fact the immigration laws are increasingly more restrictive throughout the EU. Westward movement of TE workers other than the highly qualified is bound to meet with growing resistance on the part of the incumbents, the 'front states' in particular.

The enlargement process has carefully postponed decision on this issue. It is remarkable, in this respect, that of the four freedoms of the internal market only three are relevant in the pre-accession strategy. The fourth one, the free movement of workers, has been explicitly excluded. The 1995 White Paper mentions that "this part of the Community 'acquis' cannot be considered as part of the present exercise of progressive alignment, although its importance for the establishment of the internal market after accession is beyond doubt" (European Commission, 1995b, Vol.1, p. 13). This wariness initially mirrored western concerns that the transition would immediately fuel massive westward migration. These fears now appear to have been largely exaggerated, especially in light of migration pressures originating from other regions of the world.

It is very difficult to estimate the actual or future flows of migrants. Past flows do not provide any clue as the right to leave under communism was severely restricted, and strictly regulated for some categories of the population, such as Jews. Some early estimates take into account specific factors influencing migration, such as the present economic situation and the prospects for economic recovery in individual countries (UNECE, 1992, 1997b). Though no estimates of potential flows are offered, such studies suggest that migration from TEs has on the whole been much smaller than had earlier been anticipated.

Actual figures show that for the period 1990-1995 net westward migration, mainly from Poland and Romania, the two largest TEs other than the successor states of the Soviet Union, amounted to 950,000 people (Chesnais, 1997, pp. 252-53). A new concern is migration from the successor states of the Soviet Union, however. Poland is especially vulnerable as it has a long border (some 1,300 km or 800 miles) with these states. The European Commission has been prodding Poland to harden its entry requirements for citizens from border countries, but it is very reluctant to do so, fearing retaliation against Polish minorities in these states (*Le Monde*, 3 January 1998). This too may be seen as a new, incidental condition. The issue will be more critical when the five second-round TEs will be negotiating for accession since all have a common border with the western successor states of the Soviet Union.

Unemployment and the bleak prospect for being reemployed at home offers an incentive for emigration. The relative pace of unemployment in TEs has stabilized at rates similar to those in the EU, roughly at low double-digit levels, except for the comparative 'anomaly' of the Czech Republic, where unemployment has remained surprisingly at less than half the levels observed in other TEs.

EU members are also concerned about the political and social impacts of overly large discrepancies in levels of living as compared to those prevailing in TEs. Economic theory suggests that trade, especially exports of labor-intensive goods, may be a substitute for migration; similarly for FDI, which in principle can absorb cheap labor resources in TEs, though low wages are only one factor among the motivations for foreign investors to relocate their activities from one site to another. But there are strong obstacles to a surge of labor-intensive exports as such goods belong to the so-called sensitive sectors in EU countries. In addition, there is competition from the developing countries to be factored into the equation.

How are these issues to be solved during the accession process? A major difficulty is the fuzziness with which the basic EU documents deal with the matters at stake. Freedom of movement of labor is one of the "four freedoms" and as such has been (partly and restrictively) tackled in the EAs. Migration (that is, movement of persons at large) is dealt with in the Maastricht (Amsterdam) Treaty under a different title and belongs to what is called in EU parlance the 'third pillar' devoted to justice and home affairs (see chapter 2). The enlargement process has been mainly concerned with the first pillar. As Alan Mayhew (1998, p. 341) states, "the third-pillar area is one where it is difficult to say exactly what the *acquis communautaire* is or what it is likely to be when the accession takes place." Unfortunately, migration is also a very sensitive issue both to western and eastern European constituencies.

Competitiveness

This is a vast issue that needs broader attention than I can allocate to it here. At the least one has to pose the following question: if capacity to cope with the EU's competitive pressures and market forces is a condition for accession, does this mean that anything enhancing competitiveness is good (short of undue intervention by the state)? That too may warrant a lengthy investigation, but here I want to deal only with two specific aspects of the issue. First, since the TEs are on the whole more agricultural than EU members, how can one assess their competitiveness in this sector? Also, since the TEs have until now been competitive in sectors considered sensitive, hence subject to actual or potential trade restrictions, does a request for them to become more competitive not directly conflict with the erection of barriers to their exports?

The TE-5 are predominantly industrialized. The share of agriculture in their GDP is 6 percent, more than twice that of the EU, though comparable to that of the four poorer members. For the other TEs, however, that share is about twice as large. The differences in the shares of agriculture in total employment are even more striking: as compared to 5.3 percent for the EU, it is 22.5 percent for the TE-10. The integration of the latter into the EU would more than double the EU's present agricultural labor force; integration of the TE-5 would increase it by 45 percent.

The EU is afraid of eastern agriculture. The main present concern is to withhold the full benefits of the present CAP from TEs. One obvious way to accomplish this is by reducing the advantages to present beneficiaries, which may well be required in any case under the negotiations slated to commence in 1999 under the WTO's auspices. If and when the TEs are to benefit from the CAP, it will definitely not be to the degree thus far enjoyed by EU members. Current discussions within the EU revolve around the reduction of the EU's support prices (for example, those for grain and oilseeds crops would be reduced by 20 percent in 2000/01) and to compensate farmers for only half of the losses due to support-price reductions. As a consequence, the present gap between TE and EU agricultural prices, which is still significant,[8] would shrink and entail less costs if the renewed CAP were to be extended to the TEs.

Are the fears about TE competition justified? The situation of the agricultural sector in TEs has been rapidly deteriorating. Privatization has been impeded in Hungary, and still more in Bulgaria and in the Czech and Slovak Republics, by the restitution of and compensation for land confiscated under communism. When decollectivization is achieved, it often amounts to splitting up large estates into a large number of small farms that are not viable in global competition. Small farms do not have access to credit for modernizing their operations either because it is too expensive due to a stringent monetary policy or not available at all.

Relying on evidence from agriculture in the Czech Republic, Hungary, and Poland, Alain Pouliquen (1998) shows that the EU's apprehension about potential TE competition based on low prices and low-cost labor is not warranted. He shows that the only potentially competitive component of the sector is grain, once farm restructuring will have been accomplished via FDI and the acquisition of best-practice technology and knowhow, and the excess farm labor has been laid off. His conclusion is that the EU should primarily worry about the social consequences of the huge unemployment likely to occur in the farm sector, a danger that might be partly offset by special structural aid aiming at supporting subsistence farming.

Whatever the merit of the above findings, agricultural issues have already entered into the deliberations during the early phases of the accession process. An example is the conflict about apple exports that emerged between the Czech Republic and the EU. The Czech authorities had imposed a discriminatory tariff on apple imports from the EU above a quota of 24,000 tons per year, claiming that apple exports from the EU (40,000 tons in 1997) were heavily subsidized while Czech apple exports to the EU were restricted (*Financial Times*, 5 May 1998). Though the dispute has been temporarily settled, similar conflicts may crop up again.

In most TEs the share of industry in overall output sharply contracted with the inception of the transition. By contrast, the output of services significantly expanded in absolute terms and as a share of GDP. The structure of output in these countries is now comparable to that of developed countries. Given their level of development, however, the Czech Republic and Poland appear to be overindustrialized, a legacy of communism. This suggests that these countries have yet to eliminate inefficient industries, which previously were geared primarily to CMEA, especially Soviet, markets.

In industry, the initial export specialization of the TEs was geared by the distress of the early phases of the transition and the CMEA's collapse as the TEs tried to sell whatever was at hand. These distress exports were mainly sensitive goods (besides foodstuffs, some chemicals, footwear, clothing and textile, and iron and steel products). The role of these sectors in the TEs' economic structure has been rapidly shrinking, however. The chemical industry, developed on the basis of cheap Soviet oil, has no future at world energy prices. Processed agricultural goods have been crowded out in local demand by the role of the transnational retail chains supplying their stores with their own goods procured from their usual suppliers. There is not much of a future in such exports, except perhaps for items such as alcoholic beverages. Textile and clothing look more promising, but basically only when treating TEs as a subcontracting workshop for EU producers: about two-thirds of the imports of clothing from TEs into the EU in 1992 were already due to outward-processing trade (Corado, 1994).

Nevertheless the EU sees a potential surge of such exports following accession as a danger. What alternatives are at hand? The identification of other, more competitive exports in less sensitive sectors is not easy. The structure of the TEs' exports to the EU has remained stable for several years now (see chapter 7). It remains heavily concentrated. The data (UNECE, 1997c, pp. 57 ff.) show that for each TE the five largest commodity groups in the three-digit Standard International Trade Classification (SITC) accounted for 47 percent of total exports to the EU in 1992 and 45 percent in 1996. The list of these commodities has remained largely unchanged, except for Hungary, which succeeded in increasing the share of nonsensitive goods in its exports, with equipment and machinery replacing chemicals and agricultural goods. Clothing was on the list of all ten TEs.

This suggests a vicious circle: if the TEs turn into dynamic, competitive economies, upon accession they will tend to jeopardize declining sectors in the EU; if they keep exploiting their present revealed comparative advantages their trade deficit with the EU will widen, which will somehow have to be covered, including through assistance from their more developed partners. Neither way seems to be the favored strategy "to cope with market forces within the Union."

Conclusions

In this chapter I have examined the formal, less formal, and tacit conditions for accession. Virtually all are very fluid and fuzzy. From this we may infer that they will be met if and when there is on both sides the political will to adjust and interpret the conditionalities with a generous pinch of salt. In the end, the TEs will be admitted to the EU once the present EU membership for political reasons deems such an expansion to be desirable. There are signs that EU states have been trying to slow down the enlargement process, which is very easy due to the way conditions for entry are expressed. There is plenty of room to extend the negotiation schedule, and to introduce long delays in implementing some provisions once the accession becomes a reality. This will undoubtedly require further changes in the TEs as prerequisites for making entry into the EU feasible.

How long that adjustment process will take and how much good will the TEs will need to mobilize in the years to come are questions deserving appropriate analyses that transcend the confines of this chapter. Let us just mention here that even before the TE-10, in their present definition, will become members of the EU, other issues are looming, such as the European future of Albania and the successor states of the former Yugoslavia other than Slovenia, or some successor states of the former Soviet Union. Croatia and Ukraine are already claiming that they belong to "Europe," and can credibly make that claim because of their geopolitical position, which ought to raise EU concerns about their economic potential and security (see chapter 9).

For the time being, however, it is easy to dismiss the above-cited claims: the trade and cooperation agreement of Croatia with the EU is stalled and there is no association agreement in sight, in spite of what Croatian policy makers claim presumably for domestic public consumption (see chapter 9). Ukraine has for now very few opportunities indeed for transforming its 1994 Partnership and Cooperation Agreement (PCA), as discussed in more detail in chapter 9, into an EA.

Just the same, however, the problem of further eastward expansion of the EU remains and continues to pose nettlesome questions. Though the EU in general and the Commission in particular have thus far deftly skirted the core of the many issues at stake, the problems are clearly visible and advancing toward Brussels's doorsteps. They will undoubtedly have to be dealt with at some point in the not-too-distant future.

Notes

This is a revised and updated version of Lavigne, 1998.

1 A 'white paper' in the EU's practice, as in the United Kingdom, designates a document prepared by the European Commission in which it reports information or states proposals on a particular issue. This is different from a 'green paper' since that is a draft for discussion among technicians and policy makers before its policy matters and implications are brought to the attention of the parliamentary bodies.

2 This should be understood as the five countries with an EA not included among the TE-5.

3 This should not, of course, be confounded with the German-inspired Stability and Growth Pact associated with monetary union and defined by the European Council's regulation of 17 June 1997 (EC/1466/97). This makes it compulsory for all EU incumbents to present convergence programs every year. Of course, the regulation will formally apply to the TEs only once they join the EU. But there are likely to be implications for the macroeconomic policy behavior of TEs already prior to that stage.

4 Note that this went into effect on 1 January 1999.

5 WTO agreed to admit Latvia in October 1998 and the country entered in early 1999. In April 1999, it agreed to admit Estonia once it will have changed several aspects of its trading regime. Entry is forecast for late 1999 at the earliest.

6 It had earlier been suggested that the Commission would draw up annual 'reports,' such as those in *Agenda 2000*, for the TE-10, including the five not endorsed for fast-track accession negotiations. Since it might be politically touchy to adjudicate suitability in such a comprehensive fashion, the Council decided that the Commission should draw up 'annual

reviews' in which progress toward suitability for membership is recorded (OA, 1998).

7 This stands for *Pologne/Hongrie—assistance à la restructuration économique* for reasons examined in chapter 9.

8 The gap differs according to countries and products. For example, the producer price for wheat amounted in 1995 to 50-70 percent of the EU price; for beef to 30-44 percent; and for milk to 28-65 percent (Cacheux, 1996b, p. 297).

Chapter 4

IGC96—'Deepening' vs. 'Widening'

Jozef M. van Brabant

With the June 1993 decision of the European Council in Copenhagen, subsequently refined in terms of entrance criteria in particular at the Essen Council in December 1994, to entertain the future entry into the EU of up to ten TEs, as well as Cyprus and Malta but not other applicants,[1] a new crucial step on the road to remaking Europe was set. The commitment made at Essen, and reiterated in subsequent European Council sessions, notably at Cannes (June 1995) and Madrid (December 1995), was to begin accession negotiations soon after the 'successful' conclusion of IGC96. As a result, interest in the latter's preparation and policy deliberations, including that of the TEs, soared markedly. 'Widening' was thus again on the EU's agenda. Even more than on the four earlier occasions, such a fifth enlargement, and indeed beyond, was from the beginning predicated on 'deepening' integration. That should in part have received a new impetus from the solutions to obdurate integration obstacles that many, if not all, EU members expected the IGC96 to lead up to. Disappointment set in, including among TE policy makers, when it became clear around the end of 1996 that major conflicts among the members were unlikely to be resolved by the time IGC96 had to be concluded in June 1997, largely for internal political reasons in several EU members.

This chapter discusses the salient aspects of the run-up to IGC96, of the deliberations that lasted for well over a year, and of the results obtained at the Amsterdam Council (16-17 June 1997) as well as the further refinement thereof during the Luxemburg Council (12-13 December 1997). But I do so largely from the angle of what is required in terms of political will and institutional adaptations to engineer yet another enlargement, this time toward the eastern part of Europe. That is to say, the emphasis here is on whether these deliberations have facilitated the eventual accession of TEs. Finally, I deal with the core issue: has sufficient progress been booked with deepening integration, including in updating the core institutions and their decision-making mechanisms, as well as in addressing the integration challenges reaching well beyond issues around EMU (see chapter 2), to permit eastward expansion without potentially undermining core elements of what the EU in its various incarnations has been all about since the early 1950s? Or is expansion intrinsically bound to undermine the EU as we know it?

   After setting forth the fundamental relationship between deepening and widening EU integration and the core problem areas that necessarily informed the IGC96, I detail the background of and expectations voiced in the run-up to the latter's opening in Turin on 29 March 1996. Next I look at the formal agenda entrusted to IGC96 in some fashion at the latter meeting. Thereafter I briefly recall the mechanics and results of the negotiations. Before concluding with the salience of IGC96 for aspiring members in particular, I examine the outcomes attained, including the Amsterdam Treaty, with the emphasis on whether they facilitate the eventual accession of primarily the ten TEs with an EA, whence they derive a privileged status with the EU (see chapter 9).

Reconciling 'Deepening' and 'Widening'—the Fundamentals

One must be crystal clear about the terminology applied to EU policies and related concerns. Two key concepts are at stake at this juncture. In its very essence, 'deepening' in EU-speak means consolidating the achievements made since the integration process first got under way, arguably in May 1950 (Brabant,1996a, pp. 47-48). But it also means forging ahead with new integration endeavors as enshrined in the EU's quasi-constitutional documents. In addition it calls for ensuring that those integration matters on which broad consensus among members exists but whose implementation has not yet been completed move ahead expeditiously. Finally, it implies embarking at a measured pace on bringing new areas of common concern into the *acquis* so as to enhance the dynamic leading toward the EU's *finalité politique*. Regardless of the controversy surrounding its precise meaning, the idea is that the EU's constitutional makeup should eventually take the format of a modified federal transnational 'state.' Modified in the sense that the EU ultimately will *not* consist, as in the quintessential democratic nation state, of a common legislature, executive, and judiciary at the EU level mirroring to some degree these separate powers in the member states. Some admixture of intergovernmentalism and supranationalism in the federal mode is likely to emerge eventually and must continue to prevail for as long as EU members insist on safeguarding their own identity and protecting major components of their national sovereignty. But which mix it will ultimately turn out to be remains unknown. Even so, this aspiration and the EU path traveled so far suggest unambiguously that the EU represents a sui generis case of 'regional integration.' It is best treated that way for otherwise it will prove difficult to grasp the ongoing frictions and debates, even those that affect the ability of TEs to join the EU.

By contrast, 'widening' in the EU's lexicon simply means extending the geographical remit of the single market and other forms of common activities eventually to all European countries that comply with the fundamental premises laid down in the Rome Treaty and that desire to join. Conditions for accession enshrined in the above-cited quasi-constitutional instruments revolve essentially (Brabant, 1995, pp. 452-68) around three features: a credible aspirant must have a pluralistic political system, a market-based system of resource allocation, and a European vocation. These can be refined into various other groups, calling for democracy, absence of major internal conflicts as well as outstanding claims on members and other countries, the capacity to play a useful role in the EU's type of integration, and membership leading up to a tolerable division of costs and benefits among the new entrant(s) and existing members as well as over time. None of these elements is clear-cut, however; certainly there are no ready-made entrance criteria against which the preparedness of an aspirant can be checked off (see chapter 3). Even the notion of 'European vocation' remains ill-defined as the eastern and southeastern borders of a credible Europe remain fluid. Often they have been understood to encompass countries with a western Christian heritage. Even on that score matters are far from settled, however (see chapter 9).

Another set of considerations derives from principles that are not enshrined in the quasi-constitutional documents but that can be derived from the application of the fundamental elements of the *acquis* and of the EU's precepts on solidarity, subsidiarity, cohesiveness, sharing a common destiny, and gradual federalization of core governance tasks. New accessions must therefore be affordable, possibly considered over an extended time span. This refers not only to the total net cost, but also the time path of the redistribution of costs and benefits over the existing membership. András Inotai[2] (1994, pp. 15-17) has argued and repeated often (for example, Inotai, 1998a, p. 430), that earlier accessions were simply a political matter, but that the TEs are being given discriminatory treatment. The first argument is clearly wrong and not very helpful in grasping what is really at stake in the debates on TE accessions, even when it is recognized that politics has always played a considerable role in deliberations about expansion—could it conceivably be different in the case of the TEs? But first and foremost the applicant must be able and willing to come to grips with the complexity of functioning on the terms that delineate the SEM's arena and increasingly the sphere of communautarianism[3] in other areas of common EU endeavors. His charge of discrimination refers to the principles first enunciated in Copenhagen in mid-1993 to the effect that, among other things, new accessions must be affordable to the EU membership. True, that precept had perhaps never been explicitly stated in earlier accession deliberations. But it most certainly figured among the core considerations on whether to move ahead with expansion or not in every one of the four previous enlargement exercises.

The essential problem with 'widening' versus 'deepening' integration hinges on the arguably incontestable fact that widening should not encroach on the fundamental objectives cherished by existing members both as pursued in fact and as aspirations for policy developments yet to be shored up. Opting for extending the geographical remit of EU integration is likely to slow down the pace of deepening for two reasons. One is that the EU's capacity to foster greater regional cooperation is limited. So is the energy that policy makers are able to muster and willing to expend on regional matters as opposed to the attention required for their national political concerns. Widening may also jeopardize deepening because by extending the geographical remit the number of participants increases, the diversity of interests in central integration matters is almost bound to widen, and it is by no means evident that the new entrants will be fully able and willing to subscribe to the prevailing 'philosophy' on EU integration, including the full range of the existing *acquis*.

At the same time, it must be clear that deepening core common issues cannot realistically be pursued by leaving behind some of the present members or by engineering another enlargement—essentially a sham—by giving the new entrants a de facto second-class status in the EU. The entire debate of the early 1990s phrased around such images as variable geometry, concentric circles, multi-phase, or à la carte integration, as well as the more recent "flexibility option[4]" now taken up in the Amsterdam Treaty, has, in my view, been misguided when the discussion is about membership. None of the various configurations offers a compelling alternative to EU practices adopted since 1950.[5] Forms of association that do not represent membership are, of course, always possible and these can be designed in an entirely ad hoc manner. But when it comes to membership there is little choice between adhering to essential common policies and going one's own way. One must be clear about these distinctions.

Let us consider variable geometry as the other proposals are even less credible. If it means gradualism in accession, both for existing members and new entrants, spreading of costs and benefits of integration over time, or enabling some members to join in some particular program (such as Eureka) that is not part of the core of EU integration, the problem is at best semantical. Variable geometry (or another such faddish catchword) as a constitutional issue needlessly complicates the debate on vital matters. Indeed such gradualism and flexibility in adjusting toward the common core have been the practice of the EU from its very inception. There is no reason why this should not be continued, notably in smoothing the accession of new members and in allowing some to move faster and farther with their integration than others in matters that are not at the heart of EU integration.

If on the other hand variable geometry means that there will be permanent exemptions from core agreements among EU participants, such as on monetary union, that would seem to be irreconcilable with the EU's essential ambitions as enshrined in its quasi-constitutional documents. I extend this verdict to misguided interpretations about the allegedly new willingness of the EU founders to explore flexibility. My reading of the entire policy debate on engineering more flexible approaches to deepening integration and how the principle of 'EU flexibility' has been enshrined in the Amsterdam Treaty is that it permits some members able and willing to move ahead with some aspects of integration while others will abstain from new areas or follow suit in areas already committed to at a later date. But there can be no permanent deviation from the very essentials of the Treaty of Rome without irretrievably altering the EU's ambitions laid out there. I am not aware that there is presently a consensus, or even a majority, on working toward such an incisive constitutional modification in the EU. That does *not* mean that all integration endeavors at all times will have to be fully supported by all members. But a Europe à la carte or with a permanently differing geometry or multiple paths, let alone a pick-and-choose Europe, without a convergence being in sight in essential areas of the *acquis*, in my view, simply cannot be reconciled with the EU's prime purposes.

It is, then, useful to distinguish more rigorously between the essential parts of EU unification as broadly envisioned in the Rome Treaty, even though it may well need further specification as progress is made, and other common areas of interest. The focus should be on competition in open markets based solely (at least primarily) on genuine productivity performances while ensuring the appropriate scope for raising productivity levels and prosperity throughout the EU. This includes without exception *all* aspects of the single market, notably EMU. Although not all members will have to move at the same pace, there can be no permanent exemption from that fundamental commitment without altering the very ambition of the Rome Treaty. More specifically it means that, on current commitments, the EU's future cannot be about intergovernmentalism or free trading as such.

More voluntary areas of regional cooperation in economic and other matters can be entertained, as indeed they have been in EU activities in the past. Examples are legion: Eureka, the technology-cooperation program, or the European space program. They need not involve all members. Judicious use of an appropriate subsidiarity rule (Brabant, 1995, pp. 480-88) can pragmatically validate this division of labor in these and many other conceivable areas. Conflicts in other cases will then need to be resolved through can-do political compromise.

One may, of course, counter that some members have received 'permanent' exemption from some integration initiatives (such as Denmark and the United Kingdom from joining monetary union). Those exemptions were pragmatically conceded in view of political realities *but* in the full expectation that they would not remain permanent. For as much as I can gauge, that aspiration continues to hold at this stage.

In other words, the fundamental problems of deepening cannot be avoided by resorting to some form of variable geometry with staggered levels of increasingly closer integration. The reason is simple: because there cannot be independence in most endeavors between what, say, core countries do and what the next tier or tiers may wish to subscribe to, it is virtually impossible to maintain a semblance of coherent coordination among and within those groups. This is clear for monetary union, for example: those joining the union will not tolerate wanton exchange-rate movements of members that cannot join the union or do not wish to do so (Brabant, 1996a, pp. 102ff.). That is to say, if the EU's ambitions are to be preserved, an EMU of core countries, for example, would be incompatible with its location within a larger free-trading area, precisely because the latter's commitment to anything but the features of at most a customs union would offer them free-riding opportunities not available to those constituting the core. One such example is that those remaining outside the monetary union, if not subject to constraints, would find themselves in a position to gain advantages in trade through competitive currency realignments, which their core partners would, legitimately, consider 'unfair.' But there are other opportunities for free riding that would be intolerable to those constituting the core.

Juxtaposing the issues around widening and deepening reveals a number of problems. In reality, the convoluted tasks at hand can be tackled only jointly. However, some primacy needs to be given to implementing essential elements of deepening for successful widening remains predicated on achieving just that. Only in this manner can the EU's membership be widened without hollowing out the integration ambitions stated in the EU's quasi-constitutional acts. It is paradoxical that almost the reverse has recently prevailed (Giscard d'Estaing, 1995). Although it is conceivable to consider moving ahead with deepening at the expense of widening, the reverse option is only feasible at the cost of losing the EU's raisons d'etre. In other words, widening and deepening cannot provide an easy mixture of policy objectives and paths to walk along. It could never have been otherwise.

In the case of TE accessions, the core of the conflicts from early on consisted in reluctance on the part of existing EU members even to contemplate enlargement before mid-1993 in spite of, or perhaps precisely because of, strong political pleas from the leadership of several TEs. On the one hand, EU policy makers perceived the gaps in institutional capabilities and in levels of development, technology, and trade participation of these TEs to be very considerable, and difficult to overcome in the short run (see chapter 2). These continue to pose a palpable obstacle for smoothly merging the TEs into the SEM and Europe-wide competition along established rules. Participating effectively in the SEM necessarily requires the capacities to take an active part in IIT and specialization, something that so far has not been high among the policies pursued in most TEs (see chapter 7). On the other hand, with the tumultuous changes in the eastern part of Europe since the late 1980s, the danger that attention would be diverted from solidifying the achievements made to date and forging ahead with agreed-upon integration plans remains real.

Indeed, deepening in the EU context concerns in the first place undertaking fundamental changes in the institutional and governance structures within which the fifteen members pursue common policies of various degrees of intensity. The instruments and institutions at hand to forge ahead remain essentially those embraced for the six founders with minor modifications made over time under pressure of circumstances rather than as the outcome of a strategic deliberation about how best to arrive at efficient decision making. Matters cannot continue in this mode even abstracting from the problems likely to surface with any further enlargement of the EU's remit. As noted, deepening also calls for building upon present achievements and moving further toward realization of the *finalité politique*, even though the latter's precise contours remain to be defined. The issues to be addressed concern democracy, efficiency, subsidiarity, openness, transparency, and accountability not only in the present EU integration domains but, perhaps even more, in areas that a widening compass would capture.

Backdrop to IGC96

To better comprehend the tasks set for IGC96, the way in which the deliberations were prepared, the manner in which these negotiations progressed and in the end failed to evolve, and the very disappointing outcome it is necessary to bear in mind several key features of the early 1990s. Among them, pride of place accrues to three bundles of policy problem. One stems from the inability of the negotiators in 1990 and beyond to assemble a sufficiently coherent and mature package of measures to reform the EU's fundamental governance instruments, and get on with the critical tasks at hand, as detailed in chapter 2. In an understatement of sorts the European Commission (1995a, p. 59) has observed that IGC96 "was initially intended to introduce [EMU], as a complement to the single market. Consideration of further steps toward [EPU] then became unavoidable, in response to the major upheavals that struck Europe at the turn of the decade. The Treaty undoubtedly shows signs of these mixed origins." Neither was there sufficient agreement to advance the EPU's agenda beyond very broad, largely nonbinding commitments.

As a result, the Maastricht Treaty became a sort of quasi constitution by default but with a number of key specifications left ill-defined at best, especially as concerns the EU's *finalité politique* and the wherewithal to govern these and related integration processes more efficiently, with greater transparency and accountability, and democratic commitment. Some EU members certainly had envisaged moving forward with such fundamental constitutional issues and were keen on ensuring that, in spite of the obstacles encountered in the early 1990s, the longer-term purposes of the EU and how to advance with them despite trenchant political opposition would not get lost. They therefore insisted at the time on enshrining in the TEU a commitment to convene a Review Conference by the mid-1990s.

Under the final dispositions of the Treaty, as stated in article N(2), it was agreed that "a conference of representatives of the governments of the Member States shall be convened in 1996 to examine, in accordance with the objectives set out in articles A and B, those provisions of this Treaty for which revision is provided" (European Commission, 1993, p. 56). In other words, from the very nature of the call, unlike earlier such meetings, IGC96 was never intended to lead to a new treaty ab ovo. Rather, it was from the beginning designed to clarify the fundamental, and in some cases truly hard-core constitutional, issues of the EU's final goal as well as the modi operandi of moving toward it. Thus, a renewed, streamlined, more comprehensive, and more coherent TEU should have materialized. In the end, only a slightly revised treaty crystallized and was endorsed for reasons spelled out toward the end of the chapter.

Not only was article N peculiar—a treaty providing for its own revision within such a short period of time—but also its somewhat cryptic stipulation suggests that virtually any issue pertaining to the EU's objectives and means could in principle be addressed at IGC96. Nonetheless, it was generally understood prior to the latter's ceremonial opening that the review exercise would focus more specifically on two problem areas of 'deepening' integration: (1) matters coming under pillars 2 and 3, and conceivably transferring responsibilities to the communautarian from the intergovernmental level, and (2) streamlining EU governance as a result of fine-tuning institutional and decision-making matters, notably by simplifying the division of powers among the EU's institutions and moving away from unanimity to majority decision making under the special features characterizing the EU.

Second, the euphoria about EU integration that prevailed among politicians, economists, and even the wider public in Europe since the mid-1980s took, in the early 1990s, another rather dramatic turn toward pessimism and stagnation. That too had several origins, including the much larger than anticipated difficulties in bringing about monetary union, the infusion of a good deal of obstacles in advancing with integration and its underpinnings due to the fallout of German unification, the growing realization that assimilating the most recent newcomers into the EU fold was proving to be more cumbersome than earlier thought in part because of unanticipated governance problems, and the severe recession in 1992-1994 with only a weak recovery that faltered prematurely in late 1995, albeit for only a short period of time. The upshot of all these developments was a marked erosion of popular and political support for intensifying integration and indeed for further broadening the membership. To assess the implications thereof a review of these four developments is in order, but I must necessarily remain brief here (see Brabant, 1996a).

When the Treaty was negotiated it had been taken for granted that foreign-exchange markets for most of the member currencies would continue to function smoothly and remain fairly stable, at least as far as the reciprocal rates of most EU members were concerned. That expectation was based on more than a decade of monetary cooperation within the ERM, which had been quite successful since the mid-1980s. It was also based on the underpinnings of the European Monetary System (EMS) and the convergence process toward broadening participation in the ERM, although the ERM, unlike the EMS, has never encompassed all EU members, and on the gradual shift toward phases 1 and 2, and convergence toward phase 3, of monetary union (Brabant, 1996a, pp. 102ff.).

Nobody seemed to have reckoned at the time with the potential strength of private markets to test the resolve, and indeed the ability, of EU policy makers, individually and collectively, to stabilize foreign-exchange markets. In retrospect, this is surprising given the intrinsic inconsistency between fixed exchange rates, capital mobility, autonomous fiscal policy, and only partly coordinated monetary policy with limited resources for intervention purposes. This inevitably entailed credibility problems, thus inviting private financial markets to test and challenge the determination and capacity of policy makers to support and sustain fixed exchange rates. Precisely that scenario was enacted in the fall of 1992 and again in the summer of 1993. Consequent to these eruptions, several countries withdrew from the ERM and the latter's fluctuation margins were widened from 2.25 to 15 percent either side of parity. In other words, the ERM as originally conceived had to be abandoned for all practical purposes, even though the so-called 'core countries' of the original ERM managed to emulate the earlier system, after a comparatively brief interval, by late 1993 (Pisani-Ferry, 1995, p. 449). They did not, however, restore the easy intervention mechanism as the trigger for activating the support mechanism would henceforth be the new fluctuation margins.

Moving toward monetary union implied subordinating national monetary, and by implication fiscal, policy to the commonly agreed framework of macroeconomic policy until the establishment of monetary union, when the scope for national monetary, and by implication fiscal, policy would be severely compressed. This most EU members had consented to in the TEU precisely at a time that the optimistic expectations of the mid-1980s surrounding the discussions of the future European architecture, seemingly justified by the actual implementation of most of the provisions of the SEM (see chapter 2), gave way increasingly to deep-seated skepticism. The europessimism since the early 1990s has led to rising political opposition against subordinating national priorities, notably on unemployment and/or welfare provisions, to regional, let alone supranational, objectives in virtually every single member state. This has been focused especially on issues of democracy, efficiency, subsidiarity, transparency, and accountability in the workings of the European institutions and the comportment of policy makers and

Jozef M. van Brabant

eurocrats. Apprehensions about further integration, as well as genuine fears that yielding hard-won national priorities to EU mandates would jeopardize welfare at home, have come to the fore in public debate all too often, albeit frequently in a rather disingenuous manner. The prevailing popular concerns and doubts about creating a common currency even at this stage, although misgivings have abated considerably since May 1998, when major dispositions on enacting monetary union in early 1999 were enacted, are symptomatic of these wider anxieties about 'deepening.'

These apprehensions spilled over into and were polarized by the most visible repercussion of the economic recession and sociopolitical pessimism: the rapid rise in the level and duration of unemployment to magnitudes not seen since postwar stabilization. As a result, considerable pressure built up to include explicit provisions on employment in the revised Treaty, and thus in the evolving agenda of IGC96. In fact, the various issues around unemployment have been impinging more and more on the policy debate—they have been relentlessly stressed notably by French and German policy makers—and they have been moved to the top of the list of priorities for EU policy debates.

But broader pessimism arose also from the serious chasm between expectations, as part of the optimism regarding the 'construction' of Europe in the late 1980s, and actual developments. At the time of the transition's inception, policy makers, pundits, commentators, and broad layers of the informed electorate had taken it for granted that the political changes since 1989 in the eastern part of Europe would be irreversible, that the economic transformation of TEs would proceed much more smoothly than in fact it has, and that with the first steps toward EPU taken at Maastricht it would be fairly easy to move ahead with stabilizing and reinforcing pillars 2 and 3 of the European architecture. The evolution of events, not in the least the drawn-out crisis in the former Yugoslavia and the difficulties of integrating the smaller TEs into a broader framework of European security, also demonstrates how complex it has become to extend integration beyond the spheres in which the earliest EU efforts were quite successful. Partly as a result of these developments, EU enthusiasm for enlargement toward the eastern part of Europe has waned considerably, not always for reasons germane to the real problems and likely effects, economic as well as others, of such a relocation of the EU's geographic remit (see chapter 9).

Finally, the unprecedented shifts in the eastern part of the continent changed fundamental parameters of the debate about deepening integration. This occurred not just because one suddenly found on the EU's eastern fringes countries desirous of abandoning communism and planning, and opting instead for pluralistic political decision making with market-based resource allocation. Indeed the very implosion of the Soviet Union and the shaky political and security situation engendered in the process suddenly confronted European decision makers with daunting tasks for which they had really never prepared themselves. At best some vapid commitments to extending the EU to all of Europe had occasionally been aired, but this had hardly played any role in the two IGCs of 1990-1991. Elaborating further on the Maastricht Treaty, including through the IGC96 process, would have squarely confronted EU decision makers with deepening integration. Yet, the claim lodged in particular by the smaller TEs to "return to Europe" infused into the EU debate once again the need to reconcile deepening with widening integration, a matter the EU's twelve, later fifteen, members had earlier thought to have put to rest with the fourth enlargement, which itself was reluctantly consented to (see chapter 2).

In preparing IGC96, the above three sets of developments provided a crucial impetus to the multiple contending forces that in the end informed the preparations and indeed a good part of the actual negotiations. While many organizations, each with its own agenda, were involved in paving the path toward IGC96, it is useful to distinguish among precepts of the European Commission, the interests of the European Parliament, the preparations on behalf of the European Council organized in the so-called Reflection Group, and the varying preferences of groups of member countries. This I do in the next section. The issues tabled revolved, however, around five broad problem areas.

First, finding ways and means of overcoming the lethargy about moving ahead with integration—deepening in other words—that set in soon after the TEU's endorsement ranked very high. Shaping Europe's *finalité politique* was a priority from the outset. At the very least, a clear recommitment by members to the goals set earlier was required to restore confidence in and regain momentum with the integration process. Continuing the drift of the early 1990s could only undermine relations within the EU. At the very least progress with governance reform would have ensured advancing with some deepening, hopefully enough to prepare a broader constitutional conference.

Second, the continuing string of difficulties in progressing with matters concerning both economic and monetary union could not but weigh on IGC96 although these paramount integration endeavors were not explicitly considered for inclusion on its agenda. Nevertheless, fluctuations in policy commitment to the integration enterprise, as noted earlier, the intermittent turmoil in currency markets since late 1992, and the slowdown in the pace of economic activity in key members in 1995-1996 so precipitously after the preceding deep and protracted recession, including among the core of those constituting a critical mass for a viable monetary union, simply could not be brushed aside if only because they would markedly complicate meeting the so-called Maastricht convergence criteria (see chapter 6). This in turn would encumber the SEM's completion in practice.

Third, many EU members hoped to negotiate satisfactory solutions to Europe's multiple issues of governance (democracy, subsidiarity, efficiency, transparency, accountability, and so on) not only among the existing twelve, and later fifteen, members but also in light of expanding membership diversity, which increasingly became something that EU policy makers would have to address comprehensively—after IGC96, of course. This called for institutional reforms to ensure a more streamlined division of powers among the four core EU institutions. It also was predicated on agreeing on reform in decision-making rules and in representing both the members and the citizenship at large in the various institutions. Straightforward majority decision making, even if politically acceptable, notably by the small members, would simply not fit the EU's sui generis character.

Fourth, although not on the agenda, it was clear from the outset that the EU's various transfer programs had to be refashioned to permit in particular TEs to join the EU, and also to keep the EU budget manageable in spite of fiscal stringency in most members. Budgetary matters per se were not to be the subject of intensive political debates until discussions on a new budget agreement in 1999 for the period 2000-2006 would be held.

Finally, it was becoming clearer that a coherent assistance and cooperation program for other TEs, and indeed for nonmember countries in general, needed to be formulated, perhaps by reexamining the EU's multitier preference system. Those tasks too were not explicitly on IGC96's debating table. But the questions involved could not be completely ignored there. Any further preferential arrangement would necessarily affect asymmetrically the existing members, the new members, as well as other countries that enjoy some preferential arrangement with the EU, as I detail in chapter 9. Furthermore, most if not all of these preferential arrangements could usefully be reviewed and updated to ensure greater coherence and efficiency, given the changed world after the end of the cold war.

These five clusters of broad economic, political, security, social, and other concerns undoubtedly offer a very complex set of issues from which a concrete negotiating agenda had to be extracted. The members and the European institutions at the time held widely diverging views on what the most central agenda topics should be. Some underlined their commitment to forging ahead with the integration process by moving toward EPU, and perhaps other objectives, within a reasonably coherent EMU. At the same time the political imperative of expanding membership was never far from policy concerns. This in spite of the practical problems of accommodating more and more diverse members and indeed of the many and perplexing obstacles ahead for years to come in ensuring the smooth functioning of TEs within the SEM.

Expectations on the IGC's Eve

The broad range of contentious policy matters arising from the TEU and from developments in European, and indeed global, affairs since then quickly gave rise to a wide diversity of precepts on how best to proceed with IGC96. This came almost immediately to the fore in the forum—the so-called Reflection Group—that should have ironed out most of these and related obstacles prior to embarking on serious concrete negotiations at the IGC. That working party had been set up in mid-1994 to address in detail the issues of concern in the broader setting of preparing the IGC96. That this decision was taken at the time in conjunction with the problems around governance that somewhat surprisingly cropped up with the fourth enlargement was not at all coincidental, of course.[6]

The Reflection Group consisted of one senior official or policy maker from each EU member, one from the Commission, and two from the European Parliament. Its mandate, defined at the Corfu Council meeting (24-25 June 1994), was to examine and elaborate ideas relating to: (1) provisions that the Maastricht Treaty identified as subject to review; (2) other possible improvements in democracy and openness, based on an assessment of the results obtained during the TEU's implementation; (3) options on institutional questions relating to the EU's prospective enlargement, focusing, among other matters, on the weighting of votes, the threshold for qualified-majority decisions, and the number of Commissioners and their selection; and (4) any other measures deemed necessary. The group was called upon to submit a report in time for the Madrid Council (15-16 December 1995).

At the same time the European Commission was requested to submit to the group by mid-1995 a report on its views regarding the agenda of IGC96 (European Commission, 1995a). That report set out three broad topics for the Conference. The first encompasses the four specific areas mentioned in the Maastricht Treaty: (1) the scope of codecision procedures (largely between the Council and the European Parliament); (2) security and defense or pillar 2; (3) energy, tourism, and civil protection as parts of pillar 3; and (4) the hierarchy of Community acts. The Council added: (1) the number of commissioners, the weighting of voting in the Council, and the measures required to facilitate the work of the institutions and ensure their efficient operation, and thus transcend the problems that surfaced with the fourth enlargement, as noted above; and (2) the institutional arrangements required to enable the EU's smooth functioning in the event of any further enlargement.

Finally, the European Parliament, the Council, and the Commission agreed to place two other subjects on the agenda: (1) the operation of budgetary procedures, notably as regards the classification of expenditures; and (2) the arrangements for exercising the executive powers conferred on the Commission to implement legislation adopted under the codecision procedure.

For most of 1995 the Reflection Group met to identify the core issues for IGC96, to assess the extent of prior agreement, and to clarify the areas of disagreement among the members. In addition to the persons directly involved in the negotiations, the group had access to a large number of reports containing widely diverging opinions on integration matters and expectations regarding IGC96. Some were tabled by individual or groups of member governments. Others, as reported, were submitted by the EU's governance organs. Many civil society organs as well as professional organizations formulated their own partisan views on the tasks for IGC96 and the expected or desired outcomes.

Coming to grips with this diversity of expressed attitudes toward an exceedingly wide range of daunting integration issues could never have been an easy assignment. All the more so because the negotiators were being increasingly bound by the inward turning of key member governments, hence national priorities, or their attention was diverted by matters extraneous to the proper setting for an IGC. Nonetheless, as called for, the group tabled its report (Reflection Group, 1995) for the Madrid European Council in December 1995. That is structured around four agenda topics: (1) the citizen and the EU; (2) collaboration in justice and home affairs, internal security, and free movement; (3) foreign and security policy; and (4) the institutional system.

The report's suggestions are mainly concerned with the spirit of the group's mandate and, by and large, simply register the existing disagreements among EU members about virtually the entire range of problems to be tackled—a lengthy catalogue of issues indeed with few areas of agreement. Three features stand out, however. First, it provides an overview in easily accessible language of most of the obstacles facing further EU integration and it discusses institutional and policy matters with a view to making the EU far more transparent, citizen friendly, and democratic. Second, it provides an inventory of critical integration hurdles; all questions for incisive reform for which consensus would have to be mustered later on since the report notes virtually at every twist and turn the prevailing dissent. Finally, the report failed to offer a ready-made text for negotiations, leaving this task up to IGC96 itself, even though many of the participants in the Reflection Group became negotiators in IGC96 (European Commission, 1996a).

Perhaps surprisingly, the report does not explicitly consider the important matter of enlargement. In fact, it strongly favors, although by no means unanimously, "the separation of the Conference exercise from the study of the impact of enlargement in relation to future development of common policies" (Reflection Group, 1995, para. 21 of the Annotated Agenda). In other words, the Reflection Group recommended that the impending IGC be concerned with deepening integration to enable subsequent widening, if feasible at all.

The Turin Mandate

Until the ceremonial opening of IGC96, there was no agreed agenda for its deliberations. Whereas in Turin the Council conferred a sort of mandate, it too failed to set a concrete agenda for the deliberations (European Commission, 1996b). That was left up to the Council of Ministers of Foreign Affairs after the preparatory meetings of their assistants. The latter commenced their deliberations immediately after the Turin Council. From the evidence at hand, the preliminary agenda remained limited to scheduling a set round of negotiations around clusters of key concerns: (1) a citizen friendly EU, (2) firming up the EU's external dimension, and (3) institutional reform (European Commission, 1996c, d).

The Turin mandate was issued by way of the "Presidency's Conclusions" in a rather oblique manner. The envisaged procedure, later confirmed by the course of the deliberations, was to structure the debates around: (1) bringing the EU closer to the citizens, (2) making the institutions more democratic and efficient, and (3) strengthening the capacity for external action, again laying the prime accent on deepening integration. The overriding instruction to the negotiators was: "It is essential to sustain the very nature of European construction, which has to preserve and develop its features of democracy, efficiency, solidarity, cohesion, transparency and subsidiarity" and to finalize its deliberations by adopting "a general and consistent vision throughout its work" so as "to meet the needs and expectations of our citizens, while advancing the process of European construction and preparing the Union for its future enlargement" (European Commission, 1996b). The concrete steps mentioned in the rather general mandate rely on the Reflection Group's report "without prejudice to other questions which might be raised during the Conference."

As regards bringing the EU closer to its citizens, respect for nondiscrimination, democratic values, human rights, and equality were to inform IGC96 and urge the participants to deliberate about how best to "strengthen these fundamental rights and improve the safeguarding of them." IGC96 was requested to produce on these issues better methods and instruments, ensure better protection of the EU's citizens against international crime, especially drug trafficking and terrorism, develop coherent and effective asylum, immigration, and visa policies, and remove divergent views on jurisdictional and parliamentary control of EU decisions as far as matters coming under pillar 3 are concerned.

The second topic under this heading was unemployment. IGC96 was requested to examine how the EU could provide the basis for improving cooperation and coordination in order to strengthen national policies with a view to reaching a high level of employment while ensuring social protection. Next on this part of the agenda was the compatibility between competition and the principle of universal access to essential services in the citizen's interest. In addition, it was to examine the status of outermost regions, of overseas territories, and of island regions of the EU. Moreover, it was asked to work toward improving the environment by making environmental protection more effective and coherent at the EU's level. Finally, it was to improve the application and enforcement of the principle of subsidiarity to provide transparency and openness in the EU's activities, and "to consider whether it would be possible to simplify and consolidate the Treaties."

On institutional issues, IGC96's overriding task was to look for the best means to ensure that the core institutions function with greater efficiency, coherence, and legitimacy. In that context, IGC96 was called upon to examine the most effective means of simplifying legislative procedures, making them clearer and more transparent, widening the scope of codecision in "truly legislative matters," and looking into the role of the European Parliament other than its legislative powers, as well as reflecting upon its composition and a uniform procedure for its election. In addition, it was to examine how national parliaments can become more closely involved with the EU. It was furthermore asked to ameliorate the functioning of the Council, including by pondering changes in majority voting, the weighting of votes, and the threshold for qualified-majority decision making. As regards the Commission, it was to contemplate means by which its fundamental functioning could be rendered more efficient, including with regard to its composition and its representativeness. Also matters concerning the role and functioning of the European Court of Justice and the Court of Auditors were to be taken up. Particular emphasis was to be allocated to achieving greater clarity and quality of legislation and the ways and means of fighting more effectively against fraud. Finally, it was asked to study whether and how to introduce rules "to enable a certain number of Member States to develop a strengthened cooperation, open to all, compatible with the Union's objectives, while preserving the acquis communautaire, avoiding discrimination and distortions of competition and respecting the single institutional framework"—in other words, 'flexibility.'

As concerns strengthening the capacity for external action to ensure that the EU's political weight will be commensurate with its economic strength, IGC96 was invited to identify the principles and areas of common foreign policy, to define the actions needed to promote the EU's interests in these areas and according to these principles, to set up procedures and structures designed to improve the effectiveness and timeliness of decisions in a spirit of loyalty and solidarity, and to agree on suitable budgetary provisions. In that context, it was to study the feasibility and desirability of creating a post for a "super Mr. CFSP[7]" or foreign-policy coordinator with clout acting on behalf of the European Council, in advancing pillar 2 matters. Moreover, IGC96 was called upon "to better assert the European identity in matters of security and defence," paying particular regard to the future of the Western European Union (WEU). In that context the EU's operational capacity to discharge the so-called Petersberg tasks (military participation mainly in humanitarian and peace-keeping missions) and the desirability of greater cooperation in armaments were emphasized.

Even this condensed summary of the much more detailed wish list underlines the broad range of controversial matters on which members had for years exhibited widely diverging views. The question of enlargement looms behind every single statement made, though it is mentioned only in passing, and even then obliquely at best—again the primacy of deepening over widening. The mandate did not, however, specify a concrete agenda for the negotiations. That was a strategic mistake for having an agreed agenda in place and seeing to it that the negotiators stick to the agreed-upon schedule are by no means trivial matters, as the experience with earlier IGCs had amply demonstrated. Niels Ersbøll, who was for years at the center of these deliberations as either a representative or a highly placed EU official,[8] has underlined this in unmistakable terms: managing the agreed-upon agenda, once put in place, ranks "amongst the most important and most difficult tasks of the presidencies concerned" (Ludlow and Ersbøll, 1996, p. 11). In other words, the rotation of the Presidency on a biannual basis requires not only effective management at any given time, but also effective transfer from one member state to the next.[9] As described in detail in the remainder of the chapter, it was precisely this failure on the part of virtually all Presidencies from the beginning of IGC96 until its conclusion and follow-up that ultimately prevented the conclusion of a "successful IGC." The consequences of this ominous failure are still being felt, including in negotiations for TE accessions.

The Mechanics and Outcome of the Negotiations

Although an IGC is as a rule opened and concluded in full diplomatic summitry mode, and IGC96 proved to be no exception to this tradition either in Turin or in Amsterdam, the operative deliberations take place elsewhere and in different fora. Two such instances are critical. One is the regular meetings, usually monthly, of the Council of Ministers of Foreign Affairs, where actual negotiations about agenda items are to be settled. This is an interactive process, however. On the one hand, the Council negotiates selected topics of the IGC's agenda only after they have been thoroughly examined and prepared by frequent, usually weekly, meetings of their assistants. In turn, these assistants or deputies, as they are often referred to, receive instructions, guidelines, and negotiating room directly from this Council. Much of the legwork, therefore, of an IGC is performed by the representatives of the ministers of foreign affairs of the EU members who usually have ministerial, cabinet, or ambassadorial rank. They are joined in their deliberations by the President of the European Commission. Periodic examinations of progress made with the negotiations at each regular European Council (usually held in June and December) are by now standard procedure. Even high-level negotiations over items that elude the ministers or their assistants may be brought up there for political compromise, thus providing a new impetus to the IGC negotiations.

Once the negotiators reach consensus, the agreement is passed on to the European Council. If consensus eluded the negotiators, the IGC can then be declared a failure by the Council. Or the latter may itself try and work out a compromise. That may include declaring the IGC a success when in fact the vast majority of its objectives failed to be reached. In any case, once the European Council endorses the agreement the members submit the text(s), if any, hammered out to their respective parliaments for ratification in accordance with the national constitutions.

Originally, the negotiators had planned (European Commission, 1996e, p. 3) to have sufficient material for a 17 May 1996[10] round of negotiations on drafting a preliminary report for the Florence Council. That schedule slipped as meetings on the 'external dimension' (that is, pillar 2 matters) were held well into June 1996 (European Commission, 1996d). Even the aim to have an interim or progress report ready by 17 June for a special session of the Council of Ministers of Foreign Affairs to prepare for the coming Florence Council (21-22 June 1996) and thus endorse a communication to that Council (European Commission,1996f, p. 1) had to be abandoned.

Apart from the largely ceremonial opening festivities in Turin (March 1996) and the complex negotiations at the conclusion of the IGC during the Amsterdam Council (June 1997), the evolution of the deliberations on substantive matters can be separated into three distinct periods. The first started in early April 1996, right after the conclusion of the opening ceremonies, and lasted until about the Florence Council. As per the agreement reached by the Heads of State and Government in Turin (European Commission, 1996b), the ministers of foreign affairs and their personal assistants were to start work immediately on the core issues in a series of meetings scheduled up to late June 1996. During the second quarter of 1996 the plan was to hold weekly deliberations in Brussels per basic topic of the mandate by the deputies and to examine the results approximately every month by the Council of Ministers of Foreign Affairs, and then to prepare part of the agenda of the regular European Council.

Note that the assistants of the ministers of foreign affairs for IGC96 consisted of deputy ministers of foreign affairs, state secretaries of foreign affairs, or high-level confidants of the ministers of foreign affairs, usually the EU member's ambassador in Brussels. Six were their country's permanent representative (ambassador to the EU) in Brussels (European Commission, 1996a) and more than half had earlier participated in the Reflection Group. At least this was the case during the first rounds of negotiations for the composition of the group changed with the turnover in national governments, particularly for those members whose representative came directly from the ministry.

The deputies met almost weekly prior to the Florence Council. Two rounds of first two and then one meeting were devoted to the three mandated broad topics cited earlier. The deliberations consisted essentially of making a broad *tour d'horizon* of the assigned tasks and the positions taken by the representatives with a view to identifying areas of agreement, near-agreement, and dissension. In this, a major effort was made to move beyond the positions hammered out, after protracted and difficult debates, by the Reflection Group. This encompassed nothing more than yet another attempt at finding the common ground that had proved to be so elusive during the deliberations of the Reflection Group, however.

In any event, the plan had been to extract from these deliberations a first assessment of what could conceivably be accomplished at the IGC in time for the Florence Council. The latter would then have issued more concrete recommendations to and instructions for the negotiators to move the IGC expeditiously along. Not surprisingly, the outcome proved to be quite disappointing to virtually all concerned, including those who had been most opposed to viewing the IGC as anything expansive in terms of modifying the substance of EU cooperation. Indeed, by mid-1996 it had become crystal clear that progress remained elusive on virtually all issues. Instead of tabling an interim IGC report for the Council as originally planned, it was on the Italian chairman's (Silvio Fagiolo) personal initiative and in his own name that a 'review' of the deliberations among the ministers of foreign affairs and their deputies (European Commission, 1996g, p. 1) was submitted (European Commission, 1996h).

This report made it abundantly clear that it had remained impossible to reach even a modicum of common ground on the core governance tasks on which the success of IGC96 became increasingly predicated. Recall that from the very beginning the European Commission had been keen on confining the IGC's deliberations primarily to institutional reform and the governance of the core EU institutions. Rather than proceed with the original purposes of the Review Conference, the deliberations tended to be confined more and more to the number of commissioners, majority voting, the number of members of the European Parliament, and the distribution of weights in the various decision-making organs. This is understandable given the IGC's original purposes as stated in the TEU and the entrenched positions of some members, the United Kingdom under Mr. John Major in particular (United Kingdom, 1996). Moreover, these matters by themselves were sufficiently daunting, given the persistent lack of agreement among the Fifteen on the future of EU integration with its consequences for institutional underpinnings and decision making—regional governance in other words. In the end, however, it proved impossible to focus the IGC's attention even on these narrow issues owing to the pall cast over the IGC by the range and complexity of the problems the EU was then, as now, facing.

In fact, the Italian Presidency deferred the substantive negotiations to the Irish Presidency, which began in July 1996. This set the tone for the second stage of the deliberations. At the time observers expected the Irish Presidency to work swiftly toward a concrete agenda for approval by the Council of Ministers so that progress with the negotiations on substantive issues could be booked. When that proved to be illusory almost from the assumption of the Presidency, the EU members agreed to impart a major impetus to the deliberations via an Extraordinary Dublin Council, at first scheduled for 19-20 October 1996 but later held on 5 October 1996, devoted to the IGC as overriding topic. Its principal purpose was to try to see whether core policy makers could infuse new life into the deliberations by setting out positions on key issues to enable the negotiators to forge ahead with their tasks.

From what emerged directly from the meeting, and even more from subsequent events, there can be little doubt that the deliberations failed to set a new stage for IGC96. At least no new initiatives on the 'grand' issues of deepening seemed to have been hammered out to provide a new impetus to the ongoing IGC. This could have been predicted for the scaled-down dimensions of the Extraordinary Council

from two to one day already suggest that there was probably insufficient commonality on most of the issues confronting IGC96 for substantive progress to be
booked. At that stage it was decided, on the initiative of the Irish Presidency, to
prepare a draft revised TEU for the regular Dublin European Council in
December,[11] whence new instructions to the negotiators could emanate. The Council of Ministers was thereafter expected to reach for a rump agreement sometime
by mid-1997 (European Commission, 1996i, pp. 1-2) under pressure of upcoming
elections in several member states.

And so, IGC96 dutifully reconvened and sought to hammer out the smallest
common denominator on the core institutional-governance issues mentioned
above. Increasingly attention of the negotiators became almost exclusively focused
on the four or so institutional issues, including the number of commissioners and
how to allocate them among the member states; issues on which majority voting
would be condoned and how large this should be to ensure that the 'small'
countries would never outvote the 'large' ones, and that indeed the interests of the
former would not be completely trampled upon; limitations of the number of seats,
and hence the key for reapportioning the seats either among existing members or
to accommodate further expansions of the European Parliament; and the distribution of voting weights in the various governance organs, but especially in the
European Council and Council of Ministers.

For the remainder of the year the negotiators sought to bridge substantial gaps
between large and small, rich and poor countries on these issues, but failed to find
sufficient commonality to come to any acceptable conclusion. Nonetheless this
slightly more enthusiastic approach toward refashioning EU integration may have
lasted until the regular Dublin Council (13-14 December 1996).

By early 1997 at the latest it had become crystal clear that advancing with any
of the issues, except on the number of commissioners and europarliamentarians,
was becoming more and more hopeless without the decisive intercession of a
paramount policy maker. Not only would he have to be willing to yield on essential issues but also possess the stamina to persuade other policy makers, including
other paramount ones, not to forfeit the chance for anchoring the foundations for
remaking Europe by refraining from using the veto power. Alas, this did not come
to pass.

And so IGC96 conferees continued in a somewhat desultory fashion to examine
the issues in nearly weekly sessions at least until the U.K. elections in May 1997
brought a new government to power, one that seemed more congenial to pushing
along EU integration matters than Mr. Major's trenchant opposition to any kind
of 'supranationalism.' But no new points of agreement appeared feasible, not even
after the Extraordinary Council at Noordwijk (23 May 1997) following the British
elections, in time for setting a constructive negotiating agenda so that the
forthcoming Amsterdam Council (16-17 June 1997) might have successfully
concluded the IGC, as originally called for.

The Amsterdam Council—A Major Setback

Recall that the regular European Council as a rule has a much broader agenda than, as in this case, the narrow institutional-governance issues that in the end preoccupied the IGC96 in conjunction with a few other matters, including 'democracy,' 'openness,' and 'security' in its several meanings. The Amsterdam Council had originally been expected to deal primarily with concluding the 'successful' IGC96, including endorsement of a revised TEU, and making preparations for the issuance of a negotiating mandate during the Luxemburg Council (12-13 December 1997) for commencing accession negotiations mainly with TEs. As happened on so many occasions when the supreme arbiter on EU integration meets, the agenda as a matter of course got overloaded with issues that should have been settled earlier or selected for a special Council Session. Among the first, too much time and prominence were allotted to moving toward monetary union. And opening up a different agenda, such as the new French government's emphasis on an EU-wide employment pact as a counterpart to the German-sponsored 'stability pact' in the context of monetary union, was not conducive to cutting the knots into which IGC96 had become tied.

None of these 'special interest' topics was easy to come to grips with during the normal duration of a Council, which is scheduled for one day and a half. Because of the priority to deal first with the most urgent and political matters at hand, much time in Amsterdam was not spent on considering the core issues left unresolved during IGC96. In the end, far too little room remained for the Heads of Government and State to resolve *in extremis* the inconclusiveness of those deliberations especially with respect to all too many obdurate deepening aspects through real-time, face-to-face political negotiations. Extending the second day's Council into a marathon night did not at all help matters (EPC, 1997); it may in fact have further encumbered the integration enterprise beyond the fifteen months' impasse into which IGC96 had landed almost before its inauguration. That in itself had reflected fundamental disagreements about the future of the EU brought into the open since the TEU's initial endorsement (see chapter 2), and any hope that these would in the end be resolved in a high-poker tradeoff in a matter of hours was misguided. It would have been more constructive to declare failure for the IGC than to do the politically more correct reverse against all odds, thus tarnishing credibility.

It would carry us too far afield to look at the details of the achievements and failures of the Amsterdam Council.[12] Let me first note some of the accomplishments. One element of the Amsterdam agenda was the incorporation of the 'social agenda' into the revised treaty, to which the new U.K. government consented. Likewise, some kind of agreement in principle, albeit a weak one, was attained for installing a foreign-policy coordinator at the EU's level, that is, "Mr. CFSP," but acting fully on behalf of the Council in cooperation with the Commission's President. Finally, the members expressed willingness to embrace some kind of reinforced cooperation among states desirous of moving ahead with integration provided other states would not object to this kind of multiple-track approach to 'deepening' EU integration and that the latter would not preclude the others from joining when they so wished.

This was a rather meager accomplishment, however. Indeed fundamentally neither the core issues of deepening nor the difficult institutional obstacles to governing appropriately with fifteen, let alone with an expanded membership, received any impetus whatsoever. Instead, on the latter issues in Amsterdam the policy makers decided to defer these matters until they could no longer skirt them with another enlargement once accession negotiations seemed to lead up to such a move. Even on the apportioning of commissioners no agreement could be worked out. The real policy issues of the multiple pillar EU edifice, notably everything but pillar 1, and even then chiefly limited to issues around EMU, failed to receive any substantive resolution. Not even principles for hammering out institutional reform could be agreed upon. Amsterdam was in fact all but a complete failure and a sad reminder of how quickly intergovernmental deliberations can go awry when sovereign states are facing the need to yield on their national prerogatives and sovereignty in the interest of advancing in common toward a goal that, at least in its vaguest connotation, has been beyond dispute. One must be clear about the latter's meaning: by virtue of the fact that member states subscribe to the Rome Treaty as further refined in Maastricht and Amsterdam, they de facto agree to cooperate at a different level from sheer intergovernmentalism. Paradoxically elevating this into a de jure position can be accomplished only through constructive intergovernmentalism. Precisely that was sadly missing from IGC96.

Failures certainly outweighed the successes at Amsterdam. As far as they are relevant to TE accessions, however, it is appropriate to bear in mind seven classes of internally unresolved accomplishments with their failures. First of all, it should be recalled that the Corfu Council (24-25 June 1994), at which IGC96 had been launched by appointing the Reflection Group, had made it clear that "[t]he institutional conditions for ensuring the proper functioning of the Union must be created at [IGC96] which, for that reason, must take place before accession negotiations begin" (EPC, 1997, p. 2). This had often been repeated in a weaker form, namely, that accession negotiations could commence only after fulfilling a number of conditions, including the successful conclusion of IGC96. The meaning of the call for success was given very different interpretations over time. At the very least, a successful IGC96 should have led to the institutional streamlining that both the TEU and the preparatory meetings of the IGC had held out. At Amsterdam, the leaders ritually declared that there had been a "successful conclusion" (European Commission, 1997d, p. 1) of the IGC96 process. That assertion may well have pleased the TEs, and perhaps even some EU members. But it could hardly disperse the thick clouds of uncertainty and indecisiveness hanging over the expansion process as a result of the fundamental failure to put the EU's house in order.

Second, some major changes in the pillar structure and the respective contents of each were introduced. As concerns pillar 1, some elements were strengthened, including the framework for outsiders and those willing to participate in the revised ERM II and work toward membership in monetary union at a later date than the first cohort. Also the social compact earlier opposed by the United Kingdom was incorporated into pillar 1, though only some of its elements fit there comfortably (see chapter 2).

Third, a revised TEU (Draft Amsterdam Treaty) was approved in principle, with the details left for experts to innovate a legally coherent text. This necessary editorial and organizational streamlining was deferred to the Commission for quick action, since the reworked draft was to be tabled for a special signing ceremony in October 1997, where the Amsterdam Treaty was subsequently approved.[13] It is perhaps useful to reconsider the pillar structure in this context. Especially as concerns pillar 3, EU leaders managed to agree on lifting border controls (thus incorporating the Schengen agreement into the mainstream EU policy, including with respect to pillar 1, but with exemptions for at least three—Denmark, Great Britain, and Ireland), on closer police cooperation, and on EU-wide visa and immigration policies. But as concerns pillar 2, the achievement was confined to endorsement of the creation of a new planning and analysis unit on foreign and security matters. Not even the "Mr. CFSP" was appointed, as that decision was delayed, with the person now slated for office in early 1999. Bringing the WEU into the EU fold was simply ruled out. The decision on forging closer "cooperation of EU and WEU" (European Commission, 1997d, p. 1) was hardly revolutionary.

Fourth, much more serious was the failure to reform the basic internal structures of the EU's governance organs, which in the end became the almost exclusive focus of attention at IGC96. In fact, it was agreed to defer virtually all issues to future negotiations when enlargement will force a reapportionment of the Commission, of voting strengths in the Council, and of seat allotment in the European Parliament. Exceptions to this generalization are the size of the European Parliament, the streamlining of codecision procedures, closer delineation of the respective roles of the various EU institutions, the role of the Commission President, and the principle of closer cooperation in pillars 2 and 3 matters with some degree of flexibility in deepening integration. But for major issues the principle of unanimity in decision making was upheld, albeit in a peculiar manner (Nentwich and Falkner, 1997, pp. 18ff.), leading to the so-called "Amsterdam Compromise," which can be treated as the successor of the notorious "Luxemburg Compromise" of 1966.[14] Majority voting was extended to pillar 3 directly as well as by incorporating some of its elements into the pillar 1 issues. Unanimity with the Amsterdam Compromise will remain most nefarious in pillar 2 matters, in spite of the 'flexibility' gained in the process.

In this context it is expedient to pause briefly to comment on the supposed success achieved in limiting the number of commissioners to twenty (Tosi, 1997a, pp. 13-14). This is not a solution (Favret, 1997, p. 582; Gevrisse, 1998, p. 570; Nentwich and Falkner, 1997, p. 10). Neither does it open the road to expansion to at least five candidates. For one thing, if less than five enter it is unclear which of the large countries will have to yield a seat, unless all five with double seating will yield.[15] But that will occur only if voting strengths will have been revised, a hard problem. If more than five are admitted at once, the full range of issues will need to be reexamined. Also, with whatever expansion—even the magic number five—the voting strengths in the Council and the Parliament must be redrawn, and there has not so far been any agreement on how that will be accomplished.

Fifth, the Treaty of Amsterdam sets out a compelling vision of a democratic person-centered union for the future. It eloquently describes the economic, moral, political, and social values of the EU. But it demonstrably fails to spell out the practical means by which these goals can realistically be promoted. In other words, the decision makers were once again formidably visionary in specifying their aspirations but woefully uninspiring when it came to setting concrete commitments on how to carry out in real time these high-flying goals. Not only that, in spite of earlier agreements to make the EU more transparent, the Treaty itself, even in its approved version of October 1997 (European Commission, 1997f), is not very accessible or readable for the EU citizen. In many respects, it is even more obscure and arcane than the original TEU. The proliferation of protocols and declarations, all in one way or another noting derogations from the main texts supposedly approved, is worrisome for it underlines the almost bazaar-like manner in which high-level policy makers have been dealing with quasi-constitutional issues concerning the future of the EU, including expansion of its geographical compass.

Sixth, internal structural reforms are now slated to be discussed again at least one year prior to another enlargement. Would this be via another IGC? And would this then nullify earlier assessments that convening yet another would be "out of the question" (Guigou, 1995; Interview, 1996), given the difficulties encountered already in the run-up to IGC96? The agreements reached at Amsterdam and some of the attachments to the revised Treaty suggest that there will be a follow-up IGC around 2000 to settle these matters, after the next budgetary battles will have been fought. In this context one really should look into the futility of the IGC process as underlined by IGC96. Without major political initiatives taken at the highest level through hard-core compromises on sovereignty issues, it will be impossible to forge ahead with deepening, let alone with widening, by having national representatives simply reiterate over and over again their nation's point of view on all issues that truly matter.

Finally, although the EU leaders, notably at the follow-up to the Amsterdam Council for TEs on 27 June 1997, went out of their way to emphasize that the failure to complete minimal internal reforms will not delay the next enlargement process, that is a disingenuous statement, putting it mildly. The annex to the Treaty first tabled at Amsterdam by Belgium, France, and Italy and subsequently endorsed by the Luxemburg Council (European Commission, 1997g) makes it clear that there will not be enlargement prior to serious, truly incisive internal structural reforms.[16] Since the latter have proved to be very difficult, the catch-22 for present candidates should be clear: having the enlargement process not affected by the disagreements about internal reforms would amount to a veritable miracle, one that the real world of EU policy making almost definitely precludes. The squabbles about the preparation of budgetary reforms, as examined briefly in the next section, amply corroborate this generalization of the EU's governance for most of its existence.

Salience of the Amsterdam and Luxemburg Councils for TEs

Inasmuch as IGC96 should have tackled and resolved major governance aspects of the institutional and political functioning of the EU, the outcome obtained in Amsterdam, as slightly modified at Luxemburg, can at best be interpreted as yet another setback for deepening EU integration. Two exceptions to this generalization deserve to be cited. One encompasses issues around the start-up and functioning of monetary union. The other concerns the SEM's completion, that is, the establishment in full of EMU, at least the first round thereof since at least four members will not participate in monetary union either by choice (Denmark, Sweden, and the United Kingdom) or because some of the key entrance criteria cannot be met for now (Greece). That is to say, for all the hoopla about achievements in moving the integration process along, very little progress has to date been booked with deepening EU integration even in the most narrow purview as adopted for IGC96. That in and of itself has major implications for aspiring entrants.

Even more so, the repeated insistence by three members (Belgium, France, and Italy) that enlargement cannot be implemented before these major institutional aspects of governing the EU will have been resolved, has since Luxemburg been officially enshrined in the 'enlargement doctrine' issued by the European Council. This carries two kinds of ominous implications. One is that even with 'easy' accession negotiations for the fast-track TEs there is no guarantee whatsoever that simultaneously the core institutional hurdles can be quickly overcome. This all the more so since the near term will be taken up, to a large extent, by difficult budget negotiations to produce an overall agreement by end 1999, and forthcoming negotiations about further agricultural reform and indeed revising the structural-support approaches since both claim the vast bulk of 'community' funds—some four-fifths of the overall budget (Dutheil de la Rochère, 1995, pp. 101-2; Thomas, 1994, p. 475).

On the first issue, two constraints have already become clear. One is that the cap of 1.27 percent of GNP as the EU budget is unlikely to be lifted. Not only that, the major beneficiaries of budget outlays for agriculture (France and Spain in particular) and structural policies (Greece, Portugal, and Spain in particular) have already made it clear that enlargement cannot encroach upon either. Quite apart from this problem in reconceiving the CAP, France in particular, but also other members, has already staked out claims that Europe's 'agricultural policy' cannot be changed in any major way regardless of enlargement.

In spite of this up-front intransigence, budgetary revisions will almost certainly be introduced beginning with the year 2000 (European Commission, 1998g). There are several reasons for this position. One is that the EU cannot afford to continue to allocate the bulk of its funds to support agriculture and cohesion. Another is that without reforms, particularly in the latter two programs, eastward enlargement is precluded. Finally, agricultural subsidies are due to be discussed again at the global level in the WTO context in 1999, as agreed to during the Uruguay Round, then still under the GATT's auspices.

The nature, scope, and objectives of most of the current transfer programs administered by the European Commission—such as for agricultural, cohesion, social, and structural supports—will have to be reassessed against the rather inflexible budget in order for the Commission to discharge fully its mandated tasks as demands for outlays are likely to far exceed the available revenues. It should, then, be clear that if the EU is to address the vital communautarian issues through financial transfers, it cannot do so while the vast bulk of its resources continue to be captured for agricultural supports and cohesion purposes. Indeed, at the Luxemburg Council in December 1997 (Tosi, 1997b) it was decided to maintain this upper level throughout the next budgetary cycle (2000-2006). But no firm agreement on redistributing the major components of outlays in particular was reached (European Commission, 1997e; France, 1997, p. 22). That presumably was to have been helped along at the special Council organized by Austria in Pörtschach[17] (24-25 October 1998) partly in preparation for the Vienna Council (11-12 December 1998), as decided at the Cardiff Council, 15-16 June 1998 (European Commission, 1998f, pp. 5ff.). Also, the large net contributors, with Germany in the lead, have requested that their assessed shares be reduced. Although this may not succeed, given Germany's interest in eastward expansion, the démarche by several EU members does put pressure on revising budgetary procedures (European Commission, 1998e, g).

Controversy cannot be far off, however. The Commission's proposals tabled in March 1998 (European Commission, 1998a, b) for agricultural and structural reforms immediately elicited adverse reaction, notably from Spain. With at best a slowly increasing amount of total revenues (presumably on a par with GNP growth), eastward expansion, which necessarily escalates claims on community finances given the TEs' level of development, population size, and agricultural problems, must aggravate the redistribution that will occur with the adoption of any expenditure reform. This cannot but weigh heavily on the ongoing accession negotiations.

Conclusions

Does widening the EU remain predicated on prior deepening? I manifestly do not wish to impart rhetoric into a very serious issue. Even so, all too many observers of the EU scene in general and the merger of the TEs into that edifice in particular appear to see the two as separate paths at best. Some have even argued that, because forging ahead with deepening is a fundamental mistake that may undo the EU, the focus of policy attention should be on widening or, in other words, 'spreading the liberal order' to all of Europe (Garton Ash, 1998). It is ironic that those two paths—deepening integration and spreading the liberal order—can be seen as parallel tasks. Deepening integration is anything but meant to spread the liberal order. Rather its main objective is to solidify the anchor of the liberal order among EU members according to some norms upon which there was earlier agreement but growing diversity of opinion now among the EU membership, and indeed among the aspiring TEs.

It should be clear that widening is unlikely to occur without minimal deepening. At least the core issues left over from IGC96 (that is, revisions in institutions and decision-making mechanisms) need to be resolved. Deepening could conceivably be pursued without widening, but there is no political support for that approach at this stage. Hence at best some bargain is likely to be struck at the highest policy-making level—the European Council—with minimal deepening in return for minimal widening. That has ominous implications for other actual or potential candidates (see chapter 9). However, it also has deleterious effects for the EU's destiny for one must bear in mind the essence of the need for deepening.

That is to say, the political-economy reality of the present and foreseeable EU is such that there is no simple choice between 'widening' and 'deepening.' Both objectives must be pursued simultaneously, even though widening remains largely contingent on a critical minimal commitment to deepening, in such a way that any delay in integration among the present and near-term members will not infringe too much on the delivery of the economic, political, security, and other benefits that EU membership eventually holds out for a range of TEs. That poses a number of critical governance issues, which hang like a heavy Damocles sword over TE accessions and *must* at some point be thoroughly addressed.

I have touched upon only some of those topics, especially those involved in the debates around IGC96. But there are undoubtedly other, even more cumbersome, issues that will eventually need to be tackled. Indeed, as the failures of IGC96 underline, deepening can in fact not be restricted to institutional and decision-making matters referring to the rather arcane subjects, among others, of the modus of voting, the number of commissioners, the division of powers among the basic EU institutions, and the distribution of voting powers among the members. The fact that even those items could not be resolved signals that there lingers much deeper-seated disagreement among the membership about expanding the EU once again, but also on fundamental integration policies.

Notes

This chapter presents a much expanded and updated version of the latter part of Brabant, 1998c.

1. The other declared candidates are Malta, Switzerland, and Turkey. Malta suspended its request for accession in October 1996 for domestic political reasons, but revived it in late 1998, also for domestic political reasons (see chapter 1). Since the Swiss electorate rejected accession to the European Economic Area (EEA), its government is unlikely any time soon to be able to count on obtaining a mandate to negotiate for accession with the EU. Making progress at all with Cyprus's accession depends critically on finding a solution to the Greek-Turkish divisions (France, 1998, p. 6) and the current deep-freeze status of the relations between Turkey and the EU (see chapter 9).

2. I am singling him out since, at least until the 1998 change in government, he was the coordinator for the Hungarian government's preparations for accession negotiations.

3. I have elsewhere (Brabant, 1996a, p. 6) justified this terminology in preference to 'communitarianism' on the basis of what the term I prefer really means in the EU context.

4. The decision to enshrine this clause in the Treaty was, of course, preceded by a protracted and convoluted debate on reforming the EU institutions so that the pace of integration would no longer be anchored to the desires of the least interested or slowest moving member. For details of the discussions through mid-1996, see Brabant, 1996a, pp. 90-92.

5. For a legal examination of these various concepts and how they have been applied in EU practice, see Ehlermann, 1996.

6. Briefly, balancing the interests of 'small' and 'large' EU members has always been critical to governing EU integration. With the entry of three small EFTA countries, a coalition of the 'small' could block a majority of the 'large' to move ahead. The matter could not be satisfactorily resolved through the so-called Ioannina Compromise reached in March 1994 at a special Foreign Affairs Council. For details, see Brabant, 1996a, pp. 85-86.

7. CFSP stands for Common Foreign and Security Policy, the subject of pillar 2.

8. He was Secretary General of the Council of Ministers for a very long time and a key member of the Reflection Group.

9. Recall that the Presidency is assisted with the former and next-scheduled Presidencies in the *troika* format.

10. That may well have been a slip since there would hardly have been sufficient time to conduct the weekly meetings on the various topics up for deliberation in time for the wrap-up session. The date of 17 June 1996 seems more appropriate, but the cited source gives the May deadline.

11. This draft materialized but proved to be too cumbersome and too overloaded with suggestions for resolving matters on which the members remained widely divided. For details, see Griller et al., 1997a.

12. For a detailed examination of the achievements, seen through the Commission's highly partisan, hence sympathetically tinted, lens, see European Commission, 1997b. A more sober analysis is in Favret, 1997; Tosi, 1997a, b. A balanced exposé on many of the relevant issues is in Haguenau-Moizard, 1998; Nentwich and Falkner, 1997. For a more systematic and detailed examination of the draft Amsterdam Treaty, see Griller et al., 1997b.

13. For some observers (Griller et al., 1997b) this, rather than the June Council's declaration of successfully concluding the IGC, marks the end of IGC96.

14. In brief, this sought to resolve the serious constitutional crisis in EEC affairs brought about by the French government's intransigence under Charles de Gaulle. The resolution was found in agreeing to disagree: member states were urged to negotiate on touchy matters until one or more members invoked the clause of "very important," just another wording for the earlier veto associated with unanimous decision making (Brabant, 1995, pp. 183ff.).

15. The Amsterdam Treaty is ambiguous on this score. In any case, it is the constraint on revising voting strengths prior to yielding the second Commissioner for the five large countries that is likely to constitute the real constraint.

16. France in particular remains adamant on the need to accomplish institutional reforms prior to any expansion beyond the present fifteen members (France, 1998, p. 3).

17. From press reports, however, this meeting focused largely on how best the EU can cope with the global recession, maintain internal buoyancy in spite of the stringent requirements of monetary union (see chapter 5), and tackle its still very sizable unemployment problem in the years ahead. There was reportedly also some discussion of organizing Europe's defense, probably basing it on the WEU, within the context of NATO.

Chapter 5

Exchange-Rate Regimes and Monetary Policies for EU Candidates

Lucjan T. Orlowski

How best to design monetary policies and exchange-rate regimes in central European TEs forms an important, indeed an integral, component of these countries' strategies for acceding to the EU and, later, for entry into the EU's monetary union. This chapter advocates a more gradual approach in these economies to the monetary policy based on stability of their national currencies in terms of the euro. The ongoing economic transformation can be made more manageable by pursuing an autonomous monetary policy with flexible exchange rates. Under such an approach, central banks will be able to complete their long-term efforts designed to gain monetary credibility. The approach is more advantageous for capacity building and institutional strengthening of domestic financial markets in these economies (Fink, Haiss, Orlowski, and Salvatore, 1998). It is also beneficial for facilitating the ongoing, deep structural adjustments that will facilitate the smooth integration of these economies into the EU at some point in the not-too-distant future (Brabant, 1996b; Orlowski, 1995).

However, upon entering the EU, new members will be expected to begin preparations for accession to monetary union and to intensify their ongoing efforts. This practically implies that they will be expected to join ERM II, that is, set a unilateral currency peg to the euro and join the rules applying to EU members absenting themselves temporarily from the monetary union—the 'outs.' The new exchange-rate regime will imply a radical change in monetary policy from the autonomous money-based policy to one anchored to the currency peg.

This chapter elaborates on problems of sequencing, instrumentation, and economic consequences of monetary-policy adjustments in TEs on their road to the EU and monetary union. At the initial stage of preparations for EU accession, a monetary policy focused on direct inflation targeting, also known in the literature as inflation-forecast targeting, is strongly advocated. This approach is consistent with relatively flexible exchange rates. Upon joining ERM II, the TEs will be expected to apply an exchange-rate targeting system of monetary policy. Such a switch should not be engineered prior to completion in full of major structural and institutional tasks incumbent upon bringing the candidate TEs closer to the EU.

Rigorous monetary and fiscal convergence in the candidate countries consistent with the nominal convergence criteria specified in the Maastricht Treaty is not a precondition for EU accession (but see chapter 3). However, the entrants will be held to rigid requirements of low inflation and a minimum ratio of the consolidated fiscal budget deficit to GDP once they join ERM II. Even with concessions prior to joining ERM II, if they were to be permitted to accede to the EU without joining ERM II, they will be subjected to macroeconomic constraints following from the obligations stipulated in the Maastricht Treaty. Even at an early stage, however, the Maastricht macroeconomic-convergence benchmarks will serve as helpful policy guidelines in order to generate the degree of price and income stability that is essential for securing eventual entry into the EU and monetary union.

At a later stage, preparations for accession to monetary union will require strict adherence to policies that can lead to fulfilling the Maastricht convergence criteria. The final stage preceding entry into monetary union will require a change in monetary policy from a money-based one into one based on maintaining the exchange rate. This monetary-policy change is called in this study a "return-to-peg strategy." The candidates for early EU accession among the TEs are familiar with a fixed exchange-rate system since their heterodox programs of economic transformation in the early 1990s were mostly based on a pegged currency. Since then, however, they have gradually departed from fixed exchange rates in favor of pursuing more autonomous monetary policies by applying more flexible exchange rates (Desai, 1998; Orlowski, 1997a; Sachs, 1996). The strategy of returning to a currency peg will gradually shift responsibility for disinflation to fiscal policy since monetary-policy flexibility will be limited. It is therefore essential for TE macroeconomic managers to adhere to strict fiscal convergence. Since inflation attributable to backward-looking expectations is still firmly rooted in these economies, it seems advisable for the candidates to follow even a tighter benchmark than the maximum 3 percent fiscal deficit-to-GDP criterion specified in the Maastricht Treaty (Orlowski, 1997b). If the required disinflation is not accomplished, an early application of the currency peg to the euro will lead to a considerable real appreciation of the TEs' currencies, to chronic current-account deficits, and to an unfavorable risk structure of capital inflows. The real appreciation of currencies of these countries has already contributed to a gradually deteriorating "pecking order" of incoming external capital. There has indeed been faster growth of portfolio capital than of FDI inflows (Orlowski and Corrigan, 1997). Consequently, prolonged balance-of-payments problems may undermine the further economic transformation of the TEs and their integration into the EU.

The chapter is organized as follows. After an examination of present exchange-rate and monetary regimes in the TE-5, I review their prevailing monetary-policy targets and discuss some proposed policy changes warranted by entry into the EU's monetary union. Then I deal with the question of whether the candidates are likely to experience a "last devaluation syndrome" (Grauwe, 1996); that is, will they be forced to devalue their currencies at least two years prior to accession to the monetary union? In conclusion I present further suggestions for short- and long-term monetary-policy adjustments.

Fixed Exchange Rates and Exit Strategies

Both the academic literature on the economics of transition and policy makers of TEs have strongly emphasized the role of the exchange rate as a policy tool aimed at solving some of the economic imbalances inherited from central planning, such as the monetary overhang and corrective inflation, weak to nonexistent policy credibility, depleted savings, and deteriorating current-account deficits (Bruno, 1992; Sachs, 1996). To accomplish these tasks, most TEs applied fixed exchange rates at the beginning of their economic transformation. The currency peg was primarily aimed at containing corrective inflation stemming from liberalization of previously fixed or rather inflexible prices for most goods, services, and intermediate materials, causing in some TEs deep market imbalances and an excess supply of money.

Price liberalization induced a one-time inflation shock of unpredictable duration and depth. At the outset of the transformation, the new TE governments were not sure whether the disturbance would be self-correcting or more persistent. They chose to actively fight corrective inflation using fixed exchange rates as a tool of policy discipline. The currency peg helped to rebuild national savings, which had been eroded by the corrective inflation, and to restore credibility of policy makers and public confidence in economic reforms.

The modern literature on exchange-rate policies in the context of economic stabilization in emerging market economies generally supports the view that successful stabilization programs anchored to the exchange rate require a predetermined, early-exit strategy from fixed exchange rates. Such an approach was variously pursued, both in time and in the intensity of the policy commitment, by the TEs under consideration here (Orlowski, 1997a), but also in a number of other TEs, especially in eastern Europe.

Among the five candidates for early EU accession, Poland departed from the dollar peg in May 1991, after having held it for sixteen months. Following this move, the government first applied a crawling-peg strategy against a basket consisting of five currencies (dominated by the dollar) and replaced it later with a crawling-band regime, whose room for fluctuation was expanded in May 1995. This regime is still in effect. In September 1998, the dollar weight stood at 45 percent, the band at 10 percent on either side of parity, and the monthly rate of crawling devaluation at 0.5 percent compounded daily.

Czechoslovakia devalued its currency against the dollar in two rounds (in October 1990 and in January 1991) by 50 percent. As part of the January 1991 comprehensive economic reform, the authorities applied a fixed exchange rate against a basket of five currencies. After the breakup in 1993, the Czech Republic assumed a fixed exchange rate of the koruna against a basket of two currencies (the German mark and the dollar) with a narrow band (0.5 percent either side of parity) for fluctuation. The fixed exchange rate was maintained until the end of February 1996, when the band was expanded to 7.5 percent either side of parity. As a result of intense attacks on the koruna and capital outflows in the second quarter of 1997, the Czech National Bank on 27 May 1997 allowed the currency to float, implying a devaluation of the currency, albeit with a commitment to switch to a German-mark peg after reaching a 'satisfactory' exchange rate against that currency. Managed floating continues, however.

In contrast, Slovenia has consistently pursued a managed float since the introduction of the tolar in October 1991. The currency experienced considerable nominal depreciation in the second half of 1995 (9 percent in dollar terms), but it has been fairly stable in nominal terms since then. On the other extreme, Estonia has maintained a currency board at 8 kroons to the German mark since June 1992.

Finally, Hungary did not experience major problems stemming from a significant monetary overhang, and it therefore did not commit to a firm currency peg. Since the beginning of 1990 and until March 1995, it pursued an adjustable peg and since then it has followed a crawling peg. The country's central bank enacted a sharp 15 percent devaluation in January 1991. The forint has been pegged to a dual-currency basket whose specific composition and weights have changed over time. The most significant currency adjustment was enacted on 13 March 1995, when the forint was devalued by 9 percent and the crawling devaluation was introduced at a monthly rate of 1.9 percent. The dual-currency basket consists presently of 70 percent for the German mark and 30 percent for the dollar. As of September 1998, the regime provides for a band of 2.5 percent on each side of central parity with a monthly rate of crawling devaluation of 0.8 percent.

The three larger candidates for fast-track accession negotiations (the Czech Republic, Hungary, and Poland) have in the meantime joined the Organisation for Economic Co-operation and Development (OECD). One of the requirements stipulated in the accession agreements was for these countries to introduce considerable currency convertibility on capital account. From the beginning of 1999, these TEs will fully liberalize portfolio investments by domestic residents abroad and capital transfers from abroad into their economies, allowing cross-border branching in the banking sector. Estonia has maintained full current and capital-account convertibility as required by the currency board, after some initial restrictions. The Slovenian tolar is fully convertible for current-account transactions, and foreign investors are permitted to repatriate profits and capital.

In sum, the candidates for EU accession are presently maintaining a variety of exchange-rate regimes, thus varying monetary-policy regimes. They range from fixity under the Estonian currency board to the Czech and Slovenian managed floats. Also the reference currencies, whether a basket or otherwise, vary considerably. If these countries desire to join the EU's monetary union at some future point in time, their specific plans for adjusting monetary policies and exchange-rate regimes will need to be centered on reaching currency stability within narrowing fluctuation bands relative to the euro. The analytical literature on the experience with economic stability in the TEs broadly agrees that fixed exchange rates have successfully fulfilled the task of reducing corrective inflation, building policy credibility, and restoring national savings. But their anti-inflationary role ought to be deemphasized at the present stage of transformation.

A more flexible exchange rate allows TE monetary authorities to cushion real appreciation of their national currencies and, consequently, to prevent the deterioration of current-account deficits. Perhaps most importantly, by lowering expectations of a further real appreciation of the national currencies, flexible exchange rates may improve the risk structure of capital inflows by favoring FDI over portfolio-capital inflows. The advantage of such a course is particularly visible in the case of the Czech Republic, where the current-account deficit stopped deteriorating and the risk structure of capital inflows was improved as a result of the introduction of the crawling band and, later, the managed float (Orlowski and Corrigan, 1997).

Variant monetary regimes, different degrees of currency convertibility for current- and capital-account transactions, and, most importantly, diverse degrees of institutional development and of efficiency in financial markets have given rise to a variety of problems such as real currency appreciation, current-account deficits, and the inflationary consequences of capital inflows. Table 5.1 reflects the present stage of these variables in the three largest early-accession candidates.

In all three countries, inflation in 1996 was higher than the nominal depreciation of the currency, thus contributing to rising real exchange rates. The data for 1996 confirm the point advanced by Halpern and Wyplosz (1996), as well as by Begg (1996), that with quasi-fixed exchange rates (crawling pegs and bands) the primary cause of real currency appreciation in the central European TEs is high inflation; the corollary is that appreciation will stop only with the completion of the transformation.

The inflation picture changed in 1997 because the pace of inflation was slower than the nominal appreciation, at least in dollar terms. This stemmed in part from

Table 5.1: Indicators for the Czech Republic, Hungary, and Poland

Variable	Czech Rep.		Hungary		Poland	
	1996	1997	1996	1997	1996	1997
REER index[a]	142.7	144.7	109.4	121.3	143.6	147.7
Depreciation[b]	-2.7	-23.1	-18.3	-23.8	-16.5	-22.4
Reserves[c]	0.1	-2.3	-3.3	4.0	0.1	1.5
Current account[d]	-8.6	-6.6	-3.8	-2.2	-1.4	-4.3
GDP growth	3.9	1.0	1.3	4.0	6.1	6.9
Change in CPI	7.4	13.0	19.8	18.4	19.9	14.9
Investment/GDP[e]	33.0	30.2	25.0	24.9	20.4	22.9
Savings/GDP[f]	25.4	23.9	23.2	23.0	19.4	19.7

Notes:
[a] REER index based on consumer price deflators (January 1990=100) as compiled by J.P. Morgan.
[b] Nominal depreciation against the dollar in percent based on year-end exchange rates.
[c] Net inflows as a percent of GDP.
[d] Percent of GDP.
[e] Domestic investment as a percent of GDP.
[f] Domestic savings as a percent of GDP.

Sources:

International financial statistics (Washington, DC: International Monetary Fund, various issues); *World financial markets* (New York: Morgan Guarantee Trust Company, 27 March 1998), p. 52; and monthly reports of the CNB, NBH, and NBP, various issues.

the overall appreciation of the dollar in terms of other key international currencies. Yet, the slowdown of the real appreciation of TE currencies also resulted from the expanded flexibility of exchange rates, primarily in the case of the Czech Republic and Poland. It is worth noting that the real effective exchange rate (REER) of the forint increased significantly in 1997. It is possible that greater flexibility of the forint exchange rate would alleviate this rise.

The strong real appreciation of the złoty along with fast GDP growth as well as the lagging of national savings behind gross investment in Poland have all contributed to the rising current-account deficit. The Czech Republic experienced similar problems even more severely in 1994-1996, leading to a peak ratio of the current account to GDP of 8.6 percent in 1996. Halting the koruna's real appreciation by raising exchange-rate flexibility successfully reduced this ratio in 1997. Pressures on the current account in Hungary are considerably lower due to the lower GDP growth rate, the smaller gap between national savings and investment, and the previous stability of the REER. However, inflation remains excessive in Hungary and may entail further real appreciation of the currency in the foreseeable future, thus possibly worsening the current-account deficit.

The above-cited empirical evidence suggests key tasks for exchange-rate policies in TEs. Their monetary authorities are encouraged to find ways to slow down the ongoing real appreciation of their currencies in order to improve the balance of payments. This can best be achieved by applying flexible exchange rates and money-based monetary policies. At the same time, they need to pursue rigorous fiscal and monetary discipline in order to reduce inflation more decisively. As stated by Mishkin (1997), price stability is essential for financial stability of economic systems. It expands the maturity of debt contracts, thus making it easier for financial- and business-sector institutions to borrow long-term capital in domestic currency. In the end, it helps to reduce the fragility of financial systems. More flexible exchange rates also favor the development of domestic foreign-exchange markets, which are essential for the future integration of these countries into the EU's financial system. Moreover, flexible rates provide clear signals about macroeconomic-policy fundamentals. If market exchange rates are not distorted, a sharp depreciation of the nominal exchange rate normally serves as a warning sign for possible corrective policies to adjust macroeconomic imbalances. Concurrently with the application of flexible exchange rates, the candidate countries may wish to apply direct inflation targeting.

Monetary-Policy Targeting Strategies

Now that some TEs are enjoying the prospect of eventually joining the EU, the candidates have to choose among a variety of intermediate and operational targets for monetary policy because, as set forth earlier, their monetary-policy systems vary significantly, complicating the design of a uniform "return-to-peg strategy" at this juncture. However, the ultimate targets of their monetary policy show greater similarities (Krzak and Schubert, 1997). Recently published monetary-policy directives of central banks in all five countries emphasize a long-term commitment to disinflation and to safeguarding currency stability. However, the Czech and Polish central banks in their 1997 policy directives state also the goal of supporting the economic policy pursued by the government. This may be a politically desirable directive. But its bearing is rather unclear, given that the central banks of these countries are ostensibly independent. If not, moving closer to the EU will impose upon these countries the constraint of engineering a far-reaching degree of central-bank independence. Once they join the EU's monetary union, monetary policy will, in effect, be transferred to the ECB.

In the recent literature on choices of monetary regimes, the distinction between intermediate and operational targets has been disappearing, especially when the monetary authorities target money balances or directly the path of inflation (Bernanke and Mishkin, 1997; Orlowski, 1998a). The distinction is still valid, though, when short-term interest rates are chosen as operational targets. Interest-rate targeting is based on observed variables, and it is thus a backward-looking policy. The targeting horizon becomes very short and the policy is frequently reset. While applying discretionary changes of interest rates as operational targets, central banks still need to apply some intermediate targets to modulate monetary policy.

The central banks of the five TEs under discussion do not apply uniform targets for monetary policy. Moreover, there has been considerable inconsistency in their choices of monetary targets. Until the end of 1997, the Czech National Bank (CNB) claimed to aim at controlling M2 balances as an intermediate target and the one-week Prague Interbank Offer Rate as an operational target (Krzak and Schubert, 1997). Since the beginning of 1998, it has applied core-inflation targeting. The new system allows integration of intermediate and operational targets by setting a predetermined level of core inflation with a fairly narrow band of tolerance. The CNB has applied a 6.0 percent core inflation target with a 0.5 percent band on either side for 1998, and a 4.5 percent target with a 1.0 percent tolerance band on either side for 2000, which is the date planned by policy makers for entry into ERM II.[1]

The new Czech system offers an attractive alternative for monetary policy in TEs. It is a forward-looking monetary policy with a transparent commitment to disinflation. However, it can be viewed also as a temporary, more sophisticated tool of gaining policy credibility and generating price stability. The CNB is applying a managed float for the koruna as an exchange-rate policy fully consistent with the monetary regime based on direct inflation targeting. The system will have to be gradually changed into a currency peg to the euro, at the latest when the country enters ERM II.

The National Bank of Hungary (NBH) states as intermediate targets maintaining the exchange rate within the current 2.5 percent band on either side of parity and M2, and as operational target the interest-rate differential vis-à-vis European financial markets. These permit the NBH to monitor short-term capital inflows more effectively. The system indicates a backward-looking, discretionary policy of the NBH.

The National Bank of Poland (NBP) enacted a major change in monetary-policy targeting in October 1998. It now intends to target the CPI inflation forecast while holding the exchange rate within the broad 10 percent band on either side of parity (without publishing any implicit target zones, that is, internal narrower bands). The new approach was introduced after the authorities had pursued a considerable degree of inconsistency in the choice of monetary-policy targets in recent years. Specifically, the NBP followed short-term interest rates as an operational target in the first half of 1996; later, when GDP growth accelerated and the current-account deficit started to deteriorate, it moved to domestic-credit expansion as an operating target. In 1997, it formally announced targeting the monetary base and in the beginning 1998 it switched again to targeting interest rates.

Direct inflation targeting as applied by the NBP is a desirable solution considering the instability of emerging financial markets and the unusually high volatility of demand for money in Poland in the third quarter of 1998. Lessons from the experiences of central banks that have adopted direct inflation targeting, particularly the Bank of Canada, Bank of England, Bank of Sweden, and the Reserve Bank of New Zealand, conclusively prove that this approach is superior to targeting interest rates or various measures of the money supply when domestic demand for money is unstable or it is undergoing major behavioral changes, as a result of structural transformation. According to the October 1998 monetary-policy guidelines, the NBP is assuming an 8 to 8.5 percent inflation target zone (measured for consumer prices) for 1999 and a 4 percent strategic target for 2003.

The new system of direct inflation targeting is expected to enhance credibility and transparency of monetary policies in the central European TEs (Orlowski, 1998a). It will allow for considerably lower indexation of wages and prices in the countries where inflation is still running at near double-digit levels. Indexation will now be adjusted to forecasted, low inflation, while it was geared to the actually observed high inflation trend before. The new approach is likely to prepare these economies adequately for the monetary convergence and stability of the domestic currency in terms of the euro, particularly if they plan to lock their exchange rates to the euro either unilaterally, at a later stage of the pre-accession period, or through formally joining ERM II upon entry into the EU.

An early application of the euro peg is advocated by Barysch (1997), who views it as a tool for facilitating disinflation and reducing excessive volatility of currencies of the present EU candidates. However, deferring application of the euro peg until it becomes sustainable is the option advocated by this author. Relatively flexible exchange rates at the present stage of transformation are to be preferred for TEs in particular until inflation is reduced to a level where it would no longer exert upward pressure on the real exchange rate of these countries' currencies. To this observer, it seems preferable to reduce inflation while maintaining fiscal discipline and applying a monetary policy that directly targets inflation rather than using a currency peg as a disciplining tool.

Direct inflation targeting implies a forward-looking policy in contrast to the backward-looking character of interest-rate targeting. It further permits monetary authorities to concentrate on the predetermined path of disinflation, thereby enhancing the commitment of central banks to monetary discipline and to price stability. The effectiveness of the new system depends strictly on the width of the effective tolerance bands on which the deviation of actual inflation rates from those targeted is predicated. Wider bands allow more time for policy-decision lags, while shorter bands require rather quick policy responses leading to frequent discretionary reactions to observed disturbances in actual income and price levels. In this respect, the present plus-minus 0.5 percent band applied by the CNB and the smaller band (plus-minus 0.25 percent) assumed by the NBP may be viewed as too narrow. The bands of permitted currency fluctuation closely correspond to inflation tolerance bands, circumscribing the maximum allowed deviation of actual inflation from the targeted level. Specifically, a short-term increase in inflation to the upper bound of the tolerance band is normally accompanied by nominal depreciation of the domestic currency, thus moving toward the lower support level of the exchange-rate band.

At a future stage of active preparations for accession to monetary union, central banks will have to move gradually toward basing their monetary policy on the exchange rate. This will require a gradual narrowing of inflation tolerance bands and closing exchange-rate bands as the value of the domestic currency in euro terms converges to a stable level. But the close connection between the inflation path and the exchange rate implies that a stable market exchange rate can be reached only when inflation approaches a low level consistent with the Maastricht benchmark. The new system of direct inflation targeting may prove to be very effective in reaching such a low-inflation environment within a period of four to five years for Hungary and Poland, and by the year of 2000 for the Czech Republic, taking the official target commitment as given.

Moreover, the system permits the elimination of some of the questionable elements of current Hungarian and Polish monetary policies, namely, the crawling devaluation and the frequent changes in policy instruments, mainly reserve-requirement ratios and central-bank lending rates. The removal of the crawling devaluation is urgent since it is viewed as a key factor presently contributing in TEs to wage and price drift because of the indexation rules in place (Rosati, 1996). Upon entry to ERM II, crawling devaluations will have to be discontinued. The system of direct inflation targeting would seem to be effective for meeting the key prerequisites for a successful entry into ERM II.

A "Return-to-Peg" Strategy

TE fiscal and monetary authorities need to encourage changes in exchange-rate regimes and operating procedures to prepare the ground for a smooth transition toward joining the euro regime. Generally speaking, it will be beneficial to these countries to enter ERM II for as long as they cannot effectively join the EU's monetary union (Bernard, 1997); that is, for at least two years following their effective entry into the EU as full members. The governments of the three largest TEs among the early accession candidates have already expressed intentions to join ERM II, thereby reaffirming their commitment to full EU integration and adding credibility to their preparations.

However, a premature "return-to-peg" will undercut the potency of monetary policy, shifting the primary responsibility for disinflation to fiscal policy. The actual entry into the ERM II depends on the permitted exchange-rate flexibility within the new system, that is, the width of the fluctuation band. The exchange-rate band of ERM II is likely to remain wide for the foreseeable future:15 percent either side of central parity. However, TE central banks are likely to apply narrower internal bands or implicit target zones as a tool of monetary discipline.

Depending upon the specific policy approach, the moment of entry into ERM II will have to correspond to the width of the bands. With a wider band, entry into ERM II is more readily feasible at an earlier stage, as soon as inflation reaches a low, sustainable level. With a narrower band, however, entry into ERM II needs to be delayed until inflation can be effectively managed at a level consistent with the Maastricht benchmark. In any case, it is not advisable for the TEs to lock their exchange rates to the euro upon its advent in January 1999 and the decision to join the ERM II should be formulated with caution. The TEs need sufficient time to monitor their exchange rates in euro terms and to reduce the exchange-rate volatility stemming from high inflation differentials and still unstable domestic financial markets.

Several benefits accrue for the TEs from delaying entry into the ERM II. The move is likely to enhance credibility of monetary policies and to improve fiscal and monetary discipline, since these countries will be expected to adhere to strict macroeconomic convergence criteria. It will further benefit the credibility and sincerity of the whole integration approach since the candidates will show in this way that they are committed to full integration. There are also visible benefits for the ongoing transformation process and for the needed modification of exchange-rate regimes. Entering ERM II will probably reduce inflation expectations in these countries. It is, therefore, likely to reduce the inflationary effect of indexation of wages and prices, which is still considerable and contributes to the inflation inertia at the present stage of transformation. In technical terms, ERM II will prompt monetary authorities in TEs to discontinue crawling devaluations that are believed to be adding to inflation because of the automatic indexation of prices and wages (Orlowski, 1997a; Rosati, 1996). It will also encourage the NBP to change the basket of reference currencies in preparation for entry into ERM II, thus lowering the dollar weight in favor of placing the overwhelming weight on the euro. Upon entry into ERM II, the euro will have to be the exclusive reference currency. This alignment will enhance the meshing of Poland's financial markets into the EU's. The Czech Republic and Hungary have already shifted to a predominant weight for the German mark over the dollar in their baskets.

There are also some disadvantages for TEs of joining ERM II, especially when entry precedes the satisfactory completion of the appropriate institutional where-withal for ensuring the more or less smooth functioning of financial markets and constructing an efficient system of bank supervision and monitoring. As argued by Wyplosz (1997), entering ERM II at the earliest moment or shadowing it from its inception may add considerable volatility to the TEs' exchange rates in euro terms since it remains uncertain how stable the new currency will initially be. Central banks may attempt to reduce this volatility through active sterilization. But the duration of such sterilization cannot be too long, if only because of the high fiscal costs associated with it. As a result, it seems preferable to replace steriliza-tion with some degree of currency appreciation whenever conditions invite sizable capital inflows. It can be further argued that expectations of a nominal appreciation of the currency tied to the stability of the euro in combination with the ongoing inflation among the EU member that will not join monetary union from its start—the 'outs'—will accelerate real appreciation of their currencies.

The overall benefits of joining ERM II seem increasingly to outweigh the expected disadvantages as TE policy makers succeed in stabilizing prices and exchange rates, and as the euro gains stability in world financial markets. It would therefore seem advisable that the candidates join ERM II at some future point, after they become EU members and once they can sustain monetary stability, rather than early on. This timing does not relieve the monetary authorities in TEs from preparing at the earliest a comprehensive, long-term strategy for eventually joining monetary union, however. Having such a strategy in place already during the early stages of accession negotiations would be an asset to TE negotiators.

TE negotiators need to address several important issues regarding exchange-rate policies. One is the scope of application of the ECB's "safeguard clause." This permits the ECB to suspend intervention and financing in the ERM II framework if these were to impinge on the objective of price stability. Another issue for the negotiators to ponder is the need to work out rules for monitoring exchange rates to assure full transparency and compliance between EU and ECB preferences, on the one hand, and the TEs' exchange-rate and disinflation policies, on the other.

A broad and critical problem for the negotiators is to define the precise nature of and procedures for the bilateral pegging system within the ERM II framework. This system is based on bilateral currency arrangements between the 'outs' and the ECB, which makes it different in that it is asymmetric from the expiring ERM, which is symmetric. In ERM II there will be a large center in the form of the euro zone and several countries remaining outside the EU's monetary union. As a result, currencies of the 'outs' will be linked through bilateral, rather than multilateral, arrangements with the euro; hence the asymmetry within the system. The new system is frequently identified as a "hubs-and-spokes" currency system in analogy with a "hubs-and-spokes"system of free-trading arrangements.

The bilateral rates will be fixed in a confidential manner involving the governors of central banks of the 'outs,' the ECB, and the European Commission. The present band of permitted currency fluctuations of plus-minus 15 percent is likely to be sustained in order to allow for substantial room for exchange-rate flexibility of the 'outs.' However, narrower official bands or unpublished internal bands are possible, but such solutions will be based on the 'convergence situation' of each country. As the 'outs' successfully pursue the path to monetary union, narrowing bands around the euro peg can be applied if only to demonstrate the countries' ability to converge smoothly to the common currency system and to reduce fluctuations of market exchange rates.

A gradual narrowing of the official band has been advocated by Klein (1997). A similar effect can be achieved by gradually narrowing the unpublished inner bands, which would also be consistent with flexible inflation targeting. This solution seems to be preferable since the official wide band would still leave enough room for flexibility in foreign-exchange markets and thus reduce expectations of a real currency appreciation. This approach is, therefore, likely to reduce the risk of speculative attacks against the currency.

In any case, a gradual closing of exchange-rate bands is advisable and this is fully consistent with the narrowing of inflation targets proposed in our advocacy of direct inflation targeting. A careful design of the exchange-rate and monetary-targeting strategies is critical because direct inflation targeting, especially if it assumes a wider inflation tolerance band, is inconsistent with the application of the currency peg. There is hence a major contradiction between direct inflation targeting and the concurrent entry into ERM II.

The steps and procedures for approaching ERM II have been discussed in the literature by Bernard (1997) and Orlowski (1997c). At the beginning of the path leading to joining the ERM II and, later on, the EU's monetary union, the candidates are likely to restructure their currency-reference baskets, increasing the euro's weight. At the same time, they will gradually phase out crawling devaluations. At a later stage, they need unilaterally to lock their exchange rates to the euro. A direct euro peg with large bands is the most desirable solution at this stage. The move will be beneficial for reducing inflation expectations and for enhancing monetary-policy credibility. Moreover, the adjustable euro peg would entitle the TEs to receive short-term financing upon locking their exchange rate to the euro once they join ERM II. There is, however, a danger of moving TE currencies onto a unilateral peg. If one or more TEs were to experience unbalanced fundamentals and risk speculative attacks against their currency, the bilateral system within ERM II would cushion the better-balanced economies against possible contagion effects, as defined by Eichengreen, Rose, and Wyplosz (1996).

The determination of a desirable spread between domestic and foreign interest rates will be one of the most critical issues in retooling monetary policy in preparation for the introduction of the regime based on the exchange rate. Direct inflation targeting allows financial markets to generate an equilibrium spread between interest rates. Interest-rate targeting would very likely distort the alignment between the interest-rate spread and the macroeconomic fundamentals, thus causing a deviation from the uncovered interest-parity condition.

Another problem to be addressed by the TEs is the optimal accumulation of foreign reserves at central banks. At the present time, strong positive interest-rate differentials lead to a significant accumulation of foreign reserves. The excessive level of reserves may be pro-inflationary, but it is necessary to reduce the risk of speculative attacks on the domestic currency. In the future, large foreign-exchange reserves will become less necessary since the TEs will have to transfer some of their reserves to the ECB upon accession to ERM II and even more upon entry into the EU's monetary union.

Approaching Monetary Union: Greece's Experience

It is essential that TEs prepare themselves for entering the EU's monetary union by first achieving an equilibrium exchange rate against the euro. If their currencies are overvalued in real terms, they may be facing expectations of a currency devaluation at the latest two years prior to the intended accession to monetary union as per the framework set forth by the Maastricht Treaty. Recall that this requires that a currency has participated for at least two years in the ERM without a change in its central parity.

Before the final preparation for entry into the EU's monetary union, economic actors may expect that the TEs will enact one last devaluation. These expectations may lead to a number of effects and repercussions that can generally be described as "the last devaluation syndrome." Financial institutions and foreign-trade companies are likely to assume currency positions consistent with expectations that the national currency will soon be devalued. Their actions may lead to a self-fulfilling devaluation in that they will force monetary authorities to devalue the currency. For instance, exporters are likely to lobby for a devaluation of the local currency, especially if they foresee a continuous real appreciation of the domestic currency due to prolonged, excessive inflation. This scenario is likely to occur since the exporters' lobby is strong throughout the TEs. Financial institutions are likely to start lowering their assets in domestic currency and buying foreign currencies, thus causing the domestic currency to depreciate in nominal terms. This will put additional pressures on monetary authorities to devalue the currency.

A "return-to-peg strategy" can bring some unpleasant consequences for TEs if they are not able to implement far-reaching institutional changes in their financial systems soon. If TE currencies are continuously experiencing real appreciation until the final stages of preparation for entry into the EU's monetary union, the monetary authorities will be expected to arrange a final devaluation. This may prove to be disastrous when debt contracts have a predominantly short-term maturity and when substantial amounts of debt are still denominated in foreign currencies (Mishkin, 1997). Such a devaluation may induce a deep financial crisis with financial institutions no longer able to allocate funds, in principle, to the most productive investment opportunities. Such a devaluation may entail a needless recession.

Moreover, a possible devaluation may cause a deterioration of balance sheets of banks and firms in terms of the domestic currency. This may result in a bank run. The devaluation will deteriorate the gap between short-term liabilities of banks denominated in foreign currencies and medium- to long-term assets in domestic currencies. The mismatch between assets and liabilities hurts the liquidity position of banks, something that they may or may not be able to overcome. If interest-rate differentials are high prior to devaluation, meaning that domestic interest rates are considerably above foreign rates, there are strong incentives for banks to borrow short term in foreign currency and make longer-term maturity loans in domestic currency. Devaluation will make it more expensive to service the short-term debt in relation to cash flows from domestic-currency loans. In sum, an emerging market economy considering devaluation cannot afford to have a fragile banking system and large short-term debt in foreign currency. The recent experiences of some southeast and east Asian economies, for example, could usefully be heeded in modulating prospective institutional and financial policies in TEs.

A possible devaluation on the road to a currency peg may also reduce confidence in the ability of central banks to control inflation. Certainly, devaluation will induce a lagged, one-time inflation shock that ought to be contained by means of a discretionary increase in interest rates by the central bank. Under such circumstances, flexible inflation targeting is beneficial. It permits the shock to expire by itself.

Expectations of devaluation in TEs may be subdued if the candidates exercise a considerable degree of exchange-rate flexibility prior to the declaration of final preparations for entry into monetary union. This will allow for a linear depreciation of the domestic currency and for a smooth convergence to the equilibrium exchange rate. If flexibility is restrained, for instance, by a narrow band of permitted fluctuations or frequent interventions, foreign-exchange markets will likely embrace expectations of a one-time devaluation, thus a nonlinear move toward exchange-rate equilibrium. They will likely foresee even a one-time move to a considerably undervalued currency, in comparison with PPP, particularly if the underlying inflation is still high and thus contributing to expectations of a real appreciation of the currency. As argued earlier, this may devastate the financial stability of the national economy.

Even if the macroeconomic fundamentals are met and the exchange rate is in equilibrium with respect to the uncovered interest-parity condition or PPP, financial markets may still expect a candidate for accession to the EU's monetary union to devalue at the latest two years prior to the intended entry. As noted earlier, this is because of the Maastricht Treaty requirement that the exchange rate must have been unchanged within the ERM for at least two years. This precludes any sizable inflation during the two years preceding accession to monetary union. It is these expectations of a one-time devaluation approximately two years before the intended entry into the monetary union that are behind the potential for a "last devaluation syndrome." Once the TEs are inside ERM II, any devaluation will have to be approved by the ECB after in-depth consultations. In extreme cases, when macroeconomic fundamentals in a participant in ERM II are not met, the ECB may force the country to devalue its currency.

It is useful to avoid by all means the "last devaluation syndrome," especially if the banking system has extensive short-term liabilities in foreign currency coupled with longer-term assets in domestic currency. Interest payments on liabilities in foreign currency would sharply rise, causing a liquidity problem in the banking sector and exacerbating the danger of bank runs. Devaluation may induce large capital outflows from the country. It will further hurt the credibility of the monetary authorities.

If the candidate countries opt to undergo devaluation in spite of the dangers to the financial stability of their economies, they will have to plan it very carefully. The last devaluation should be unannounced so that it will not induce large speculative attacks on the currency. In addition, it would have to be supplemented by the introduction of temporary controls on capital outflows. This solution is again consistent with the requirement of bringing about undistorted currency convertibility on capital account as stipulated in the OECD accession agreement and as required by eventual accession to the EU. But that final devaluation can be undertaken only after consultation with the authorities of these organizations. Moreover, the size of the last devaluation needs to be carefully assessed. It cannot be excessive for otherwise it would cause much harm to financial stability.

It remains rather ambiguous whether the TEs will have to follow the Greek program of the final stage of preparations for monetary union. Knowing that it could not meet the Maastricht convergence criteria at the time of examination for entering the monetary union upon its inception in January 1999, the government of Greece announced in mid-March 1998 a two-year program for acceding to the monetary union. Put briefly, the deadline for entering the system was set for the beginning of 2001 and the Greek drachma was devalued 14 percent against the ecu. The inflation target for 2001 was set at 2 percent. Financial markets did not fully anticipate the last devaluation, since between the beginning of January and 15 March 1998 the drachma traded within the 285-290 range to the dollar. It fell 12.2 percent (from 288 to 323 to the dollar) within two days following the devaluation. Thereafter it gradually appreciated to 315 by the end of April. This particular experience does not prove the occurrence of the last devaluation syndrome, and there were no major speculative attacks on the Greek currency prior to devaluation.

However, if the TEs were to follow the Greek example they might encounter some market pressures on their currencies prior to the expected time of devaluation. Specifically, the Polish government has disclosed intentions to join monetary union in 2006. If the fundamentals are not fully met in 2004, currency traders in financial markets are likely to sell złoty expecting the last devaluation to take place, regardless of its size. However, the likelihood of any such development remains to be seen.

Conclusions

This chapter has clarified the relationship between exchange-rate and monetary policies in some TEs bent on entering the EU and eventually acceding to the EU's monetary union. It has detailed the present exchange-rate systems and monetary regimes in the central European TEs, reviewed currently practiced targets of monetary policy, and discussed some proposed policy changes in response to the requirements of monetary union. It has also examined whether the early-accession candidates among the TEs are likely to have to resort to a final currency devaluation no more than two years prior to acceding to monetary union.

The analysis of exchange-rate policies in TEs in preparation for joining the EU's monetary union presented here is consistent with the overall framework of monetary policy. Exchange rates are no longer direct instruments of government policy affecting trade balances and capital inflows. This role of the exchange rate evaporated with the dissolution of central planning and later with the exit strategy from stabilization anchored to the exchange rate. Exchange rates are now important market variables that provide crucial information on external balances for fiscal and monetary authorities. More flexible exchange rates are superior for accomplishing the economic stability and the institutional tasks of transformation. They help to augment monetary-policy autonomy and credibility.

Gradual preparations for joining the EU's monetary union will require a dynamic "return-to-peg strategy" for the exchange rate. Application of a monetary policy based on the exchange rate should be accomplished as soon as feasible. Fixing the TE currencies in terms of a stable and strong euro will only be feasible when inflation is reduced to a low, sustainable level and when domestic financial institutions and markets function efficiently within the new currency system. A premature rush to the euro peg would generate expectations of real appreciation of domestic currencies if inflation were to remain too high. It is likely to cause asymmetric-information and liquidity problems, and may set off bank runs for the reasons elaborated upon here.

I have emphasized that the exchange-rate policy of the TE candidates for accession to the EU could best be tied to a monetary policy that targets inflation in a flexible manner. The TEs can enter the ERM II as their inflation rates are effectively brought down to a low, sustainable level by direct inflation targeting accompanied by more flexible exchange rates. It is imperative that the TEs not enter into ERM II too early so that they will take full advantage of the benefits of direct inflation targeting and flexible exchange rates for stability in their prices and current-account positions. However, after official entry into the EU, functioning within the ERM II framework will bring a number of advantages to their stabilization efforts, including enhancing policy credibility, expanding access to euro-zone credit markets, and augmenting fiscal and monetary discipline.

Governments of the candidate countries will be well advised not to delay preparations of specific plans for gradually moving toward joining the EU's monetary union and designing an optimal "return-to-peg strategy." Such plans ought to be incorporated in an overall, comprehensive strategy for full integration into the EU. They would help accession negotiators, both those of the present EU and of the candidates themselves, by ensuring consistency of specific tasks for the TEs in effectively preparing themselves for full EU integration.

Notes

This chapter thoroughly revises, updates, and modifies Orlowski, 1998b.

1. It is, of course, highly unlikely that this will actually come to pass. Perhaps the policy commitment should be understood as a determination to shadow ERM II until entry into the EU becomes feasible, which will then make it legally possible for the TEs to participate in ERM II.

Chapter 6

Nominal and Real Convergence—At What Speed?

Wladimir Andreff

Current discussions of economic convergence between TEs and the EU members focus in particular on those TEs that have been selected for fast-track accession negotiations, but much less on what is required to ensure catch-up in other TEs as well. The myriad issues revolving around convergence[1] between the EU economies and countries moving away from different systemic backdrops have been dealt with chiefly with reference to nominal variables. I do not deem this very appropriate in formulating (as in Orlowski, 1995) economic-policy recommendations that TE managers should preferably embrace during their preparation for accession to the EU, even if all the data hurdles (see chapter 3) could be overcome. Indeed, insisting on nominal convergence might well keep the country for some time in economic stagnation or recession, thus widening the gap with other growing countries as far as real macroeconomic variables are concerned. The recent experiences of the southern EU members in embracing measures that enabled all but Greece to qualify for entry into the EU's monetary union in 1999 should be heeded here. The crucial point for TEs is to assess whether nominal convergence (such as for budgets, exchange and interest rates, and inflation) to the EU countries' performances is compatible with real convergence and catch-up.

Real convergence narrows the dispersion of countries on the scale of economic development. The narrower the distribution, the lower the cost of future EU enlargement. It reduces the burden of transfers from the EU to the TEs, such as for structural, cohesion, and agricultural supports. In addition, some institutional requirements have to be met to speak meaningfully of real convergence (Cacheux, 1996a). Hence, a more comprehensive assessment of convergence must include various institutional aspects, though I can here consider only some of the more salient ones pertaining to the EU's enlargement toward the eastern part of Europe, the TE-5 in particular; but where appropriate and feasible I include measures for other TEs as well.

The chapter is organized as follows. I first lay out measures of nominal and real economic convergence, both in static and dynamic terms, basically between three groups of countries for the period 1990-1997: the present members of the EU, the TE-10, and among the latter I distinguish those slated for early accession negotiations from the other five. On occasion I broaden the horizon to other TEs, including those that will never qualify for EU membership. The empirical analyses point to several convergence dilemmas. I examine next their implications for the assessment of the economic policies that the TEs embraced in the recent past, especially those that focused on macroeconomic stabilization. I do so in particular with a view to identifying the requirements for growth recovery and policies buttressing some measure of catch-up during the negotiations and the first phase of accession. Before concluding, I point to a select set of institutional aspects of convergence between the TEs and the EU that are by their very nature at the core of the current negotiations in light of the strategy pursued by the EU.

Measuring Nominal and Real Convergence

In referring to convergence criteria, the immediate reflex of most economists is likely to be in terms of the specifications in the Maastricht Treaty regarding the conditions for qualifying for membership in the EU's monetary union. The appropriateness of these criteria for ensuring a functioning monetary union, from the economic rather than the political point of view, has been debatable from the very beginning. In any case, these criteria apply to joining monetary union and are therefore not immediately relevant to the conditions the TEs will have to meet in order to accede to the EU. As regards the latter, the only official statements are those embedded in the EU's quasi-constitutional treaties as slightly rephrased at the Copenhagen European Council in June 1993. These are qualitative criteria, as emphasized by Marie Lavigne (see chapter 3). Recall that nominal convergence criteria had not played any role at all in earlier enlargement negotiations, not even during the fourth enlargement, although at the time the Maastricht criteria had already been carefully crafted.

Even though nominal convergence criteria are not likely to play any important role in the formal accession negotiations of the present six candidates (the five TEs plus Cyprus), it is worth assessing the TEs' performance even with respect to the Maastricht nominal magnitudes since the TEs upon entry will be held to tight macroeconomic policies in the context of ERM II, due in 1999 together with monetary union. Another argument for doing so is speculating on whether moving toward a fixed exchange rate in terms of the euro (see chapter 5) would be sustainable for TEs (Boone and Maurel, 1998). Of course, we should bear in mind that when the TEs will be in a position to apply for membership in the monetary union, perhaps some five to ten years after joining the EU, their nominal economic situation might well be quite different from what the data for the early 1990s, such as they are, tend to suggest. For such a change to crystallize at all, however, policies have to be embraced to transform the 'real' situation.

Economic convergence, both on nominal and real variables, could be tested using alternative approaches. The methodology I have adopted here consists in calculating and comparing the mean value m and the standard deviation σ for each variable in the three country groups cited earlier for each year and the entire observation period 1990-1997. The degree of static convergence for one economic variable for any one country is assessed using the coefficient of variation, which is defined as σ/m. Static convergence between the country samples is assessed using for each year the relevant coefficients of variation. Dynamic convergence is assessed on the basis of annual variations of the mean value and the coefficient of variation of each economic variable from 1990 to 1997, compared within and among the country samples. For example, a decreasing coefficient of variation within one group of countries for the inflation rate is interpreted as a dynamic aspect of nominal convergence among those countries. A shrinking difference between mean values for two samples over time, let us say for inflation, is interpreted as reflecting dynamic nominal convergence between the two country groups. The statistical relevance of the measured differences between the means is tested by exploiting variance analysis (see below). For the most significant economic variables of real convergence in the sense of illustrating meaningful catch-up, these tests are complemented with the evaluation of *beta* (β) and *sigma* (σ) convergence, following the methodology advocated by Robert Barro and Xavier Sala-i-Martin (as in 1995).

As indicated, in testing the significance of the difference of mean values between country groups for each variable, I rely on analysis of variance.[2] The problem is to assess whether the differences between observed mean values, as explained later, is significantly related to whether countries belong to a country group. In other words, I would like to know how much of the dispersion in values for one variable can be 'explained' by the factor 'country group.' To do so, first the correlation coefficient of the variable according to the country group was calculated. This is the ratio of between-group sum of squares to the sum of squares. This measures the percentage of the variance of the variable explained by the country group. Second, analysis of variance is applied to test whether the factor 'country group' has a significant effect on mean values or not.

Wladimir Andreff

The Fisher criterion f_e is defined as the ratio of the between-group mean square to the within-group mean square. This permits estimation of the significance s_e of the test:

$$s_e = P (F_{(k-1),(n-k)} > f_e)$$ (6.1)

where $F_{(k-1),(n-k)}$ is the Fisher-Snedecor variable with *(k-1)* and *(n-k)* degrees of freedom. If s_e is large, the hypothesis that the factor 'country group' makes a significant difference cannot be accepted. Note, however, that the test results must be interpreted with caution because we have not checked whether the variable's distribution is Gaussian and whether the variances of the variable for the three country groups are statistically equal.

The Maastricht Criteria

Recall that the Maastricht Treaty specified five criteria: (1) inflation should be no higher than 1.5 percentage points above that in the three best-performing countries, (2) long-term interest rates should not exceed by more than 2 percentage points the rate observed in the three best-performing countries, (3) the budget deficit should not be larger than 3 percent of GDP, (4) public debt should not exceed 60 percent of GDP, and (5) the exchange rate should have remained within the permitted bands of the ERM for at least two years (Brabant, 1996a, pp. 103ff.). Table 6.1 shows the relevant measures of four of the above five magnitudes for the EU members and the TEs in the cited groups for the year 1993; for obvious reasons I am not testing the exchange-rate criterion. I have chosen 1993 as benchmark since it was during that year that the Copenhagen Council made it clear that the TEs with an EA could, if they wished, eventually join the EU. The same is done in table 6.2 for magnitudes referring to 1996 or 1997, depending on data availability.

Looking at table 6.1, several interesting observations can be derived. First of all, the evidence is unambiguous that none of the TEs met the four Maastricht criteria in 1993. Even the Czech Republic as the TE coming closest to the inflation indicator was still far off the mark; admittedly, the inflation criterion was not met by half of the EU members either at that time. None of the TEs came even close to meeting the criterion for the long-term interest rate; among the EU members, neither were Greece, Italy, Portugal, and Spain within reach of that target. As to the fiscal deficit relative to GDP, the picture is comparatively more favorable to the TEs as four met it in 1993. This is all the more pertinent since among the then twelve EC members, only Ireland and Luxemburg came in under the threshold. For the targeted ratio between public debt and GDP, three TEs met the requirement. Although I have not listed the exchange-rate target, it is pertinent to infer that, relative to the dollar, the Estonian kroon and the Czech koruna depreciated by only 4.4 and 6.5 percent, respectively. These currencies could have been within the permitted 15 percent fluctuation margins applicable to ERM members, a subset of EU members (without the drachma, lira, and pound sterling). The depreciations were much larger for the other currencies: 21.2 percent for the forint, 33.5 percent for the leva, 36.4 percent for the złoty, and 77.0 percent for the leu.

Table 6.1: The central European countries and Maastricht criteria, 1993

Countries	Inflation	Interest rate	Deficit/GDP	Debt/GDP
Bulgaria	56.0	63.0	15.7	111.0
Czech Republic	20.8	16.5	-1.4	29.0
Estonia	89.8	17.2	1.1	n.a.
Hungary	22.5	28.5	6.3	65.0
Latvia	109.0	27.0	-0.6	n.a.
Lithuania	411.0	108.0	4.9	n.a.
Poland	35.3	48.5	4.0	54.0
Romania	256.0	70.0	0.1	16.0
Slovakia	23.2	16.5	7.1	29.0
Slovenia	32.3	49.6	0.3	n.a.
TE-10 m	**105.6**	**44.5**	**3.8**	**50.7**
TE-10 σ	122.4	28.2	4.9	31.6
Maastricht criterion	**3.2**	**9.1**	**3.0**	**60.0**
Belgium	2.7	7.5	7.4	138.4
Denmark	1.3	9.4	4.4	79.0
France	2.0	7.4	5.9	58.3
Germany	4.1	6.7	4.2	50.5
Greece	15.2	21.0	15.5	113.6
Ireland	1.8	8.5	3.0	92.9
Italy	4.5	12.6	10.0	115.3
Luxemburg	3.5	7.4	2.5	10.0
Netherlands	2.5	7.0	4.0	83.6
Portugal	7.0	13.5	8.9	69.0
Spain	4.7	11.4	7.2	56.6
United Kingdom	1.9	8.3	9.6	53.2
EU-12 m	**4.3**	**10.1**	**6.9**	**76.7**
EU-12 σ	3.6	3.9	3.6	33.5

Sources: EUROSTAT; IMF, 1997b; and UNECE, 1998.

Looking at the data in table 6.2, by 1997 no TE had met the inflation target, which for the EU had come down from 3.2 percent in 1993 to 2.8 percent in 1997. But the Czech Republic, Estonia, Latvia, Lithuania, Poland, Slovakia, and Slove-

Table 6.2: The central European countries and Maastricht criteria, 1996

Countries	Inflation[a]	Interest rate	Deficit/GDP	Debt/GDP
Bulgaria	578.7	481.0	8.0	n.a.
Czech Republic	9.9	12.5	0.5	12.0
Estonia	12.3	13.7	1.4	n.a.
Hungary	18.4	24.0	3.5	72.1
Latvia	7.0	25.8	0.7	n.a.
Lithuania	8.5	21.6	3.5	n.a.
Poland	13.2	23.3	2.7	51.0
Romania	151.7	71.0	5.4	n.a.
Slovakia	6.5	13.2	1.4	n.a.
Slovenia	9.5	18.3	0.6	n.a.
TE-10 m	*81.6*	*70.4*	*2.8*	*n.a.*
TE-10 σ	171.0	137.8	2.3	n.a.
TE-5 m	**12.7**	**18.3**	**1.7**	**n.a.**
TE-5 σ	3.2	4.7	1.2	n.a.
Maastricht criteria	**2.8**	**7.8**	**3.0**	**60.0**
Austria	1.3	5.7	2.8	66.1
Belgium	1.6	5.8	2.6	124.7
Denmark	2.1	6.3	-1.3	67.0
Finland	1.2	6.0	1.4	59.0
France	1.3	5.6	3.1	57.3
Germany	1.5	5.7	3.0	61.7
Greece	5.6	10.0	4.2	109.3
Ireland	1.4	6.4	-0.6	65.8
Italy	2.0	7.0	3.0	123.2
Luxemburg	1.4	5.6	-1.6	6.6
Netherlands	2.0	5.6	2.1	73.4
Portugal	2.0	6.5	2.7	62.5
Spain	2.0	6.5	2.9	68.1
Sweden	1.7	6.7	1.9	77.4
United Kingdom	1.9	7.2	2.0	52.9
EU-15 m	**1.9**	**6.4**	**1.9**	**71.7**
EU-15 σ	1.0	1.1	1.7	284.7

Note: [a] 1997.
Sources: EUROSTAT; IMF, 1997b; and UNECE, 1998.

nia and marginally Hungary, came closer to meeting the criterion even than the Czech Republic in 1993. This suggests that there was some nominal convergence toward the Maastricht criterion, but without reaching it. On average the TE-5 performed better than the other five, but this is primarily due to the surge in inflation in Bulgaria and Romania. Recall, however, that Slovakia, which was the best performer in terms of inflation, is not included among the privileged five.

As to the interest target, which was also down like the inflation target, from 9.1 percent in 1993 to 7.8 percent in 1996, in 1996 Latvia and Slovakia were nearer to the criterion than Portugal and Greece in 1993. But no TE met the required interest-rate criterion.[3] And not a single one was able to curb its interest rate below Greece's, the worst EU performer. This is both a consequence of rather high inflation and of the still-incomplete restructuring of the banking and financial systems. Nonetheless it bears stressing that between 1993 and 1996 the gap between TE and EU interest rates shrank appreciably.

Table 6.2 also suggests that most TEs, as well as on average, by 1996 had converged to the criteria of fiscal deficit and public debt. Of the TE-5 only Hungary's ratio of the fiscal deficit to GDP exceeded the Maastricht benchmark of 3 percent; so did Latvia's and Slovakia's. Public debt decreased for the Czech Republic and Poland, but in Hungary it remained above 60 percent; even that high level was well below that for Belgium, Greece, Italy, the Netherlands, and Sweden in 1997, however.

Whatever the intrinsic economic merits of the Maastricht criteria, the data in tables 6.1 and 6.2 show that the TEs with an EA, and particularly the privileged five, do not perform badly at all when compared to EU members. Bulgaria and Romania, of course, are special cases, given the setbacks with transformation policies incurred in recent years and the still incomplete reversal since mid-1997. It is now important to look into the overall process of economic convergence through which the TEs can be expected to move closer to the EU's economic performance. I cannot, of course, predict what may happen in the years ahead. But it is of interest to examine carefully what occurred between the two sets of observations with a view to inferring about the dynamics of adjustments in the TEs.

Before doing so, however, one may question whether the Maastricht criteria make sense for TEs. For one thing, it should be clear that the restrictive monetary policy used as the principal tool for narrowing the gap between inflation rates is likely to push up interest rates and hinder efforts to compress the public deficit and debt. The evidence shown in tables 6.1 and 6.2 regarding the different performances in terms of inflation and long-term interest rates illustrate this proposition. On the other hand, a nominal convergence that is not tightly linked to real convergence, made feasible notably via economic restructuring and approximation of EU legislation and institutions, would compel countries to adhere to short-term stabilization policies that are inimical to economic and institutional restructuring. To some extent, nominal convergence can even mask the absence of, or poor progress with, structural adjustment. The Czech Republic, with its 'good' nominal indicators through 1995 and rapid deterioration thereafter, provides a case in point. It has since early 1997 been engaged in reducing public expenditures. Although the nominal convergence criteria for EU members may encourage these countries' monetary authorities to embrace policies that dampen economic buoyancy, such a deflationary policy bias toward slow growth should be completely unacceptable to TE policy makers and indeed inimical to accomplishing the tasks ahead in fostering economic restructuring. But it should be noted that some TE economists (see Csaba, 1997) argue that the current distance of inflation and interest rates in TEs relative to EU performance provides an important reference for the EU candidates.

Table 6.3: Test of convergence of inflation rates, 1990-1997

Samples	1990	1991	1992	1993	1994	1995	1996	1997
TE-10								
m	125.2	142.9	364.3	107.3	48.4	27.6	29.5	132.3
σ	221.5	90.9	433.3	121.6	39.3	15.0	32.5	319.7
σ/m	**1.77**	**0.63**	**1.19**	**1.13**	**0.81**	**0.54**	**1.10**	**2.41**
TE-5								
m	238.5	94.2	271.8	40.3	26.0	21.5	17.0	12.4
σ	269.2	60.5	409.0	25.3	13.2	8.7	6.4	3.8
σ/m	**1.12**	**0.64**	**1.50**	**0.63**	**0.51**	**0.41**	**0.38**	**0.31**
EU-15								
m	6.5	5.9	4.7	4.0	3.3	3.0	2.4	2.0
σ	4.9	4.4	3.4	3.1	2.3	1.9	1.8	1.1
σ/m	**0.75**	**0.75**	**0.73**	**0.78**	**0.69**	**0.64**	**0.74**	**0.57**
CIS								
m	5.6	109.8	1016.8	2176.4	2905.0	299.5	77.4	25.9
σ	0.6	22.0	320.3	1272.8	5958.1	219.0	116.3	25.5
σ/m	**0.10**	**0.20**	**0.32**	**0.58**	**2.05**	**0.73**	**1.50**	**0.98**

Source: UNECE, 1998.

Nominal Convergence

Whatever the intrinsic merits of the Maastricht criteria, they or a variant thereof are likely to play more than a trivial role in the ongoing enlargement negotiations, at least in formulating the EU's stance with respect to TE accessions. It is therefore of more than marginal relevance to inquire more systematically into the nature and achievement of nominal convergence between the TEs, especially the TE-5, and the EU. In what follows I discuss only tests for inflation and interest rates, because the fiscal deficit in TEs depends critically on growth recovery (see below) and public debt reflects the inertia of fiscal deficits incurred in the past. In addition, measurement of the budgetary position in TEs is not at all straightforward as the quality and comparability of the available data leave a lot to be desired. Indeed the less visible forms of fiscal deficits directly depend on progress with structural reforms (Kosterna, 1998).

As concerns static convergence for inflation (see table 6.3) as assessed via the coefficient of variation in each sample, the trend is weaker among the TEs than among the EU for every year in the sample, except 1991 and 1995. This suggests that the big policy issue for the TEs is not only that, among themselves, they are more inflationary than the EU members, but also that their performances are more diverse. Until 1993, they were even more dispersed than the CIS countries; this can be observed also for 1997 due to high inflation during the crisis in Bulgaria and for the year as a whole in Romania. This impression is confirmed even when we focus on the TE-5. Within that group, one can observe stronger convergence than within the EU every year, except 1990 and 1992. That is to say, the TEs in 1997 fall into two groups: the less inflationary countries (the TE-5, Latvia, Lithuania, and Slovakia) and two economies that are not yet stabilized.

Within the EU, in dynamic terms, the average inflation rate was sharply reduced by two-thirds between 1990 and 1997, while the coefficient of variation remained rather steady from 1990 up to 1993 and thereafter it decreased, except in 1996. Thus, the overall picture suggests convergence toward lower inflation rates in all EU members. One can observe the same dynamic convergence for inflation among the TE-10 from 1992 to 1995, but thereafter this process halted on account of the serious slippage sustained in Bulgaria and Romania. On the other hand, the TE-5 among themselves were converging even faster and closer than the EU countries—the coefficient of variation fell to 0.31 in 1997 as against 0.57 for the EU—even though inflation remained at the two-digit level (roughly 12 percent), basically due to still strong inflationary pressures in Hungary and Poland. Such a slight convergence sharply contrasts with the CIS countries, whose coefficient of variation tended to rise after 1991 because some countries (Armenia, Azerbaijan, Moldova, and Russia) have curbed inflation with some measure of success while others are still mired in rather high inflation.

The results of variance analysis for the three country groups and between the TE-10 and the EU are shown in tables 6.4 and 6.5. The first test suggests that the inflation rate is rather strongly correlated with the group a country belongs to for 1991, 1992, 1993, and 1995; but in these four years the significance of the test is very weak (lower than 1 percent). We cannot thus conclude that there was significant convergence of the inflation rates in the overall sample of thirty-seven countries. For the test between the TE-10 and the EU, belonging to some country group influences inflation rates only in 1991 and 1995, with a rather significant difference between mean values (the test's significance is below 1 percent), thus indicating that there has been no convergence in inflation rates.

Table 6.4: Test of the difference of mean values among the country groups

Variables	1990	1991	1992	1993	1994	1995	1996	1997
Inflation								
ρ	0.17	0.60	0.69	0.65	0.14	0.54	0.19	0.09
f_e	3.6	25.5	37.7	32.0	2.7	19.7	3.7	1.7
s_e	5%	<1%	<1%	<1%	10%	<1%	2.5%	>10%
Interest								
ρ	n.a.	n.a.	0.36	0.73	0.93	0.48	0.57	n.a.
f_e	n.a.	n.a.	5.1	31.7	166.6	12.8	17.4	n.a.
s_e	n.a.	n.a.	1%	<1%	<1%	<1%	<1%	Na
GDP growth								
ρ	0.45	0.64	0.26	0.31	0.71	0.03	0.10	0.01
f_e	13.7	29.9	5.9	7.6	42.3	0.6	1.8	0.1
s_e	<1%	<1%	1%	<1%	<1%	>10%	>10%	>10%
Productivity								
ρ	n.a.	n.a.	0.23	0.30	0.66	0.45	0.07	0.02
f_e	n.a.	n.a.	5.2	7.4	33.7	44.0	1.4	0.4
s_e	n.a.	n.a.	1%	1%	<1%	<1%	>10%	>10%
Unemployment								
ρ	n.a.	n.a.	0.43	0.47	0.45	0.41	0.36	0.35
f_e	n.a.	n.a.	12.6	14.8	13.7	11.6	9.4	9.3
s_e	n.a.	n.a.	<1%	<1%	<1%	<1%	<1%	<1%

Notes:
ρ: correlation coefficient.
f: Fisher criterion (see text).
s: significance of the test.

Basically the same picture emerges from the calculations on long-term interest rates (table 6.6). The coefficient of variation is rather stable (between 0.35 and 0.52) throughout the observation period in the EU, while interest rates are declining. Among the TE-10, dynamic convergence is more marked for interest rates than for inflation rates, which probably stems from increasingly open credit markets inducing interest rates to level off throughout the TEs; this is confirmed by the slight difference between the calculated mean for interest rates in the TE-5 and the TE-10 in 1995-1996, on the one hand, and between the coefficients of variation in the two groups of countries, on the other hand. But the interest rates are more dispersed within the CIS after 1994 and are obviously at much higher levels. The variance test (see tables 6.4 and 6.5) shows that belonging to a country group influences the interest rate in 1993, 1994, and 1996, though the hypothesis that the three mean values are equal must be rejected. There is no interest-rate convergence among the EU, the TE-10, and the CIS countries. The test between

Table 6.5: Test of the difference of mean values between TE-10 and the EU

	1990	1991	1992	1993	1994	1995	1996	1997
Inflation								
ρ	0.15	0.58	0.29	0.30	0.44	0.61	0.29	0.09
f_e	4.0	31.5	9.5	10.0	18.1	36.2	9.6	2.3
s_e	5%	<1%	<1%	<1%	<1%	<1%	<1%	10%
Interest								
ρ	n.a.	n.a.	0.36	0.42	0.53	0.60	0.57	n.a.
f_e	n.a.	n.a.	9.6	15.2	24.8	33.5	28.0	n.a.
s_e	n.a.	n.a.	<1%	<1%	<1%	<1%	<1%	n.a.
GDP growth								
ρ	0.64	0.84	0.38	0.14	0.01	0.03	0.00	0.01
f_e	39.0	122.8	14.2	3.7	0.2	0.7	0.00	0.10
s_e	<1%	<1%	<1%	5%	>10%	>10%	>10%	>10%
Productivity								
ρ	n.a.	n.a.	0.21	0.04	0.04	0.19	0.20	0.20
f_e	n.a.	n.a.	6.3	0.8	1.1	5.4	5.6	5.5
s_e	n.a.	n.a.	<1%	>10%	>10%	2.5%	2.5%	2.5%
Unemployment								
ρ	n.a.	n.a.	0.00	0.00	0.00	0.00	0.01	0.00
f_e	n.a.	n.a.	0.05	0.00	0.00	0.00	0.10	0.00
s_e	n.a.	n.a.	>10%	>10%	>10%	>10%	>10%	>10%
Savings rate								
ρ	n.a.	0.06	0.03	0.03	0.01	0.01	0.02	n.a.
f_e	n.a.	0.5	0.3	0.4	0.1	0.1	0.2	n.a.
s_e	n.a.	>10%	>10%	>10%	>10%	>10%	>10%	n.a.

Notes:
ρ: correlation coefficient.
f: Fisher criterion (see text).
s: significance of the test.

the TE-10 and the EU yields a similar result: The mean value of the interest rates is correlated with belonging to a country group since 1994 and the difference between mean values cannot be rejected. There is, then, no nominal convergence between the TE-10 and EU countries.

On the basis of the evidence presented here, we may conclude that there is no significant nominal convergence between the TEs and the EU. There might have been very slight nominal convergence within the TE-5 and Slovakia. In that respect, these six TEs appear to present a more homogeneous group today than at the inception of the transitions, most likely because all embarked at some point on a more or less severe stabilization policy. In most cases, this was backed up with

Table 6.6: Test of convergence of long-term interest rates, 1990-1996

Samples	1990	1991	1992	1993	1994	1995	1996	1997
TE-10								
m	266.5	314.4	76.6	43.0	37.3	26.6	21.6	132.3
σ	237.7	381.3	73.5	28.7	19.1	9.2	7.3	319.7
σ/m	**0.89**	**1.21**	**0.96**	**0.67**	**0.51**	**0.35**	**0.34**	**2.41**
TE-5								
m	266.5	314.4	76.6	30.3	27.2	23.9	19.0	12.4
σ	237.7	381.3	73.5	11.8	8.9	8.4	6.2	3.8
σ/m	**0.89**	**1.21**	**0.96**	**0.39**	**0.33**	**0.35**	**0.32**	**0.30**
EU-15								
m	14.1	14.0	13.9	11.9	10.1	9.8	8.4	2.0
σ	4.9	5.6	4.9	5.2	5.3	4.3	4.1	1.1
σ/m	**0.35**	**0.40**	**0.35**	**0.44**	**0.52**	**0.44**	**0.49**	**0.60**
CIS								
m	n.a.	n.a.	21.0	141.5	194.5	118.1	66.7	25.9
σ	n.a.	n.a.	9.0	57.3	37.5	94.5	41.3	25.5
σ/m	**n.a.**	**n.a.**	**0.43**	**0.41**	**0.19**	**0.80**	**0.62**	**1.00**

Source: UNECE, 1998.

IMF conditionality. But not in the Czech Republic and Slovenia, which, however, embraced their own version of restrictive policies (Andreff, 1998b), although an impetus for such a policy stance may have emanated from the circumstances surrounding the rendering of assistance by the EU and indeed from the incentive of eventually being able to join the EU. In marked contrast, such policies were not pursued consistently, if at all, by Bulgaria and Romania, in spite of IMF programs, EU assistance, or the prospect of EU accession.

From an analytical point of view, however, nominal convergence in itself does not suffice to adjudicate the appropriateness of economic policies. Some commentators have suggested that nominal convergence, even among EU members, is not necessary. I maintain that, especially in the case of the TEs, convergence in nominal magnitudes is directly a function of real economic convergence. Consider that nominal convergence refers chiefly to prices (including interest and exchange rates), which are not independent of the dynamics of real variables, except perhaps under a strict quantity theory of money. On the other hand, attaining nominal convergence would not suffice to ward off aggressive speculation against the weaker currencies of the countries exhibiting nominal convergence. That perceived weakness often results from lack of real convergence, as in the case of the southern EU members until recent years, or from a lack of credibility of economic policies due to weak real convergence (Yvars, 1997). Among the TEs, truly pertinent examples of weak real convergence in recent years are Bulgaria, the Czech Republic, and Romania.

Real Convergence

A number of studies have in recent years focused on real economic convergence, thus providing a welcome counterweight to the earlier excessive attention to nominal criteria (Nguyen, 1996; Richez-Battesti, 1994). The empirical evidence at first sight suggests that there is static divergence between the TEs and EU countries as regards macroeconomic and social variables; in other words, a wide gap between their respective levels of economic and social development. A catch-up process in the TEs toward levels typical of the EU for economic and social development can be construed as dynamic convergence.

Nevertheless, the precise meaning of real convergence is less clear than that of nominal convergence. Let us define it as in the Maastricht Treaty: reducing disparities in levels of living within the EU. This necessarily encompasses social welfare and economic development. The variables required to assess such a long-run process far exceed what we could possibly accommodate within the space of this chapter. Even if the notion of real convergence were defined solely in terms of macroeconomic variables, we would still have to monitor and assess a wide range of variables, such as economic growth; changes in productivity, employment, and unemployment; shifts in investment and savings; levels and changes in income distribution, private and public consumption, energy consumption, inward FDI, and foreign-trade balance; and transformations in the sectoral composition of aggregate output (Andreff, 1997a; Drumetz, Erkel-Rousse, and Jaillard, 1993). Considering the theory of endogenous growth (Grossman and Helpman, 1991; Lucas, 1988; Romer, 1986) the list should be extended to R&D and science and technology networks (Andreff, 1997b), existing infrastructures, education and health expenditures, and some indicators of poverty, life expectancy, and so on. Documenting all of the enumerated variables would amount to a gigantic task, one far exceeding what I can possibly accomplish here. In what follows, I therefore confine myself to a more modest test of real convergence between TEs and EU members.

The core variable in any study of real convergence is GDP growth, and in what follows I focus my convergence tests on this aggregate. GDP growth permits the derivation of an indicator of labor productivity. I shall assume that this indicator in some sense captures the effects of endogenous factors on economic growth. Unemployment is also crucial as a real convergence variable. In the case of the TEs it signals the depth of economic restructuring and of the functioning of the emerging labor market. On the other hand, unemployment rates for TEs are indicative of the potential magnitude of the future westward labor mobility from

TEs, insofar as the Schengen Agreement is now part and parcel of the *acquis* (Csaba, 1997). Finally, I consider the rate of gross domestic savings to GDP. Raising and effectively mobilizing domestic savings are crucial in embarking on sustainable catch-up growth because domestic investment must on the whole be financed by domestic savings rather than FDI. This has been corroborated by economic growth theory and econometric tests of regional convergence (Barro and Sala-i-Martin, 1991).

Should one expect that the TEs diverging least from the EU in nominal terms are also converging in real terms? The Washington financial organizations tend to provide a positive answer: there can be at worst a time lag between short-term nominal stabilization and medium-term real recovery of economic growth, followed by long-term real catch-up to levels of total factor productivity, output, income, and so on of developed economies. Following this paradigm, several commentators have tried to document that the most successful TEs in terms of compressing inflation have experienced lower contraction of GDP and rapid growth recovery (Brenton, Gros, and Vandille, 1997). Also, the Maastricht Treaty (art. 104c) presumes that there is a link between nominal and real convergence. Indeed, the Fund for Social Cohesion provides assistance to EU members subject to the condition of abiding by agreed budget commitments, a nominal variable, as prescribed by various EU bodies on the recommendation of the ECOFIN Council, one of the important subordinate bodies of the EU (see chapter 2). This linkage between nominal and real criteria of convergence can be viewed as a compromise between the economists' approach, according to which monetary union must follow real and structural convergence, and the monetarists' approach, which advocates monetary union as the engine of convergence.

In light of the above, one should verify whether the TEs' experiences in recent years confirm the hypothesis of nominal as well as real economic convergence, if only to avoid repeating some questionable policies pursued recently in the EU for the sake of being able to join the EU's monetary union from its inception. In the case of Spain, for example, it was not practically possible to reconcile the catch-up process with macroeconomic convergence to EU nominal performances when the country joined (Fayolle, 1996a). The period 1986-1992 was basically one of catch-up, but since 1992-1993 nominal criteria have gradually prevailed in macroeconomic policy, thus braking the consolidation of real expansion. More generally, the first half of the 1980s was characterized by real economic divergence among EU members, with the less developed ones (Greece, Ireland, Portugal, and Spain) trailing behind, primarily because of the overall economic slowdown (Neven and Gouyette, 1994). Catch-up resumed in the second half of the 1980s and lasted until 1992. This was followed by a break in real convergence in 1993-1994 and thereafter a resumption of catch-up in the four cited EU members. Just the same, real convergence has remained quite uneven, with Ireland well ahead and Greece lagging behind. Not only that, the speed of convergence appears to have slowed down recently because of restrictive stabilization policies, aiming at nominal convergence (Larre and Torres, 1991; Nguyen, 1996) in preparing for entry into monetary union.

The process observed in the cited countries appears to consist at first of strong catch-up of the lagging economy, followed by a period of higher inflation than in the more developed EU members, leading to an unsustainable trade deficit. That also characterizes the experiences of the TEs since the turnaround in output decline. In other words, there may be a tradeoff between nominal and real convergence as observed in the less-developed EU members, except Ireland, where inflation and interest rates as well as the fiscal deficit have remained rather low (Silva and Lima, 1997).

There may be not only a contemporaneous tradeoff, but a tight stabilization policy adhered to for years may delay economic recovery and the start of the catch-up process. This suggests that the persisting gaps between the less developed and the richer northern EU members derives in part not only from the former's catch-up itself but also from diverging economic, especially fiscal and monetary, policies. More generally, pursuing catch-up tends to be accompanied by persistent inflation for less-developed countries. This is known as the Balassa effect (Balassa, 1964), whose pertinence and robustness are beyond doubt (Busson and Villa, 1996). A shrinking productivity gap in the production of tradables allows for more rapid wage increases in the catching-up countries, which will spread in time to the nontradable sector, where lower productivity gains do not warrant such a wage shock, thus exacerbating inflation. If at the same time catching-up countries are compelled to adhere to nominal-convergence criteria (such as the pace of inflation and the fiscal deficit), only real divergence or a slowdown of the catch-up process can prevail. Considering this evidence, one may well question whether the same, or similar, restrictive policies should be pursued by the TEs, let alone imposed by the framework of the ongoing negotiations for EU accession, as in the members of the EU's monetary union. Before inquiring into this, I interpret several tests of real economic convergence between the TEs and EU members.

A first test of real convergence considers GDP growth rates (table 6.7). The data show on the whole a similar trend for the TEs: negative growth from 1990 to 1992 (except in Poland in 1992); growth resumption in all TEs by 1994-1995; and continued growth in 1996-1997 in most of the TE-10, the exceptions being Bulgaria and Romania. The coefficient of variation suggests convergence for all TEs during the economic slump in 1990-1992, except for the slight recovery in 1992 in Poland. In 1992-1993, however, the coefficients show a far greater differentiation in growth performances among the TEs. This began to diminish rapidly in 1994-1995. In 1996-1997, however, convergence was interrupted, due largely to the economic slump in Bulgaria in 1996-1997 and in Romania in 1997. Lack of real convergence extends to the TE-5: they diverged in 1992 and much more in 1993, with positive growth in three TEs but a decline in Estonia and Hungary; thereafter, one observes convergence among these TEs and at a more rapid pace than occurred for EU members because of higher growth in the TEs.

Table 6.7: Test of convergence in GDP growth rates, 1990-1997

Samples	1990	1991	1992	1993	1994	1995	1996	1997
TE-10								
m	-5.4	-11.2	-11.5	-5.1	2.7	4.2	2.6	2.8
σ	4.0	2.1	12.2	10.0	2.2	2.6	4.7	5.3
σ/m	**-0.75**	**-0.18**	**-1.06**	**-1.97**	**0.83**	**0.63**	**1.84**	**1.89**
TE-5								
m	-6.5	-9.9	-4.7	-0.3	2.8	4.6	3.7	4.9
σ	3.7	1.8	5.4	4.4	2.6	1.9	1.6	2.7
σ/m	**-0.57**	**-0.18**	**-1.16**	**-13.29**	**0.91**	**0.42**	**0.42**	**0.56**
EU-15								
m	3.1	1.4	1.1	0.3	3.0	3.3	2.6	3.3
σ	2.3	3.0	1.9	2.6	1.5	2.1	1.6	1.7
σ/m	**0.75**	**2.11**	**1.79**	**7.92**	**0.50**	**0.64**	**0.62**	**0.52**
CIS								
m	-3.1	-8.2	-16.5	-11.2	-15.0	0.0	-3.9	2.3
σ	5.3	6.2	20.1	8.6	8.9	16.7	15.5	8.0
σ/m	**-1.70**	**-0.76**	**-1.22**	**-0.77**	**-0.60**	**-448.50**	**-3.96**	**3.42**

Source: UNECE, 1998.

But economic recovery in the TEs, though coinciding with the resumption of growth in the EU as part of the upswing in the business cycle, has been of a different nature, namely, the emergence from the so-called 'transformational recession' (Kornai, 1994); this might well signal the starting point of a catch-up process. In contrast, the CIS countries remained stuck in the economic slump until 1994 and for several of them until today. In recent years, the continuing output decline in Moldova, Russia, Tajikistan, Turkmenistan, and Ukraine contrasted with growth recovery elsewhere in the CIS. As a result, the absolute value of the coefficient of variation is rather high, especially after 1994. In any case, average rates of growth remained significantly lower than in the TE-10 and in the EU.

Analysis of variance (see tables 6.4 and 6.5) underlines that belonging to a country group does not explain the rate of GDP growth since 1993 and the test is not significant at the 10 percent level after 1994. We can therefore conclude that there is convergence in economic growth among the three country groups, but it is stronger between the TE-10 and EU members. Beginning with 1992, the correlation coefficient (ρ) gradually decreases and falls to a very small value in 1996, meaning that the mean value of the growth rate does not depend on whether the country belongs either to TE-10 or to the EU. Moreover, the significance of the test improves, beginning with 1993, and is very high for the period since 1994. This points to rather strong real convergence, in terms of GDP growth.

Table 6.8: Test of convergence in labor productivity, 1991-1997

Samples	1991	1992	1993	1994	1995	1996	1997
TE-10							
m	-6.3	-7.4	-1.0	4.0	4.3	5.1	6.1
σ	5.7	13.5	9.7	2.6	3.4	5.3	6.1
σ/m	**-0.90**	**-1.83**	**-9.39**	**0.66**	**0.80**	**1.03**	**1.00**
TE-5							
m	-5.0	0.6	4.1	3.4	3.9	5.1	9.7
σ	4.7	6.0	1.9	3.0	1.0	2.8	5.8
σ/m	**-0.94**	**9.38**	**0.46**	**0.88**	**0.27**	**0.54**	**0.59**
EU-15							
m	n.a.	1.8	1.4	3.1	1.9	1.6	2.1
σ	n.a.	1.6	2.0	1.5	1.2	1.0	1.3
σ/m	**n.a.**	**0.88**	**1.39**	**0.47**	**0.63**	**0.64**	**0.61**
CIS							
m	-7.4	-14.1	-10.1	-14.6	-5.6	8.3	4.4
σ	4.7	17.7	9.8	10.1	7.1	16.8	17.5
σ/m	**-0.63**	**-1.25**	**-0.97**	**-0.69**	**-1.27**	**2.02**	**3.95**

Source: UNECE, 1998.

Indicators of labor productivity (table 6.8) also exhibit a tendency toward convergence since 1994 among the TE-10, and even earlier (1993) and stronger among the TE-5, given that the coefficient of variation is lower than that for the EU members after 1994. The growth of labor productivity is converging to a higher level in the TE-10 than in the EU, signaling catch-up. On the other hand, labor-productivity growth recovered only in 1996 in the CIS countries. The divergence within this group is exhibited by a high and increasing absolute value for the coefficient of variation. First signs of a catch-up, based on strong labor-productivity gains, are apparent since 1996 only in countries like Armenia, Georgia, and Kyrgyzstan. Analysis of variance (see tables 6.4 and 6.5) shows that belonging to a country group influences the mean value of labor productivity for the period prior to 1995 with considerable statistical significance. Between the TE-10 and the EU, the mean value of labor productivity does not depend on belonging to a country group, in particular in 1993 and 1994, and the test becomes significant after 1995. Hence, with convergence in real economic growth and a slighter convergence in labor productivity due to better performances in the TE-10 than in the EU, two basic characteristics of a catch-up process under way have been present already since 1993.

Unemployment in the TEs has become an inertial element of the economic transformation process. The increase in the number of unemployed is only partly a consequence of economic recession, however; indeed it basically derives from the labor shedding required to come to terms with overmanning during state social-ism. Some of this labor is not, and indeed cannot be, reemployed during the current economic recovery and will stay in the 'stagnant pool' of the long-term unemployed (Boeri, 1994). In fact, layoffs might well continue simply because the economic recovery is likely to facilitate the restructuring that did not occur during the first years of the transformation. Rising unemployment holds true also for the CIS countries, but observed levels (3.7 percent in 1997) tend to lag significantly behind those typical of the former Eastern Europe or the EU, suggesting limited restructuring under way to date. This explains why the coefficient of variation is more than twice that of the TE-10 (see table 6.9).

Table 6.9: Test of convergence in unemployment rates, 1990-1997

Samples	1990	1991	1992	1993	1994	1995	1996	1997
TE-10								
m	1.9	6.7	8.1	10.3	9.9	9.5	9.2	9.4
σ	2.1	4.6	5.4	5.1	4.5	3.8	3.7	3.4
σ/m	**1.11**	**0.69**	**0.67**	**0.50**	**0.45**	**0.40**	**0.40**	**0.36**
TE-5								
m	2.8	6.7	8.7	10.5	9.9	9.5	9.4	9.1
σ	2.5	4.2	5.3	5.3	5.0	4.9	4.2	3.8
σ/m	**0.89**	**0.63**	**0.61**	**0.51**	**0.51**	**0.51**	**0.45**	**0.42**
EU-15								
m	6.7	7.4	8.5	10.1	10.4	9.9	9.9	9.5
σ	3.9	3.9	4.3	5.0	5.1	4.7	4.5	4.2
σ/m	**0.58**	**0.52**	**0.50**	**0.49**	**0.49**	**0.48**	**0.45**	**0.45**
CIS								
m	n.a.	n.a.	0.7	1.6	2.2	2.8	3.6	3.7
σ	n.a.	n.a.	1.3	2.0	2.3	2.7	2.9	3.0
σ/m	**n.a.**	**n.a.**	**1.69**	**1.23**	**1**	**0.96**	**0.82**	**0.81**

Source: UNECE, 1998.

Although it includes an inertial component, the unemployment rate is, iron-ically, the real variable with the clearest convergence between the TE-10 and the EU. This holds for individual TEs as well, except for the Czech Republic and, to a lesser extent, for Estonia, Latvia, Lithuania, and Romania. The official rate of unemployment, which was near zero throughout the TEs in 1989, rapidly con-verged for the TE-10 to the average EU level by 1991. The gap between mean unemployment rates in the two groups has never been wider than 0.7 since 1991, while the two regional averages have fluctuated up (1991-1993) and slightly down

(1994-1997) almost in tandem. One can contend that a negative convergence[4] toward EU unemployment rates has taken place. The divergence of unemployment rates among the TE-10 and TE-5 has tended to decrease, with the coefficients of variation dropping to 0.36 and 0.42, respectively, in 1997—the lowest value for any year and any country group; it is even lower than the dispersion around the average unemployment rate within the EU (0.45). This convergence would have been even stronger without the Czech exception as regards employment management and economic restructuring. The analysis of variance (see tables 6.4 and 6.5) shows a positive, and statistically significant, correlation between belonging to a country group and the unemployment rate. On the other hand, the correlation coefficient is practically nil since 1992 in the test for the TE-10 against the EU, but the statistic is not significant. In other words, the TE-10 converged to the EU unemployment rate as soon as 1992 and then remained stuck at about the EU level, regardless of the latter's variations. Paradoxically, then, and quite unexpectedly, the strongest real convergence is the least desirable one, as if labor markets had integrated even prior to eastward enlargement!

Table 6.10: Test of convergence in savings rates, 1991-1996

Samples	1991	1992	1993	1994	1995	1996
TE-10						
m	24.9	22.9	18.4	21.0	20.7	19.1
σ	8.5	4.2	4.8	5.0	4.0	6.0
σ/m	**0.34**	**0.18**	**0.26**	**0.24**	**0.19**	**0.31**
TE-5						
m	22.0	24.4	17.6	21.0	19.8	21.4
σ	2.5	3.7	4.7	4.9	1.2	4.9
σ/m	**0.11**	**0.15**	**0.27**	**0.23**	**0.06**	**0.23**
EU-15						
m	21.5	21.1	20.1	19.9	19.4	20.8
σ	5.3	5.2	4.5	4.9	7.0	5.8
σ/m	**0.25**	**0.25**	**0.22**	**0.24**	**0.36**	**0.28**

Source: World Bank, 1997.

Domestic investment in TEs has followed a J-curve, with a collapse in the first years of transformation, due both to economic recession and uncertainties about the new rules of the game, and a strong overall recovery after 1993 in the TE-10. Recovery cannot, however, be explained by the inflow of FDI, except perhaps in Estonia and Hungary (Andreff and Andreff, 1997, 1998; Andreff, 1998e). Thus, in most TEs the capacity to invest, hence to embark on sustainable catch-up, basically depends on domestic resource mobilization. Table 6.10 shows that the rate of savings in the TE-10 is not inferior to that in EU members, except in 1993 and 1996. But it is often more dispersed among the TE-10 than among the TE-5, even when compared with the EU. This is encouraging from the point of view of catch-up insofar as in particular the TE-5 seem to converge to a savings rate that is not significantly lower than that of EU members. The data are, unfortunately, not available to assess the situation in the CIS in this regard. Nevertheless, since 1994 the rate of savings has been even negative in Armenia, Georgia, and Moldova, and lower than 20 percent in all CIS members, except Russia and Turkmenistan.

Analysis of variance for TE-10 against EU members (see tables 6.4 and 6.5) shows that the country group does not influence the savings rate, but the test is not statistically significant. Thus the savings rate fluctuates in the same range of values rather than being really converging, but its comparable levels in the TE-10 and EU members confirms that domestic saving is not yet a very important variable for the catch-up of the TEs.

In short, there is no significant nominal convergence between TE-10 and the EU. This may be disappointing when interpreted in the light of the Maastricht criteria. However, this negative result might well have made possible real convergence in terms of GDP growth, which is encouraging, and of unemployment, which is not. The good news about real convergence in GDP growth is enhanced by the, admittedly weaker, convergence in labor productivity but at a more rapid pace than for the EU, thus possibly providing the engine for sustainable catch-up. There is no evidence of convergence as far as the savings rate is concerned. But this is not because it is significantly higher in the TEs. Rather it is less stable, which is not so encouraging, given the need for catch-up.

Real Catch-Up vs. Nominal Convergence

Table 6.7 makes it clear that the changeover from state socialism and the first years of the transition, until about 1993, widened the economic-development gap between the TEs and EU members. No TE has as yet recovered its relative level of economic development as compared to the EU. Because of the divergence in growth performance, especially during the transition's first years, the gap became wider by 1993 than it had been at the end of state socialism. By 1996, Poland was the first to regain its measured pre-1990 level of GDP. Several other TEs were on the verge of recovering it in 1997. This provides some grounds for the hypothesis of a catch-up process toward the EU level, beginning with 1993 or 1994, although the gaps remain palpable.

To test this hypothesis the most common approach involves cross-section econometric regression of the rate of economic growth on the initial level of GDP per head (Barro and Sala-i-Martin, 1992, 1995). Two concepts of convergence are at stake. One is β convergence, which tests whether the gap in per capita levels of economic development is narrowing. It exhibits a negative relationship between the growth over a given period of time and the initial level of GDP per capita: the higher the initial GDP level the slower the catch-up process should be. To obtain results for the TE-10 we must therefore estimate the catch-up coefficient in a sample encompassing the TEs and EU members. A second real-convergence concept is known as σ convergence, which indicates the decrease over time of the dispersion (variance) between the values of GDP per capita within the sampled countries. β convergence is a necessary but not a sufficient condition for σ convergence because of the potential for asymmetric shocks.

The model can be formulated as follows:

$$\log Y_{i,T} = a + b \log Y_{i,0} + u_{i,T,0} \tag{6.2}$$

where:

$$b = - (1 - e^{-\beta T}) \tag{6.3}$$

and Y is GDP per capita, T the number of years included in the calculation, and β the speed of convergence. I estimated this equation for two periods: 1990-1996 and 1992-1996. For the first period, the regression is not significant ($r^2 = 0.01$, adj. $r^2 = -0.04$, with a t value of -0.47), signaling that there has been no convergence. For the period 1992-1996, the regression is significant ($r^2 = 0.59$, *adj. r^2* = 0.57). The value of b is -0.25 with a t of -5.77. The value of β is strong: at 0.072 it suggests a high speed—roughly 7 percent per year—of real convergence between the TE-10 and the EU. However, the effect of the initial situation on the growth rate diminishes when the time interval increases, and this may explain the strength of β as compared with that at about 2 percent within the EU. Table 6.11 shows the variance of the logarithm of GDP per capita in order to assess σ convergence. When the variance diminishes after 1992 in both the TE-10 and TE-5, there is evidence of σ convergence with EU countries.

Table 6.11: Sigma convergence of TEs toward the EU

Variance	1990	1991	1992	1993	1994	1995	1996
TE-10	1.06	1.19	1.97	1.50	1.30	1.20	1.20
TE-5	0.65	0.65	1.05	0.81	0.74	0.67	0.60

Source: World Bank, 1997.

Even though the results for β convergence might be biased upwards by the short observation period, there is sufficiently strong evidence to buttress the proposition that, rather than focusing on nominal convergence and being disappointed by a lack of convergence, TE governments and EU decision makers should pay more attention to real convergence and the speed of the catch-up process, for which the results are much more positive, and reassuring. Such a reassessment of the TE-10's economic performance is likely to change our views about the accuracy of stop-go policies that have replaced in good time both shock therapy and gradualism. It should also have an impact on pre-accession negotiations and measures.

The Convergence Dilemma and Policy Consequences

The results regarding nominal and real convergence reported earlier suggest a dilemma. On the one hand, all TEs are attracted by the prospect of eventually joining the EU. They are therefore eager to stabilize their nominal variables, thus giving rise to a policy bias toward dampening the pace of economic activity. This deflationary bias holds in particular for the TEs whose political leadership has staked a claim on, and is prepared to work toward, early membership in monetary union. On the other hand, once these TEs reach the cutoff criteria on inflation and fiscal deficit their macroeconomic managers are inclined toward adopting a less-restrictive stabilization policy or even a policy overtly geared toward stimulating economic growth and alleviating the social costs of transition. But such a choice is likely to weaken nominal performance of the economy in the medium term, precisely due to insufficient real economic convergence toward performances in the EU. In turn, this necessitates adopting again a more restrictive policy stance. The stop-go toward catch-up will tend to continue for quite some time, in fact for as long as TE policy makers aim at reaching both stabilization of nominal macroeconomic variables and some catch-up to EU levels of economic development because the two aims are, generally speaking, incompatible in the short and medium term, although they may be consistent in the long run.

Earlier I drew attention to a similar dilemma experienced in the southern EU members and the criticism of some observers with regard to the priority given to nominal convergence in terms of the costs of joining the EU's monetary union early on, which tends to be far larger for less- than for more-developed EU members. Indeed, the emphasis placed on nominal convergence might well exacerbate real divergence in the medium and long run (Fayolle, 1996a; Loufir and Reichlin, 1993; Neven and Gouyette, 1994; Richez-Battesti, 1994; Rollet, 1993). The TEs presently bent on joining monetary union as soon as legally feasible, that is, at least two years after they join ERM II, for which first EU accession is a prerequisite, are likely to become enmeshed in a similar tradeoff between nominal stabilization and output and employment losses. A realistic compromise for the TEs (see Hagen, 1996) could be to choose a timely accession against fulfilling all the prerequisites of participation in monetary union. Another compromise, involving most likely a growth slowdown triggered by adhering to restrictive fiscal and monetary policies (Coricelli, 1996), is the cited stop-go policy. The latter would seem to have been adopted by several of the TE-5 in particular, as underlined by the shifts in economic policy in Poland (1993, 1997), Hungary (1995), and the Czech Republic (1996-1997); but also in Romania (1991, 1996), Latvia (1995), and Slovakia (1993).

Given the start-up of negotiations for accession of the TE-5 in early 1998, it is of interest to determine where these countries stood with their stop-go approaches through 1997, in light of their policy experiences since the inception of transition. Recall that at the start of transition most TEs adopted a harsh stabilization policy, although in virtually all countries it was de facto eased beyond the bounds of strict IMF conditionality because of the social cost of austerity as well as the trade and fiscal deficits with sizable inflation. On the other hand, the TEs (such as Hungary) that initially did not resort to stiff austerity had eventually to abandon their gradual stabilization policy for some policy 'shock.' One way of looking at this contrast is that Poland partly reversed its economic policy with the advent of the post-communist government in order to mitigate the costs of austerity, while Hungary, bowing to the constraints of a double fiscal and trade deficit, was compelled to abandon its gradual pace of economic policy. Both TEs therefore converged from different starting points to some kind of stop-go policy, resulting in asymmetric catch-up. Indeed, Poland has enjoyed one of the highest rates of GDP growth in Europe, only lagging behind Ireland and Slovakia in 1995-1996 and behind Ireland and Estonia in 1997, while Hungary has been saddled with one of the lowest rates, only ahead of Latvia in 1995 and of Bulgaria and Italy in 1996. In some sense, and paradoxically so, the observed real economic convergence has been partly fueled by this belated convergence toward a stop-go policy.

Elsewhere (Andreff, 1998b, c) I have extensively discussed the need for less-restrictive monetary and fiscal policies in order to gain economic recovery and sustainable economic growth, thus catch-up. Without repeating these analyses, I deem it useful to illustrate the stop-go policy in the case of selected TEs.

Poland de facto suspended its initial shock therapy in September 1991, and the IMF blocked loans to Poland up to 1993. In 1992, social and public expenditures rose substantially while the wage tax (*popiwek*) was reduced, nominal wages rose by 65 percent so that real wages dropped by only 2.7 percent. These measures propped up growth recovery rather than stabilization. In 1993, the first signs of a slight Keynesian recovery policy emerged. The central bank lowered the interest rates in February 1993 to foster investment and sustain the growth recovery that had emerged, however tenuously, in 1992. Nominal wages were increased by 41 percent in 1993 with a resulting rise in real wages, the first one since the beginning of the transition. Growth recovery started to shrink the fiscal deficit. The new postcommunist government attempted to back economic recovery in November 1993 with a very significant rise in public-sector salaries, pensions, and family allowances. The wage tax was suppressed in 1994 and a sort of wage indexation emerged from a lax wage policy, with wage increases (41 percent in 1994, 32 percent in 1995, and 26 percent in 1996) surpassing the inflation rate. While the stabilization policy still aimed at curbing inflation, the Sejm—the Polish Parliament—adopted the "Strategy for Poland" (Kołodko, 1994) in April 1994, which was actually an economic-recovery program and thus quite distinct from the earlier shock therapy; it was brought up to date two years later as "Poland 2000" (Kołodko, 1996). The recovery policy was primarily relying on fiscal incentives to invest and export so that since 1994 economic growth has been pulled by investment instead of private consumption, as in 1992-1993. The recovery policy thus seems to have given rise to a catch-up process. The problem with the recovery policy in Poland has been a persistent two-digit rate of inflation and, even more constraining, a rising trade deficit. The crawling peg of the złoty, combined with higher inflation than expected, led to a real appreciation of the exchange rate, which has been hindering exports and triggering more imports of needed equipment, leading in turn to a trade deficit equivalent to 5 percent of GDP in 1997 (see chapter 5). With the newly elected political majority, a debate has been opened on whether to revert to a more restrictive stabilization therapy. Embracing tighter monetary and fiscal policies risks slowing down growth recovery, thus throttling the still-buoyant catch-up process under way.

Without going into quite the same degree of detail, shock therapy in the Czech Republic was alleviated sometime in 1995, resulting in one of the highest real-wage surges in TEs in 1995 and 1996, well exceeding the modest rise in labor productivity. Increased social transfers in 1995, a lax monetary policy facilitated by foreign-capital inflows, and a fiscal deficit since 1996, all contributed to economic recovery in 1995-1996; but they soon also led to a large trade deficit, currency devaluation, and a new austerity program launched in April 1997. Again a stop-go policy.

Also the Baltic states abandoned their very restrictive monetary policies after 1994. Both the Estonian and Lithuanian currency boards will eventually have to be dismantled, at the very least since they are not compatible with the *acquis*. In all three countries, since 1995 public investment expenditures, consumption credit, and wage increases above the gains in labor productivity have been intensifying. The Latvian growth-recovery program adopted in November 1995 has relied during 1996-1997 on public investment.

On the other hand, Hungary's initially gradualist strategy paved the way for inertial inflation (Andreff, 1994a, 1998d) fueled by wage increases, thus entailing real appreciation and a foreign-trade imbalance. Together these led eventually to the double fiscal and trade constraints, whose financing became in 1993-1994 the subject of a contentious battle between the ministry of finance and the central bank, resulting in less predictable monetary policy and interest rates. In the run-up to the 1994 election, a lax economic policy permitted increases in social expenditures and wages in the public sector. The fiscal deficit skyrocketed to 8.2 percent of GDP. The new postcommunist government was not able to avoid a shock-therapy austerity program in March 1995: a rise in taxes, sharp cuts in fiscal outlays, reduction of family allowances and maternity leaves, layoffs in the public sector, a ceiling of 10 percent on all wage increases per year, and a sharp devaluation of the forint; all this accompanied with a restrictive monetary policy relying on high real interest rates. By cutting the share of wages in national income, embracing disinflation, and curbing the fiscal deficit in part thanks to privatization revenues, in 1995-1996 part of the root causes of inertial inflation in Hungary were stamped out. The trade deficit was compressed in part by levying an 8 percent import surcharge. By 1997, Hungary found itself in a more stabilized economic situation than the Czech Republic or Poland and entered a period of growth recovery that should be sustainable for the near term. This outcome, once again, appears to have been the result of stop-go policies. Although there were some differences in the details of economic-policy measures in Slovakia and Slovenia, the same conclusion applies to them. So, we remain only with two bad 'students' among the TE-10, basically because economic policies in Bulgaria and Romania suffered from weaker commitment of governments to austerity and structural and institutional reforms.

Stop-go policy usually does not deserve a positive appraisal since it is less efficient in handling nominal variables than a restrictive policy and its growth impulses tend to be weaker as well. In the case of the TEs, however, an involuntary stop-go policy has enabled eight TEs to embark on a path of real convergence toward the EU macroeconomic performances even if at the cost of nominal divergence. In our view, such a policy is definitely better suited to ease eventual EU accession for the TEs than shock therapy, considering their need of catch-up to ease their entry into the EU, and than a pure gradualist strategy, which is not sustainable at any rate. The observed real convergence, albeit while jeopardizing nominal convergence, stems partly from the fact that these countries have involuntarily gravitated toward stop-go. Mainstream economists would never have advocated such a choice.

Although the policy steps prospectively to be undertaken by TEs, and indeed by EU policy makers, in order to facilitate EU accession are as yet unclear and will soon need to be concretely specified, the foregoing analyses suggest that policy makers, both in the candidates for accession and in EU members, as well as the negotiators in the accession talks, can in any case facilitate accession by stressing the primacy of real convergence over nominal convergence, especially early on in preparing the TEs for accession and smoothing their trajectory toward full access to the four freedoms. In other words, a longer transition period after EU accession will be needed for joining the euro than for integrating the TEs into the EU if the TE leadership were to target explicitly policies in real terms.

Convergence and the Bumpy Road to EU Accession

Nominal and real convergence are sometimes enhanced and at other times hindered by structural and institutional changes or rigidities. They are influenced by the restructuring of the productive sphere, the transformation of banking and financial systems, the revamping of trade ties and institutions, and the economic role the state plays. The issues of systemic transformation and transition toward a genuine market economy, *in se* the gamut of the transformation process as a whole, in each TE crop up at every step of the EU accession process. Within the scope of this chapter I can sketch only cursorily the core issues at stake. I confine myself to the question whether new institutions and regulations adopted since 1990 in the TEs are converging toward the EU's. But even then multiple approaches to formulating a rounded view would be desirable.

One way of tackling such issues is to look carefully at the remaining role of the public sector in the transformation process (Andreff, 1995), the success with privatization, and the institutional convergence toward the distribution of property and the functioning of corporate governance (Andreff 1994b, 1996, 1998a). In many cases, economic restructuring can proceed only through initiatives taken by SOEs or firms in which the state retains a large residual role. Blurred property rights or ill-defined corporate governance may then become a constraint on desirable restructuring.

Other paths toward evaluating convergence of institutional aspects of economic transformation among the TEs or between the TEs and the EU can be designed. One is more a legal concern, such as meticulously comparing new laws ruling ownership, banking, accounting, business lawyers' activity, bankruptcy, competition (antitrust law), stock exchange operations, tax systems, labor legislation, social welfare, and so on. Another is to point to difficulties or failures preventing the TEs from adopting and/or applying the *acquis* (Altmann, Andreff, and Fink, 1995). If institutional change is actually to promote real convergence, it will necessarily take time because there is a lag between adopting new laws and regulations, and their implementation, let alone ensuring their smooth functioning for stabilizing the market-economy framework. Accession of the TEs to the EU will probably occur before the TEs can bridge this gap, even though the EU requires in principle the adoption of the entire *acquis* upon accession.

The costs and benefits of accession, not just in terms of budgetary transfers, depend heavily on convergence toward the EU average (see chapter 3). This means that the pre-accession period should be protracted for some TEs and perhaps all TEs will need extensive transition periods after accession until they can benefit from all the economic advantages of full membership without overly burdening any one of the present members. The faster and deeper the catch-up achieved prior to accession, the easier it will be to harmonize the interests of TEs and present EU members, hence the greater the EU's capacity to absorb TEs and the smaller will be the often neglected necessary institutional change of the EU itself (Inotai, 1994, 1996). So bearing in mind the requirements of catch-up, not only in economic-performance indicators but also in institutional terms, real convergence should be promising in smoothing some parts of the negotiation process, while many TEs could consider nominal convergence as a set of western criteria or barriers used to brake or postpone their accession.

Another advantage of putting real convergence in the center of the backdrop to the accession negotiations is that the *acquis* itself is a moving target, and hence not completely known. Not only that, although real economic convergence is not independent of institutional approximation and harmonization, it is much more concrete and tangible than assessment of institutional approximation around the obligations ensuing from the *acquis*. In some 'sensitive' areas, like the CAP or environmental protection, a rapid approximation is not even desirable from the EU's point of view; for example, extending the CAP to TEs under prevailing conditions would encourage surplus production, thus necessitating substantial EU funds. On the other hand, both overall institution building and approximation of the *acquis* at the enterprise level (as argued in chapter 7) require an investment effort that will be more sustainable with fast economic growth than with a stabilization policy geared toward nominal convergence, which by definition is less favorable to investment.

All of the TE-10 are presently involved in working out with the European Commission a reinforced pre-accession strategy in the framework of the APA, new pre-accession funding, and the European Conference that first met on 12 March 1998 to examine the conditions for TE accession. However, this strategy does not seem to include efforts aimed at promoting a revival of economic ties among the TEs themselves (see Brabant, 1996b), as discussed in chapter 3. Pre-accession financial aid is not the most crucial issue, though €45 billion would be allocated from 2000 to 2006, with €1 billion per year for structural aid and €520 million for aid to agricultural development to each applicant country (European Commission, 1997h). Institution building will require much more qualitative assistance than financial flows. It might be wise to arrange, as part of the pre-accession strategy, for the transfer of technology to the TE-10 since that is likely to accelerate real convergence and the catch-up process, particularly in TEs where the R&D sector has all but collapsed (Andreff, 1997b). This can be achieved through FDI, transfers from the EU's public-research systems, and scientific cooperation between R&D institutions in the EU and the TEs.

Conclusions

I have tried in this chapter to operationalize the meaning of economic convergence between the TEs and EU members. Unlike the emphasis placed on nominal convergence in recent debates around the EU's monetary union, I have stressed the importance of real convergence and its compatibility with nominal convergence. Real convergence in TEs would signal catch-up toward average EU levels of income, productivity, and so on, which in turn would lower the budgetary transfers mandated by the EU programs in place and in all likelihood impose smaller adjustment costs on present EU members. Another dimension of real convergence, however, refers to the institutional catch-up required for the TEs to play a constructive role in the SEM. From all the evidence at hand, whereas there are few indications of nominal convergence, there are more encouraging signs of real convergence, at least in macroeconomic indicators. But there is also convergence in the institutional setup, although major catch-up remains to be accomplished.

The discrepancy between nominal and real convergence in the TEs provides ammunition for innovating well-targeted, rather than common or similar, economic policies within the enlarged EU because the catch-up requirements cannot be reconciled with the most restrictive nominal stabilization policy. As underlined in a recent position paper (Eatwell et al., 1997, p. 62): "If enlargement is equated with the admission of a first batch of countries which satisfy mechanistic criteria, with little flexibility and only traditional transition procedures, and with unsuccessful applicants simply excluded from the Union, then enlargement will divide rather than unite." This warning becomes even more pointed when we consider that attention to real convergence has thus far remained in the background of the accession negotiations compared with the Copenhagen criteria and sometimes, erroneously, the Maastricht criteria of nominal convergence.

Notes

1. Systemic convergence of course comprises noneconomic characteristics such as external, political, social, and technical aspects of systemic changes that I cannot cover in this contribution.

2. These tests were undertaken by Madeleine Andreff, who is assistant professor in economics at the University of Marne la Vallée (France).

3. Due to a lack of adequate data for many TEs, we have taken lending rates as the measure for long-term interest rates insofar as they are the ones with the longest maturity (one year or over). Therefore, the comparison to the Maastricht criterion is less meaningful for the interest rate than for the inflation rate.

4. For a theoretical approach toward negative convergence, called 'congruence,' see Andreff, 1992.

Chapter 7

Structural Convergence—Through Industrial Policy?

Hubert Gabrisch and Klaus Werner

There can hardly be any doubt that the EU's eastward enlargement is a prerequisite for raising in a sustainable manner, and over the long haul, welfare in the eastern part of Europe (see Baldwin, Francois, and Portes, 1997). Yet, it is unclear how the short-term[1] gains and adjustment costs of EU entry and of the full assimilation of the *acquis* will be distributed over the various present EU members and entrants, let alone third parties (see chapter 9), and whether these outcomes will be politically and socially acceptable in the various countries. The current EU members constitute a heterogeneous group from various economic, political, and social points of view. Furthermore, it has been in the process of deepening integration, moving into areas for which securing social and political acceptance in many members has become increasingly more complex and problematical. TE accessions will further exacerbate this heterogeneity since these are on the whole countries with comparatively small firms, especially in the private sector; poorly developed capacities to broach new markets, especially in advanced industrial economies; and facing for years to come wholesale transformation of economic structures that continue to exhibit strong legacies of socialist-type central planning, as well as of state socialism more generally, albeit to varying degrees in the various TEs.

The literature considers, albeit often implicitly, the liberalization of trade and factor markets as a sufficient prerequisite for overcoming the above-cited features of TEs. One can argue against this, however, that it is especially the inherited starting position that determines to a large extent the prospective development path of individual economies, deviating from which can be very costly indeed in terms of required resources, including time. Moreover, the EU encompasses not only a fairly integrated SEM. It is also advancing toward a common monetary policy around a common currency for most EU members and a rather stringent ERM II for the other members.

Seen against a backdrop characterized by path dependence, asymmetry, institutional diversity, and macroeconomic restrictions, it is impossible to predict offhand the short- or longer-term benefits and losses of joining the EU for the TEs individually or as a group. Yet one can specify the prerequisites that determine the longer-term benefits of the desired structural change. On that basis one can identify the weak elements for the TEs undergoing wholesale mutations in their economic and societal structures. In this connection, it is especially important to ascertain whether the EU's market forces are such that they themselves can conceivably set off and support the necessary structural-adjustment processes in TEs.

The objective of this chapter is to examine whether temporary exceptions from the *acquis* can usefully support the necessary structural change in TEs that wish to join the EU. Our working hypothesis is that structural convergence is a necessary prerequisite for reaping over the long haul the benefits potentially accruing from EU membership for all partners involved. EU accession, in a normative sense, must therefore trigger such convergence. By this we mean in particular the growing capability of TE firms to wage constructive competition in the SEM, given their factor endowment and cultural, historical, and social specificities. These competition conditions are not only circumscribed by the EU's *acquis* but they also result from the fact, which we deem to be important, that firms already accustomed to competing in the present SEM, let alone while that is rapidly evolving, possess greater capabilities than TE firms presently do. Improving the competitiveness of TE firms is arguably the most important challenge for the eastern transformation processes, especially when seen against the backdrop of the burdens inherited from socialist-type central planning.

The chapter is organized as follows. First we discuss changes in trade structures induced by market forces and identify those economic aspects that may entail problems, certainly in a long-term perspective. We assume that rising shares of IIT reflect structural convergence. Especially manufacturing firms in industrial economies, such as the EU, use product differentiation as a central strategy to open and defend markets. This involves essentially strengthening their market position by varying the volume and quality of their output on the basis of company-specific advantages. Next we depict the often unsatisfactory relationship between market and government intervention in common IIT models. Thereafter we discuss the actual role of governments in TEs since the transition's inception. Before concluding, we examine if and in which areas governments that embrace an activist structural policy are in conflict with EU regulations and how the potential for such conflicts can best be contained.

Emerging Patterns of IIT Adjustments in TEs

Among economists the general view prevails that strengthening IIT is in and of itself advantageous. Experiences of the EU and other integrated areas show that at the macroeconomic level the structural-adjustment processes induced by trade liberalization tend to be less disruptive if the adjustment follows intra- rather than interindustry patterns (Greenaway and Milner, 1987). Intersectoral adjustments are encumbered by the fact that production factors can be reallocated among broad sectors only to a limited extent. Moreover, changes in the distribution of wage incomes among sectors after trade liberalization turn out to be less dramatic in the case of intra-industry adjustment patterns. All in all, the political and social obstacles that may arise in making trade liberalization acceptable, when it involves primarily intrasectoral adjustments, can be anticipated to be fewer and of a smaller magnitude not only in the entering TEs but also in the present EU members.

IIT patterns have thus far been empirically analyzed chiefly for trade among industrial countries and between industrialized and developing countries. For the most part it can be shown that for trade between industrialized and developing countries, IIT is of lesser importance, although rising over time, than that among industrialized countries (Fukasaku, 1992; Lee, 1989). Similar processes can be discussed for trade between four central European TEs (Czech Republic, Hungary, Poland, and Slovakia) and the EU since 1991, that is, roughly after trade liberalization (UNECE, 1995, p. 50). We have chosen these four countries because of their free-trade agreements (FTAs) with the EU concluded as part and parcel of the EAs, but put in place already in 1992. These agreements have by now all but completely liberalized a fairly high proportion of trade between both regions. Applying comparable starting data with the sample drawn from the eighty-two chapters of the EU's Combined Nomenclature (CN), the Grubel-Lloyd index for IIT in 1996 (see the methodological annex) was already higher than that for Greece, Portugal, and Spain at the time of their EU accession (see table 7.1).

That said, it should be borne in mind that any empirical analysis of trade structures might be distorted by the aggregation of subitems. In our case a distortion arises from the changes in the trade shares of the individual commodity groups considered.[2] If the share of a commodity group with a strong IIT indicator increases then also the aggregate IIT level must rise. But this expansion may come about without trade liberalization necessarily having induced those adjustment processes at the microeconomic level, that is, in individual firms, that we consider essential for IIT to be mirroring 'modernization trends' in some meaningful sense.

Through a factoring of the aggregate indicators over six commodity groups distinguished by factor intensity the 'true' IIT indicator can be determined, as explained in the methodological note set forth in the annex.

Table 7.1: Grubel-Lloyd indices[a] for EU[b] trade with four TEs

Country	1991	1993	1996	
			Unadjusted[c]	Adjusted[c]
Czech Republic[d]	0.516	0.585	0.647	0.628
Hungary	0.564	0.590	0.720	0.520
Poland	0.292	0.432	0.465	0.439
Slovakia[d]	0.516	0.425	0.574	0.528

Memorandum: Greece (1981): 0.262; Portugal (1986): 0.529; Spain (1986): 0.673.

Notes:
[a] Calculated as a weighted average on the basis of the 82 chapters of the EU's CN.
[b] 1991 and 1993: EU-12; 1996: EU-15.
[c] See text and annex for details.
[d] Czechoslovakia for 1991.

Sources: own calculations based on EUROSTAT, 1997.

The adjusted and unadjusted values are reported for 1996 in table 7.1. The adjusted values suggest that the rise in IIT of the Czech Republic, Poland, and Slovakia is less impressive than the unadjusted values tend to suggest. In the case of Hungary the indicator takes an even smaller value than in 1991. The statistical relevance of the higher unadjusted values can be seen in the marked increase of trade shares of those commodity groups in which both countries show sizable IIT magnitudes. In Hungary these were specialized goods (see table 7.2). The economic explanation can be found in trade diversion. Following the collapse of CMEA trade relations and trade liberalization with the EU, demand and supply in these countries have become increasingly geared toward the EU.

Had the trade shares remained the same, the increase of the aggregate IIT level for the Czech Republic, Poland, and Slovakia would have been a reflection of an increased level of IIT with resource- and scale- or labor-intensive products. Labor- and scale-intensive industries are mainly characterized by mass production of standardized products. On the other hand, specialized products actually make up the core of IIT. They can mostly be found in engineering and machine-tool industries in which the competitiveness of companies is based on and strengthened through product differentiation according to prevailing demand patterns rather than by compressing costs.

The above IIT picture painted by factor intensity and technology level is consistent with Linder's (1961) hypothesis, given the substantial income differences between trading partners. Income differences between TEs and EU members tend to push IIT for TEs toward mass-production goods. With growing per capita income, a country's consumption patterns will increasingly differentiate and therefore serve as a starting point for product differentiation. But since domestic firms mainly concentrate on the internal market the pattern of product differentiation is determined by mainstream domestic demand. Accordingly, the different consumption preferences between 'rich' and 'poor' countries influence the patterns of intra-industry structural adjustment. In TEs with comparatively low per capita income the preferences can be expected to be biased toward daily needs and rather standardized products resulting from mass production rather than from expensive, research-intensive or highly specialized, products.

Table 7.2: Grubel-Lloyd indices of EU trade with four TEs

Country	Grubel-Lloyd indices			Trade shares	
	1991	1996	Change	1991	1996
Czech Republic[b]					
resource intensive	0.499	0.564	0.065	16.1	12.9
labor intensive	0.510	0.708	0.198	15.3	14.4
scale intensive	0.594	0.702	0.108	36.9	37.2
specialized supplier	0.481	0.625	0.144	26.1	30.9
research intensive	0.191	0.402	0.211	5.6	4.6
Hungary					
resource intensive	0.409	0.482	0.073	16.6	12.1
labor intensive	0.482	0.543	0.061	23.4	16.2
scale intensive	0.618	0.692	0.074	30.6	28.4
specialized supplier	0.708	0.924	0.218	24.9	39.3
research intensive	0.359	0.401	0.042	4.5	4.0
Poland					
resource intensive	0.160	0.446	0.286	47.8	17.3
labor intensive	0.399	0.353	-0.046	13.2	18.8
scale intensive	0.449	0.567	0.118	22.7	36.7
specialized supplier	0.390	0.448	0.058	13.4	23.5
research intensive	0.193	0.165	-0.028	2.9	3.7
Slovakia[b]					
resource intensive	0.499	0.422	-0.077	16.1	13.7
labor intensive	0.510	0.440	-0.070	15.3	15.9
scale intensive	0.594	0.717	0.123	36.9	41.2
specialized supplier	0.481	0.560	0.079	26.1	33.0
research intensive	0.191	0.189	-0.002	5.6	3.3

Notes:

[a] The classification follows that suggested in OECD, 1992.
[b] Czechoslovakia in 1991.

Sources: own calculations based on EUROSTAT, 1997.

It is possible that the trade arrangements between TEs and the EU have intensified that trend. Many resource-, labor-, and scale-intensive products fall into the category of the 'sensitive sectors' for which trade liberalization has been retarded as per the EA. Examples are textiles, garments, and footwear or products from the iron and steel industry. Trade with specialized and research-intensive products between the EU and TEs was liberalized early on. In contrast to orthodox or standardized goods, adjustment processes in TE firms have generally been far more restrained. Under the circumstances, one should remain rather skeptical about the future possibilities of the nature and extent of IIT between highly developed EU countries and structurally weak TEs at a low- to middle-income level. Instead, the restructuring of the capital stock in the TEs under way may be biased toward products and technologies that can in time be abandoned only at considerable, and rising, costs.

Another argument against the use of growth in IIT indicators, when one eschews probing deeper into their meaning, as indicators of structural change derives from the relationship between economic growth and the kind of product differentiation one can expect to emerge. Empirical studies (among the newer investigations, see Fontagné et al., 1996) show differences between the effects of vertical and horizontal product differentiation. Vertical differentiation rests on the exchange of basically the same goods but at different qualities, different prices, and produced by different technologies, resulting in different shares of value added in output. Horizontal differentiation, on the other hand, leads to an exchange of similar goods with comparable value-added shares that are produced at similar levels of technological sophistication within the same industry branch. The differentiation stems primarily from alternative designs, colors, packaging, or other features that individualize goods and services. Vertical differentiation, notably characterized by significant differences in the shares of value added between imports and exports, would therefore seem to be an attribute of firm specialization for countries at a fairly low level of development. By contrast, horizontal differentiation, with goods showing higher and similar value-added shares, has been characteristic of firms in countries at higher levels of economic development.

Given this apparent link between horizontal and vertical intra-industry specialization and level of economic development, the aggregate economic effect of higher IIT indicators may reflect entirely different outcomes in terms of buttressing growth and development, depending on the kind of product differentiation individual countries can access. This throws doubt on the often invoked argument cited above: growing IIT magnitudes are in and of themselves indicative of desirable changes in economic structures. Since this is not always so, one should probe beyond estimates of aggregate IIT shares and address the more qualitative elements underlying these developments, especially differences in technological sophistication and in product quality, given prevailing demand structures.

Various studies (see Forstner and Ballance, 1990, pp. 166ff.) have been devoted to testing the hypothesis that IIT between industrialized and developing countries depends chiefly on vertical product differentiation. The key difference in most of the theoretical models concerned with the relationship between vertical product differentiation and IIT lies in alternative levels of technological maturity. Those levels may coincide with differences in the endowment with physical capital (Falvey, 1981) or with highly qualified labor (Flam and Helpman, 1987).

A plausible approach to understanding vertical product differentiation in trade between heterogeneous economic regions can be found in the product-cycle model first proposed in a coherent fashion by Raymond Vernon (1966). IIT is accordingly understood to be a combination of the different phases of the product cycle. This product cycle can be characterized in the following manner: firms in industrialized countries ensure a steady flow of 'new' products through high R&D expenditures, whence they derive technological superiority over the technology utilized in the production of 'old' products. Because various obstacles—not just the ability to bolster savings—limit access to best-practice technology during the innovation phases of 'new' products, the originators of the technology, and thus the 'new' products, enjoy a monopolistic competitive advantage for that particular product. IIT takes place when the industrialized countries export the new version but import the old version. During the maturing phase of the product, imitators or emulators, possibly through the acquisition of licenses, emerge in less-developed countries as they shift the composition of their endowment with real capital relative to their labor supply. During the standardization phase, labor-intensive production processes are frequently sourced out to countries with a comparatively high, often unskilled, labor endowment.

Technological differentiation is a key determinant of the differences in economic structures. These in turn are crucial in the genesis of the distinguishing features of trade relations between higher- and less-developed countries, and appear mainly in the form of gaps between quality and price in trade. The concept usually applied to measure such quality-price differences are relative unit values (RUVs). Assuming perfect information, the rationale for using unit values as an indicator for price-quality gaps lies in the fact that goods sold at a higher price will tend to be of higher quality than goods sold more cheaply (Greenaway, Hine, and Milner,1994, p. 81). Though unit values are problematic for various well-known reasons,[3] we calculate unit values in the EU's trade with the above-identified four TEs for 1993 and 1996 in order to disentangle vertical from total IIT. As a measure for price-quality gaps, we obtained RUVs from unit values of EU imports (UVMs) from and of EU exports (UVXs) to the TEs considered.[4] Vertical IIT (VIIT) is defined as the simultaneous export and import of CN two-digit categories provided the ratio between UVX and UVM remains within a specified range; we decided to set it at 15 percent either side of unity. True, this range is an arbitrary choice. However, others have proceeded in a similar fashion when tackling the kind of questions posed here (for example, Abd-el-Rahman, 1991; Greenaway, Hine, and Milner, 1994). Furthermore, since we are primarily interested in the change of the VIIT shares over time, this should not depend on the range specified.

Table 7.3: Relative unit values[a] of EU trade with four TEs, 1996

CN chapters	Czech Rep.	Hungary	Poland	Slovakia
26 Ores, slag, and ash	0.55	1.76	0.87	2.92
27 Mineral fuels and products	0.22	0.77	0.32	0.53
30 Pharmaceutical products	0.36	0.42	0.12	2.17
33 Oils, perfumery, cosmetics, etc.	0.83	0.67	0.40	1.38
34 Soaps, laundry products, etc.	1.23	1.08	0.77	0.99
35 Albuminous substances, etc.	1.65	1.37	1.36	1.39
36 Explosives, etc.	0.87	0.44	0.54	0.22
37 Photo and cinema products	1.01	1.59	5.83	9.83
38 Miscellaneous chemicals	0.25	0.49	0.19	0.65
45 Cork and articles	0.93	2.14	0.20	0.49
46 Wickerwork and basket work	0.22	0.35	0.47	0.45
47 Pulp of wood, cellulose, etc.	0.95	1.48	0.86	1.37
48 Paper and articles	0.73	0.71	0.45	0.61
49 Printing products	0.84	0.61	0.59	0.49
65 Headgear and parts thereof	1.10	1.18	0.54	1.77
66 Umbrellas, etc.	0.71	0.65	0.77	0.45
67 Prepared feathers and articles	1.10	0.80	0.36	n.a.
68 Articles of stone, etc.	0.24	1.09	0.31	0.35
71 Pearls, etc.	0.30	0.69	0.90	0.22
84 Nuclear reactors, machinery, etc.	0.50	0.67	0.31	0.29
86 Railway or tramway equipment	0.27	0.28	0.14	0.41
88 Aircraft, spacecraft	1.68	0.17	0.18	0.43
89 Ships, etc.	1.96	2.62	0.21	13.55
90 Optical, photographic, etc.	0.38	0.35	0.30	0.18
91 Clocks, watches, and parts	0.64	1.16	0.44	n.a.
92 Musical instruments	0.40	0.90	0.17	0.34
93 Arms and ammunition	0.78	0.36	0.50	4.96
95 Toys, games, sports appliances	0.76	0.71	0.55	0.72
96 Miscellaneous manufactures	0.41	0.18	0.33	0.21
97 Works of art	0.11	0.04	0.56	1.72

Notes: [a] Defined as UVM/UVX for all-but-completely liberalized trade.
Sources: own calculations based on EUROSTAT, 1997.

In addition, we decomposed VIIT indices by identifying all those CN chapters that show an RUV higher than 1.15. In this case, the TE has a price advantage in its EU exports. The reverse holds for an RUV lower than 0.85. We consider all these items with an RUV exceeding 1.15 to be 'high quality' VIIT imports of the EU from the TEs. Finally, we selected all two-digit CN categories whose trade has been nearly completely[5] liberalized immediately after the FTA with the EU came into effect. In total, thirty of the eighty-two CN categories considered in this study belong to the group of commodities whose trade was completely liberalized in this sense from the very beginning.[6]

The results can be summarized as follows. First of all, the calculated RUVs in most categories turn out to be outside the specified range. This is especially true for items whose trade was completely liberalized in 1996 (see table 7.3). Only a few commodity groups qualify for our classification of horizontal IIT. In all other cases, the indicators remain substantially below 0.85, suggesting a strong price-quality gap to the disadvantage of the TEs and a combination of low-quality imports by and high-quality exports from the EU can be assumed. For comparison, Landesmann and Burgstaller (1997) compared unit values of the TEs in their exports to the EU with similar magnitudes for the EU's total imports (or exports from the rest of the world to the EU). In 1994 UVXs for TEs ranged from 52 to 83 percent of the EU's total UVMs.[7] Mechanical engineering, for example, was between 55 and 81 percent. In our calculation for 1996, UVXs of the CN chapter eighty-four, which is comparable to the category specified by Landesmann and Burgstaller, was between 29 and 67 percent. That is, the price-quality gap was even higher.

Table 7.4: IIT and VIIT shares in EU trade with TEs, 1993 and 1996

	Czech Rep.		Hungary		Poland		Slovakia	
	1993	1996	1993	1996	1993	1996	1993	1996
IIT (GL) indices	0.585	0.647	0.590	0.720	0.432	0.465	0.425	0.574
relative VIIT[a]	89.6	92.6	90.2	88.4	93.5	90.5	95.3	73.1
relative hq VIIT[b]	3.9	3.4	10.0	6.7	7.5	5.8	7.1	7.1

Notes:

[a] In percent of IIT.
[b] 'High quality' VIIT in percent of VIIT.

Source: Own calculations based on EUROSTAT, 1997.

Second, in unadjusted total IIT (TIIT), between 89 and 95 percent was vertical in 1993, using the specified 15 percent range for RUVs (see table 7.4). In 1996, this share even rose for the Czech Republic. The share was lower in 1996 for trade with Hungary, Poland, and Slovakia but remained at fairly high levels of between 73 and 93 percent. For comparison, Abd-el-Rahman (1991) calculated that the VIIT share for France amounted to about one-third of TIIT for the period 1985-1987. Greenaway, Hine, and Milner (1994) calculated for the United Kingdom a 70 percent share of VIIT in TIIT in 1988. Both studies employed the same methodology as specified here. However, they used more disaggregated data (six- and five-digit, respectively) and only SITC groups five to eight (excluding the CN chapters sixteen to twenty-seven in our study). Direct comparison between our and their results is therefore not quite straightforward.

Table 7.5: VIIT shares in percent of all-but-completely liberalized trade

Year	Czech Rep.	Hungary	Poland	Slovakia
1993	99.7	99.2	97.1	99.7
1996	98.4	98.4	98.7	99.1

Source: own calculations based on EUROSTAT, 1997.

Third, the cases in which the EU's UVMs in trade with TEs are higher than the UVXs are very rare indeed. Only in these few cases a negative price-quality gap applies for the EU in trade with TEs. The share of such 'high quality' imports by the EU remains between 3.4 and 10 percent in 1996. In all other cases, the VIITs actually consist of high-quality exports by and low-quality imports from the EU.

Finally, almost 100 percent of the EU's IIT with TEs in all-but-completely liberalized commodities was vertical in 1993, and this share had not changed significantly by 1996 (table 7.5). To put it differently: TEs can realize 'high quality' exports in VIIT and high horizontal IIT predominantly in incompletely liberalized trade.

Summing up the above analyses, while the evidence points overwhelmingly toward the finding that trade liberalization between the EU and TEs has bolstered IIT, one cannot detect any strong sign of structural convergence. Instead changes seem to have taken place that, if sustained, might entail diverging economic structures. Indications thereof are that intra-industry adjustments are mainly taking place for standard goods of labor- and scale-intensive production technologies; and there is wider use of production methods with fairly low levels of technological sophistication, as compared to best practice in global trade and production. There is accordingly a growing risk that the TEs may be committing themselves to production processes yielding 'low-quality' products in the sense invoked here.

The consequences of such a development, if not reversed, should be clear: vertical product differentiation leads less developed countries to specialize primarily in goods with small shares of value added in total output. The income distribution that stems from such a division of labor is less favorable to the TEs, it tends to worsen in the context of what is likely to occur when they accede to the EU, and it furthermore hinders the process of catching up economically with the more developed EU members. If investment continues to be concentrated in low- to medium-level technologies, the TEs could find themselves in a technology-gap trap. Emerging therefrom could be very expensive indeed. It is therefore necessary to investigate how such a longer-term development could be forestalled by redirecting the course of structural change in the TEs and moving it onto a path leading to the desired convergence.

IIT Models and the Role of an Activist Government

Theoretical as well as empirical models (see especially Helpman and Krugman, 1985) seeking explanations for IIT specify demand- and supply-side factors as well as country- and industry-specific factors. Government activities in these configurations appear only when the impact of explicit trade barriers is considered (Fukasaku, 1992; Lee, 1989). It is simply assumed that trade liberalization offers a better opportunity to compete for outlets in a larger market. The trade-inhibiting role of transport costs is lowered and/or increasing returns to scale can be reckoned with. But trade liberalization does not only promote adjustment in industrial structures by way of larger markets, it also promotes horizontal product differentiation. The reason for this is simple: if transportation costs are high due to the geographical distance between the production site and the location of sales' outlets, they mainly affect the competitiveness of specialized goods since competitive products are as a rule not produced on a large scale. The effect of high transport costs can be eased through increasing returns to scale if liberalization provides access to larger markets, thus enabling longer production runs. In the case of trade barriers, countries must concentrate on less-specialized goods for which transportation costs and returns to scale have little meaning. As a rule, these encompass chiefly mass-produced goods or raw materials, but also orthodox labor- and capital-intensive products.

The suggestion that the economic role of the state should be limited primarily to internal and external market liberalization in order to trigger intra-industry adjustments overly narrows the complexity of economic processes. Indeed, it neglects the existence of noneconomic and implicit barriers to market entry. Among the noneconomic barriers to market entry that cannot be eliminated through trade liberalization consider in the first instance missing institutions that are crucial to the proper functioning of markets or problems with the social acceptance of the consequences of trade liberalization. Among the implicit barriers to entry, a number of economic factors hindering the technological upgrading of less-developed countries can be identified.

A traditional argument for contemplating an active role for government in economic affairs revolves around the infant-industry case. Its core idea is to erect temporarily protective tariffs or to defer a contemplated lowering of existing trade barriers so that investments promising declining marginal costs over the longer haul are undertaken. An argument against infant-industry protection is that those investments should be financed via the capital market and not via higher prices (Siebert and Rauscher, 1991, p. 3). True, EU membership will improve the TEs' access to international capital markets and spur on the inflow of foreign capital into TEs because of stabilization of the basic institutional conditions, including notably those embedded in living up to the obligations ensuing from the *acquis*. It is therefore often stated that higher international mobility of capital would reduce the impact of the relative factor endowment of a country on its trade structures (Kantzenbach, 1997).

But technical progress in communications and expansion of the transportation infrastructure may confine the room for capital mobility. In the case of open borders new market outlets can easily be supplied from already installed production locations, such as has been typical of developments since 1990 in the 'new' Länder in the context of the larger Germany: firms located in western Germany have been supplying the east's markets instead of, as had earlier been anticipated, moving their production facilities toward the east. The inflow of long-term capital could come to a halt if the sum of transportation and risk costs falls below the transaction costs for establishing a foreign subsidy. Despite lowering trade and capital barriers, intra-industry adjustments would follow the pattern of relative factor endowment, which in turn would lead to vertical product differentiation in trade between industrialized and other economies. FDI flows required to measurably transform inherited structures would have to be attracted by granting subsidies or erecting protective tariffs and other trade impediments.

Also information asymmetries cannot be overcome through trade liberalization. They explain why companies oftentimes have only limited access to modern technologies. Even if firms in less-developed countries, including TEs, can purchase up-to-date technologies or investment goods embodying such new technology, or acquire the relevant licenses in an affordable manner, this does not necessarily guarantee that the firms in question or their local competitors can build further upon the technology obtained in this manner in order to keep pace with ongoing modernization trends in the global economy, hence to face up to the ever-changing conditions of international competition. In the absence of indigenous technological developments and capability building, the purchase of technology must be repeated whenever 'global technology' changes in order to overcome information asymmetries. The danger here is that firms will not be purchasing the most modern capital goods and that imitating technology and obtaining licenses can lead to modifications in the structure of trade toward vertical product differentiation. State activity may then become necessary in order to reduce that information asymmetry. Examples of such successful activities can be found in the developmental institutions in several of the successful east and southeast Asian economies, including Japan, Korea, and Taiwan.

Again, foreign capital, particularly FDI, can contribute to reducing information asymmetries, especially through international cooperation, transnational corporations (TNCs), and strategic alliances. The latter also increase the mobility of technological change embodied in physical and human capital. However, recent experience in ever more liberalized capital flows has demonstrated that the expanding role of TNCs is generally limited to countries that are already fairly developed. The increased presence of TNCs in developing countries in the 1990s has been only temporary (UNCTAD, 1997). Not only that, in the end the stream of technological progress embodied in the stock of human and physical capital within a corporation depends on the extent to which production processes can spatially be separated from R&D processes. The automobile sector provides a ready example of the separability option, whereas the aircraft and space industries illustrate the limits of such an option. If spatial separation is feasible, again an IIT pattern emerges that gives rise primarily to vertical product differentiation: R&D remains in the highly developed countries where the TNCs are headquartered, whereas the standardized production is mobile worldwide as it is primarily attracted by low unit labor costs. Facing new and generally accessible communication technologies, there is no need to relocate technology embodying human capital within the TNC in order to ensure high returns of the goods produced outside the country. Due to technical progress, formerly spatially inseparable research and production processes can now be split up among 'separate' markets. The country that succeeds in supporting a high pace of modernization tends to find itself in a more favorable position in terms of its ability to realize a higher share of value added in its cooperative production than is the case for other countries.

When discussing the potential role of an active government stance in TEs, one should bear in mind that when the TEs are likely to accede to the EU their transformation processes will not yet have been completed, even though the *acquis* may then have become fully applicable. One may fix the drift of the argument by referring once again to the experience of the eastern Länder of Germany. With unification, western Germany's *acquis* became fully applicable from the first half of 1990. Yet even at this stage in late 1998, the economy of the eastern part of Germany for all practical purposes continues to exhibit many features of a TE. This is so because adopting the rules of the game is one thing; ensuring appropriate mutations in the behavior of economic agents is another matter altogether. Systemic transformation cannot possibly be confined to adopting or changing formal rules. It must also call forth a significant mutation in the attitude of all economic agents, whether private or public. As the example of the eastern Länder illustrates, the prerequisites for functioning markets are not yet fully in place in TEs (see Landesmann, 1993; Radosevic, 1997).

Considering the prevailing risks, investors and consumers cannot yet formulate firm and reliable long-term expectations. Since this generally applies to all goods and factors, a special argument for bolstering IIT is necessary: the production of specialized goods is essential since it permits in the longer run horizontal product differentiation for which a transition to production in larger series is essential. The same applies to research-intensive production, given the limited divisibility of capital. Especially the latter types of products but also specialized goods will be more strongly affected by malfunctions in the price regime than is the case for labor- and resource-intensive products. For the latter, reasonably transparent world market prices allow the formation of rather reliable expectations. For specialized and research-intensive products, on the other hand, world market prices for similar products offer only a weak orientation for structuring competition. This has consequences for the privatization of assets: if there is a lack of reliable expectations about future returns current prices of a capital-intensive production line can become a strong source of resource misallocation.

Structural Activism by Government During Transformation

The promise that trade liberalization will eventually induce the proper intra-industry structural adjustments is much too vague a proposition for the TEs to preclude from the outset activism in economic affairs on the part of the state. Trade liberalization can trigger negative structural effects when the international economy, as well as that of the TEs, is characterized by limited capital mobility, information asymmetries, and poorly functioning markets. Technological modernization may, therefore, be contingent on an activist government bent on pushing through desirable changes in economic structures. Doing so would not necessarily, and indeed should not, hark back to the type of state-socialist planning and administrative steering that, in the end because of the fundamental inability or unwillingness of the leadership to adapt, proved to be so ruinous for these countries.

The reality in TEs since the inception of the transition, however, has revolved, at best, around weak structural-policy commitments and government initiatives to 'guide' modernization in a purposeful manner. The system of subsidies, which during state-socialist planning was primarily directed toward subsidizing prices and central transfers for financing investments, was drastically modified and shifted toward direct enterprise subsidies, costly borrowing, and self-financing. The average subsidy (excluding tax benefits from early depreciation allowances) measured for the TEs of primary interest here has plummeted to 3.3 percent of public spending, thus roughly equaling the EU average between 1992 and 1994 (European Commission, 1997k, p. 39). The structural policies pursued under state socialism have not been replaced with elements of structural policies that are common in and compatible with practices in industrial economies. Neither did the authorities implement a system for promoting exports, such as through government-guaranteed insurance as in the EU. Nor was a viable concept for the promotion of technological change introduced. Instead the share of expenditures for R&D in GDP has shrunk, thus depressing the R&D sector more generally (Balázs, 1995; Jasinski, 1994; Paasi, 1998). Additionally, government expenditure in support of infrastructural projects has plummeted precipitously; it is at present roughly comparable to the share of such expenditures in GDP in OECD members. But note that the TEs have reached this level with a considerably poorer infrastructure endowment (EBRD, 1995, pp. 72-73).

The reduction in public expenditures stems by far not solely from the stringencies imposed by macroeconomic stabilization efforts and more rigid budget constraints. Economic pressures might have justified such a development. One cannot, however, ignore that TE governments are lacking experience with the formulation and implementation of effective structural policies. Furthermore, their administrative capacities, especially those required to harmonize structural policy under rules of the emerging market economy, was very sparse during the early transformation phase. An example of these three aspects can be found in the concept developed by the Hungarian government in 1993. This initiative failed because it did not set priorities, the envisaged interventions could not be financed, and it ignored the weak capabilities and performance of the country's public administration (OECD, 1995, p. 10).

Of even greater importance, however, is that the new élites in most TEs to this day remain under the impression that, in a market economy, state-conducted structural policy can be justified only on the basis of entrenched ideological positions. There is, however, an important economic argument for the conception of a 'minimal state': the obviously inefficient factor allocation during state-socialist planning with all of its legacies. Many reasons can be cited for this: a one-sided emphasis on capital-intensive production in sunset industries (especially heavy industry), a lopsided regional distribution of production, and unfavorable company size with little external specialization as firms tended to be self-reliant. Especially at the beginning of the transitions, international opinion, included that supported by prominent economists but with little experience or interest in, or empathy for, the history and politics of these TE societies, emphasized that all assets inherited from state socialism were worthless.[8] This blatantly ignored that most of these assets in most TEs were generating positive value added. Not only that, these commentators, who exerted considerable influence over the structuring of western assistance and the approach to transformation, also stressed that the reconstruction of a competitive capital stock should preferably be left solely to the market.[9]

The emphasis during transformation on moving quickly toward the minimal state neglects that in a complex market economy the state takes over a number of economic functions in which it can as a matter of principle (such as in the case of public goods) or at least temporarily (such as for network industries) be more efficient than the private sector. The idea of the minimal state also underestimates the positive role governments have played in advancing long-term economic development in general and industrialization in particular—indeed in fostering the market economy—since the fifteenth century. Furthermore, one should not ignore that without the promotion by government of research-intensive activities, such as the aviation and space industries or renewable energy and with it environmental protection, the modernization trend in structural change witnessed over the long haul would have been crystallizing and progressing much more slowly. Technology policy understood as demand promotion permits the use of scale advantages and learning-curve effects. It also creates impulses for the further development of products and the diffusion of technical progress. Additionally, an active government not only sets the ground rules, such as the regulatory regime, through its economic policy for the market economy; it is also better qualified than the 'market' to deal with the social-acceptance problems that tend to arise with the restructuring process, especially when opening up to foreign capital or coming to grips with the social consequences of structural reforms. All this is far more difficult in TEs than in mature market economies.

A transformation phase is also characterized by a special interactive relationship between the private and public sector. At least during the first phase, which is of great importance for the path to be traced into the future, the relationship usually is a close and symbiotic one (Bhaduri, 1994; Laski and Bhaduri, 1997, pp. 115ff.). If the latter is neglected, the dynamic development of the private sector can be significantly impeded or steered in the 'wrong' direction. An example of this is the negative attitude governments in TEs have taken toward SOEs. The transfer of thousands of SOEs to new owners was and continues to pose one of the biggest structural-policy challenges for which TE governments with their civil-service infrastructure definitely lacked the necessary capacities and obviously were not seeking to maximize revenues in the interest of society as a whole. The withdrawal of restructuring subsidies or hasty divestment without even seriously contemplating the feasibility of restructuring (as in the Czech Republic) in reality led to techno-logical retardation and declining competitiveness in many industries. Since the private sector was closely linked to SOEs through supply and sales' relations during the early transformation phase, its own development was highly dependent on the health and future prospects of SOEs even once privatized.

A purely anti-government perspective overlooks that the decline of SOEs also leads to a shrinkage of demand for economically profitable, newly founded firms. It is not by chance that SMEs in TEs are today primarily located in the service and craft sectors. Similar developments pertain to firms with foreign-capital partici-pation. For example, 24 percent of the existing incorporated firms in Poland in 1997 were in industry (albeit with an average of only nine employees), but 36 per-cent were in trade and crafts; of the 28,000 limited liability companies with foreign capital 27 percent were in industry but 53 percent in trade (GUS, 1997b). Dynamic developments for private firms in manufacturing are hindered since the competi-tiveness of the new enterprises falls behind those of foreign companies (for example, as a result of too slow a decline in unit costs due to limited sales) and/or because of lack of state support for R&D and for export promotion.

Hungary is a possible exception: instead of a hasty and fruitless privatization, microeconomic restructuring, especially of the enterprise sector, was attempted by applying the bankruptcy law. The legal enforcement of automatic bankruptcy led to large-scale liquidation and restructuring during 1991 and 1992. Approximately 22,000 firms, some private but mostly SOEs, were in the process reorganized, restructured, or liquidated (Gray et al., 1996). As a result, the development condi-tions for the whole enterprise sector, public as well as private, improved. That strategy seems to be an appropriate one for a TE especially when considering the burdens inherited from state-socialist planning and the still limited ability of government and public administration to undertake privatization in anything like an efficient manner.

Turning to trade policy, the component of industrial policy affecting a country's external-trading position at first sight would seem to offer a different picture from that suggested by the discussion so far. At the transformation's inception, policy makers in TEs were inclined toward engineering extreme trade liberalization as an urgent policy goal. Trade quotas were abolished altogether or strongly reduced soon after the transition's inception. So was the average level of tariff protection. At times the average nominal tariff level was set even below the EU's. The Baltic countries and some other TEs (including Bulgaria and Poland) actually discriminated against their own agricultural sector despite the fact that the EA allows for fairly high levels of protection for such activities (Frohberg and Hartmann, 1998). Soon, however, as a rule at most after the first two years of transition with extreme trade liberalization, the average tariff level was raised and new quantitative restrictions were introduced in one form or another. These measures were not, however, directly linked to a consistent industrial policy or even motivated by a coherent concept of intervention. Instead the stance taken by policy makers can be understood as a reflex reaction driven by tactical considerations around impending negotiations with the EU and the negotiations for accession to or normalization of relations with the GATT, and later the WTO, the erection of barriers against formerly fraternal CMEA partners (Gács, 1994), and the pressures exercised by interest groups in affected sectors and occupational groups.

The introduction of temporary and gradually decreasing protective tariffs on imported automobiles from the EU, either until the beginning of 2001 or, as in Poland, until 2002, does not constitute an exception in this context. The Czech Republic, Hungary, Poland, and Slovakia did not introduce that protective tariff out of a genuine industrial-policy motive, but because the international automobile companies were not willing to participate in privatization and invest in the restructuring of the automobile industry without being granted this level of protection (Kämpfe, 1996). The alternative to that development most probably would have been the collapse of the automobile sector in TEs with the latter's markets supplied primarily from western Europe. This example shows that the introduction of temporary import limitations may spur on the technical and organizational upgrading of industries (Becker, 1997).

Structural-Policy Options and Potential EU Conflicts

Whereas it appears desirable that TE governments retain structural-policy options, this may provoke conflicts prior to and after EU accession. Ushering TEs into the EU sets off a redistribution of investments and other resources against the backdrop of an overall, now expanded, European market horizon. Present EU members whose firms compete in similar market segments with firms from acceding TEs will insist on equal competition rules; they will certainly deny any major, possibly just any, derogation for newcomers or apply for similar exemptions or for financial compensation. The central political conflict between new and present EU members will be between the imperative of the EU's common competition policy and the need for embracing a national structural policy that will in time underpin constructive competition on the part of most economic agents of the TE entrants. And so one may ask whether temporary exemptions for the entering TEs could conceivably be condoned technically and, above all, politically while implementing the *acquis*.

Among the EU policy instruments, competition policy is generally granted priority, although the EU itself pursues common structural-policy goals and allots a considerable part of its budget to supporting them. There are two areas of the EU's structural policy in which explicit injunctions exist that are bound to exert considerable political influence over the upgrading of economic structures in TEs and moving them broadly in the directions pointed out earlier. One is the area of trade policy from which there can be no room for derogation in the SEM. The FTA parts of the EAs will be completed prior to any TE's formal accession; the same is bound to be the case for trade in agricultural products. Temporary import tariffs, for instance, as some of the TEs have introduced for the automobile sectors, will then no longer be feasible.

The second field is the EU's attitude toward state subsidies, especially those that actually do or threaten to distort competition in the SEM. The latter are as a matter of principle prohibited (art. 93 of the Treaty of Rome). The Treaty itself, however, provides for numerous derogations, such as in the case of subsidies for social causes related to individual consumers, as long as they are granted without discrimination favoring the origin of the consumer good, or subsidies for dealing with natural disasters or similar 'unusual events.' The derogation rules of the Treaty of Rome go even further: the promotion of projects of Europe-wide interest or projects directed at eliminating considerable disturbances within any member's economy is considered compatible with the single market's uniform competition rules. The same goes for supporting the economic development of disadvantaged regions or economic branches. This approach constitutes the foundation of the EU's structural policy (see chapter 8). It holds especially for infrastructural, regional, and technology policies. To the extent that the EU's common structural policy offers financial resources, the entering TEs will almost certainly underpin programs that fulfill the appropriate criteria.

Shortly after their accession, the TEs could find themselves locked into a situation in which the EU's dominant approach toward structural policy will fail to offer adequate solutions for the kind of problems specific to the transformation agenda. At present, a large share of manufacturing—for example, 30.5 percent for Poland in 1996 (GUS, 1997a)—is still in state ownership in one form or another. This applies in particular to 'sensitive' industries, such as steel, shipyards, and synthetic fibers. Even in the Czech Republic, after the second round of voucher privatization, still one-tenth of industrial workers were employed in SOEs in 1996 (ČSÚ, 1997). Other parts of industry, even when privatized, have not yet been sufficiently reorganized and restructured. These particular features will most probably not have been eliminated sufficiently by the time the TEs will be admitted into the EU.

Promoting technological upgrading and infrastructural investments seems to be a reasonable and desirable option within the context of structural policy since such undertakings will most likely elicit positive external effects for TE firms. But as long as the former SOEs that have not yet been reorganized cannot depend on reaping the benefits of such industrial-policy measures, major results will not crystallize. This assertion can be illustrated with reference to privatization and restructuring experiences in the eastern part of Germany. Offhand these suggest[10] that an approach tailored to the needs of firms offers better opportunities for coming to grips with the structural problems induced by the ongoing transformation than the EU's regional-policy approach, which does not address problems at the firm level. A firm-focused approach would better suit the desirable transformation's requirements since the problem of low profitability coupled with privatization, restructuring, and access to financial means plays a dominant role.

Furthermore, enterprise-focused structural policies are especially appropriate to strengthen horizontal IIT as they enable firms, as distinct from regions or individual branches, to prepare themselves better, and indeed get ready, for full-fledged competition in the SEM. One objective of any step set in that direction would be to strengthen the TEs' comparative advantages by offering individualized and research-intensive goods. Individual advantages may be special technical knowledge, outstanding management skills, a special acquaintance with certain markets, qualification of the labor force, or product innovations. An effective instrument to mobilize those skills might be subsidies in the R&D area, promotion of medium-size firms, subsidies for restructuring SOEs about to be privatized, or supports in the form of investment allowances, such as accelerated depreciation programs.

Enterprise-focused structural programs that include subsidies can be reconciled with the EU's competition rules. The European Commission has very often approved financial assistance for investment measures, especially in the case of SMEs; for the promotion of R&D projects; for support of consultants advising firms on restructuring; and for transfers in order to create new jobs and vocational-training opportunities for the unemployed (Lenz, 1994, pp. 561ff.). However, conflict-free adaptation of enterprise-focused structural programs must be aligned with the EU's regulations on state subsidies.

Generally the Commission assesses whether subsidies are linked to microeconomic aspects. The intended goal must demonstrably be to reinforce the enterprise's competitiveness while at the same time protecting the interests of competitors on other markets against any adverse implications of the subsidy. It is for that reason that the Commission does not approve privatization contracts containing market-entry barriers for suppliers in up- or downstream production activities of the enterprise in question. When in the course of privatization government subsidies are granted only if the buyer of the SOE agrees to purchase a certain amount of intermediate goods from local suppliers then the Commission will prohibit subsidization, as the experience of the new Länder has underlined on more than one occasion.

Additionally, it is crucial to respect the so-called notifying obligation for only then can an assessment procedure be initiated in order to determine whether the subsidy is in line with the EU's regulations on state subsidies. Meeting this obligation is especially important for the TEs since a large number of their firms are still in state hands in one form or another. Capital increases or compensation for losses by the state as owner, which are considered a subsidy according to EU rules, must be reported and will be prohibited if any other than microeconomic goals are targeted. Shortcomings in reporting state subsidies by member governments have been a source of recurrent friction within the EU. For example, 17 percent of the subsidy cases investigated in the EU in 1996 had originally not been reported (European Commission, 1997c, p. 103).

An important aspect when designing enterprise-focused structural policies is the separation of sensitive from nonsensitive areas. In the case of nonsensitive areas countries may obtain so-called general approval for subsidy programs through the Council of Ministers. Proceeding in this way has the advantage that, by accepting the program's basic approach, the European Commission need not approve every individual subsidy. In the case of sensitive areas (such as steel, shipbuilding, synthetic fibers, the automobile industry, farming, and forestry), the restrictions on subsidies are much more stringent. In fact, they are in principle altogether forbidden. Since 1997, this prohibition has been applied also to the TE-10. Nonetheless exceptions do exist. The potential for conflict can be reduced if the TEs are allowed a general exemption provided the subsidy is eliminated over time and the scope of its application is narrowed as the subsidy is gradually being phased out. Such general exemptions, which have been common to almost all treaties with acceding countries (but especially in the cases of Greece, Portugal, and Spain), shift the negotiations and the approval procedure of sensitive areas to the European Commission. If no exemption is granted, the country must refer the intended subsidy program to the Council of Ministers, which can grant approval. This is a rather ineffective way of proceeding, however, as it calls forth yet another bargaining process in which the national interests of other EU countries necessarily come to the fore. The experience of the new Länder provides a good example: since they form a constituent part of Germany, they cannot obtain a general exemption for subsidizing sensitive areas. New members can, however. The Treuhandanstalt and its successor had to solicit approval by the Council of Ministers on a number of occasions, such as for various shipbuilding, steel, and automobile subsidies, with at best mixed results.

Conclusions

We have focused in this chapter on critiquing the prevalent thesis in debates about transformation in the TEs that trade liberalization, and indeed entry into the EU, will in an of itself bring about the desired changes in economic structures of these countries. Logical and empirical arguments, referring to various IIT measures, were buttressed to underpin the finding that to date trade liberalization in the central European TEs has not yet led to the kind of structural adjustment that is needed for the TEs to compete constructively within the SEM while moving ahead with their modernization. The persistent evidence of vertical IIT or intersectoral trade is worrisome in this regard. The apparent slow progress with aligning firms' trade and production profiles closer to the EU's patterns has various origins.

In addition, we have looked at the potential contribution of a more active role for government in spurring on this structural change and whether this can be rendered compatible with the EU's competition rules. In our view, given the considerable risk of market failure in TEs, appropriate structural-policy measures and temporary exemptions from the *acquis* can bolster the competitiveness of the enterprise sector in TEs through purposeful modernization, preferably with greater involvement of foreign capital and technology. Moreover, the EU's framework allows for structural policies beyond common regional approaches since subsidy programs can be designed that will not violate the prevailing competition rules. The experience of the eastern part of Germany has shown how difficult it is to obtain approval for those programs if the applying country does not hold a general exemption. TEs should therefore aim at embodying such rulings in their accession treaty. There is, however, a real dilemma for them in insisting upon such exemptions: general-exemption rulings are required to 'depoliticize' negotiations on enterprise-focused programs but the chances for quick entry into the EU are compromised if too many requests for general exemptions are lodged.

The solution to this dilemma lies in the necessary but still very uncertain reform of the EU's institutions and governance mechanisms, which has to be completed before any enlargement. In this case, extending the scope of majority voting, in depth as well as in breadth, and enhancing the Commission's competence might diminish the impact of political bargaining of present member states and may strengthen a European view on enlargement issues.

Annex

The Grubel-Lloyd index Y of an individual commodity (group) i at a certain time of observation t was calculated on the basis of the following equation for any observation period t:

$$Y_i = 1 - |X_i - M_i|/(X_i + M_i) \qquad \text{(A.1)}$$

where X_i and M_i are the values of exports and imports of any commodity group i. The individual index can take on values between 0 and 1. The former indicates complete intersectoral specialization or the reference country exports goods that differ from its imports, while the latter indicates complete intra-industry specialization or the reference country exports and imports goods in the same product category.

Individual indices calculated according to equation A.1 for any reference period were aggregated using the weights of each commodity group in overall trade as follows:

$$Y = \sum_i a_i Y_i \qquad (A.2)$$

where a is the share of any of the n commodity groups in total trade:

$$a_i = (X_i + M_i)/\sum_i (X_i + M_i) \qquad (A.3)$$

In contrast to the individual index, the aggregate index can take on values between 0 and 1 only when overall trade is balanced. Much of the literature dealing with the measure concerns the advisability of adjustments to account for imbalances in overall trade. In most applications, however, a correction for trade imbalance is not recommended (for a detailed discussion see Vona, 1991). This study follows this path.

The magnitude of the index is also determined by the degree of aggregation of the applied commodity nomenclature. For the present study it was calculated on the basis of the CN's 82 chapters. Differences with other calculations (such as those reported in UNECE, 1995) result because the latter depend on sections 5 to 8 of the SITC in which the COMTRADE database is kept; this excludes, for example, products of the food-processing industry.

The impact of changes in trade shares over time can be calculated by analyzing, for any observation period t, the (unadjusted) TIIT indicator as in equation A.4:

$$\Delta Y = \sum_i (b_i \Delta Y_i + Z_i \Delta a_i + \Delta Y_i \Delta a_i) \qquad (A.4)$$

where b and Z are the starting values of a and Y, respectively. The first element on the right-hand side is the sum of the 'true' intra-industry effect. The second one measures the impact of changed trade shares on the volume of IIT at the next higher aggregation level; it actually represents an interindustry effect. The third element is the joint effect, which always appears mathematically when the analysis is carried out in discrete time. It can be distributed to the two separate components only under mathematically confined conditions. Moreover, its economic significance is very difficult to interpret.

Table 7.6 details the influence of the various effects on TIIT for the four selected countries. At first sight the interindustry structure factor seems to be exercising a considerable effect on the overall IIT level in three of the four observed TEs. But it is also noticeable that the joint effect in three of the four cases is sizable. This finding seems to be a reflection of the time span under which structural change has been taking place in the TEs. Normally structural change is spread over a long time span so that, as a rule, the joint effect can be assumed to be negligible. At least in the Polish case the joint effect is so strong that the explanatory power of the two separate components becomes negligible.

Table 7.6: The influence of various effects on TIIT, 1991-1996

(in percent of the aggregate effect[a])

Country	Intra	Inter	Joint	Total
Czech Republic	97.0	1.8	0.9	99.8
Hungary	72.2	14.2	13.8	100.2
Poland	94.5	44.4	-38.9	100.0
Slovakia	70.1	18.5	10.8	99.4

Note: [a] due to rounding, the sum of the components does not add up to 100.
Source: own calculations based on EUROSTAT, 1997.

Notes

This chapter expands in major respects on and updates Gabrisch and Werner, 1998.

1. We define 'short term' as the path extending from the present to a situation in which aggregate welfare and its regional distribution are determined by general-equilibrium conditions. Of course, these conditions are not automatically met with accession.
2. We disregard the potential problem of unbalanced trade, as explained in the Annex.
3. For a more detailed discussion of unit values, see Greenaway, Hine, and Milner, 1994, p. 81.
4. Recall that exports are denominated free on board (f.o.b.) whereas imports are inclusive of cost, insurance, and freight (c.i.f.). This has implications for using mirror statistics, as in our tests for the TEs.
5. 'All-but-completely' means that only minor items at the eight-digit level of the CN category are not liberalized in the observation year.
6. We used in particular CN chapters 26, 27, 30, 33-38, 45-49, 65-68, 71, 84, 86, 88-93 and 95-97.
7. The indices according to Landesmann and Burgstaller (1997, table 1 in the annex) are: Czech Republic: 0.72, Hungary: 0.81, Poland: 0.60, Slovakia: 0.55.
8. For a more extensive discussion of this position during the early privatization debates with ample source references, including to prominent western 'advisers,' see Brabant, 1992, pp. 184ff.
9. For an overview of the literature, see Brabant, 1998a.
10. We rely here on the experiences gathered during the negotiations on subsidies with EU organs of the Treuhandanstalt and its successor, the Bundesanstalt für vereinigungs-bedingte Sonderaufgaben. We obtained especially useful insights from interviews with the latter's managers.

Chapter 8

Enlargement—Conflicts and Policy Options

Paul J. J. Welfens

In mid-July 1997 the European Commission (1997h) issued its so-called *avis* regarding the suitability of the applicant countries for accession to the union in the context of its *Agenda 2000*, which also contains the Commission's recommendations for the economic and fiscal orientation for EU policy during the next budget period 2000-2006. Both are interrelated in the sense that the Commission urges incisive institutional and economic adjustments in the applicant countries, which would then render the economic and fiscal constraints underlying the projections more realistic. Recall that the TEs are all poor, have a large share of agriculture with low productivity, and falling industrial employment with only sluggish productivity growth. The Luxemburg Council adopted these recommendations in December 1997.

One of the major challenges of eastward enlargement derives from the increasing economic divergence in the EU, given the comparatively low levels of development and modernization in TEs (see chapter 7), which contributes to heterogeneity in political preferences. Thus, the disparity in the present EU in 1995, the average being 100, ranged from 67 for Greece and 116 for Denmark, ignoring Luxemburg for now. With enlargement toward the TE-5, at present levels, this disparity would range from 31 for Poland and 116 for Denmark, ignoring the anomaly of Estonia just like I ignored the outlier Luxemburg. Not only that, one should remain cognizant that income differentials along the EU's central European fault line are higher than the cited averages since Austria's and Germany's income levels are above the EU's average. Sustainable enlargement, both politically and economically, therefore requires speeding up economic convergence. Whereas a quick, purely market-driven convergence process remains rather unlikely, one should not rule out a successful convergence (see chapter 6) in the medium term, provided the TEs adopt pertinent domestic policies and the EU a more appropriate cohesion policy than it has so far.

I focus here on the starting conditions for enlargement in the EU as well as in TEs. Then I discuss the institutional challenges. Thereafter I examine how the theory of integration is relevant, both theoretically and empirically, to enlargement issues. Before concluding, I specify policy options for sustainable enlargement, given that the major economic benefits of enlargement especially for the TEs are associated with considerable risks for the efficiency of future EU decision making and the potential conflicts of widening economic divergence among the TEs.

The EU and Monetary Union

The adjustment dynamic induced by the SEM is fully at work in the late 1990s. In combination with the ongoing economic globalization and a sharper international innovation race, this is fueling an economic upswing during the prelude to the inception of monetary union, which will reinforce market transparency and reduce EU internal transaction costs so that competition will intensify further.

Due to the convergence pressures associated with meeting the requirements for entry into monetary union, most EU countries have achieved considerable progress with respect to key macroeconomic variables and medium-term prospects for converging more fully toward the debt-to-GDP ratio in particular, provided no adverse shocks hit the euro participants, are promising. The elimination of intragroup exchange-rate movements and the switch to reduced money-supply volatility in the relatively large monetary union suggest that higher investment-to-GDP ratios might emerge in the euro area (Jungmittag and Welfens, 1998), thus providing a positive growth impulse that should more than offset the negative welfare effect associated with the loss of the exchange rate as a policy instrument. The proviso is important if the participants in monetary union exhibit strong dissimilarities. Since the exchange-rate instrument is no longer available major problems could arise from asymmetric economic shocks in the presence of low labor mobility and wage rigidity. While monetary union has potentially large economic benefits (Kenen, 1998), it is unclear whether intensified competition within the union and more integrated and competitive financial markets will bring about the required social-security, labor market, and government reforms.

Because the *acquis* in the late 1990s is far more encompassing and complex than at any previous enlargement, the EU has decided to provide technical and financial support to TEs already prior to accession. Although upon entry into the

EU these countries do not have to join monetary union, even if they could according to the established rules and desired to do so, they will be held to introducing central-bank independence, submitting to multilateral surveillance as regards convergence indicators, and applying measures to adhere to stability and growth roughly aiming at fulfilling the Maastricht fiscal criteria as embedded in the rules governing the EU's monetary union (see chapters 3 and 6). This includes the stipulation that the ratio of the fiscal deficit to GDP should not exceed 3 percent except when an extreme economic downswing or special adverse shock occurs. Given the TEs' enormous investment needs, including for infrastructure, this ceiling implicitly restricts public investment to the extent that one can consider loan financing of investment as a natural strategy to share investment costs between present and future generations. A solution to the problem could be to increasingly rely on private financing and operation of certain infrastructures, such as through toll highways, private airports, and privatized telecommunication networks (EBRD, 1996).

Given the double problem of high EU unemployment and unsustainable social-security systems, reforms of the public sector in the EU have to compress the level and widen the dispersion of total labor costs if full employment is ever to be regained. High unemployment creates political reservations against labor mobility and EU enlargement. In that respect, it is worth noting that, unlike some TEs, such as Hungary and Poland, the EU has found it extremely difficult to reform its social-security systems.

Both of the above points, as well as other considerations on the present policy stances of EU members on net contributions to the EU budget with their distributional conflicts (see chapter 4), lead the observer to reckon with EU budgetary conflicts in the years ahead. Those cannot but impinge on the climate for enlargement negotiations and the feasibility of expeditiously ushering the TEs into the EU. If eastward enlargement were to be feasible only in the presence of a major rise in the EU's budget (say, raising the 1.27 percent GNP ceiling on the members' contribution), serious distributional conflicts between net contributors and net recipients would be unavoidable.

Even without raising the budget ceiling, distributional conflicts are in the offing one way or the other. The biggest recipient countries will see their net gain erode; the large net contributing countries will also see their net cost rise, and some will switch from being net recipients to net contributors with eastward enlargement. Given restrictions on domestic budgets arising from the obligations assumed under the monetary union, EU countries might have to face stark choices in the appropriation of their fiscal revenues. Not only that, as argued in chapter 4, there are bound to be asymmetries in the gains that an eastward enlargement will bring to the present EU members, with Austria, Germany, Italy, and Sweden probably being the larger beneficiaries. Curbing their net contribution to the EU budget will therefore hardly be acceptable to EU members that stand to gain less from TE accession.

In light of the above arguments, eastward enlargement is almost bound to call forth difficult distributional issues among EU members. The largest uncertainty derives arguably from the size and distribution of the economic benefits that can be expected from enlargement, if only because they are so much less visible than the budgetary costs of EU membership. Invisible benefits accrue through higher trade and investment levels so that the countries concerned will have more rapid economic growth and hence larger fiscal receipts. To obtain some idea of the potential benefits of eastward enlargement, it is important to bear in mind the socioeconomic situation in the TEs now and in the foreseeable future.

The TEs after the First Transformation Phase

Privatization of the economy, macroeconomic stabilization, economic opening-up, and institutional changes in factor markets as well as in economic policy were the main steps in the transformation process, which is now largely completed in the TE-5; other TEs lag behind to varying degrees for a variety of reasons. Competition and R&D policies are crucial for transformation and growth (Fingleton, Fox, Neven, and Seabright 1996; Slay, 1995). It has been adopted in all TEs although to date only Hungary has an independent, credible antitrust authority. Efficient corporate governance also remains a crucial problem, which derives in part from the mode of privatization chosen, the rules for the capital market, and the most common incentive schemes for managers (Jasinski and Welfens, 1994; Valbonesi, 1995; Welfens, 1992).

Facing declining internal demand and the transitory difficulties of switching over to the gradually emerging market conditions, many TEs encountered more or less severe problems with their banking system, in part because of the comparatively high share—20 to 40 percent during some periods in some TEs—of nonperforming assets, chiefly on account of the fact that SOEs, even many that had been ostensibly privatized, found it difficult to service their loans. Even in the TEs bent on addressing the problem, formulating, approving, and implementing solutions took time. Thus, in the Czech Republic the share of nonperforming assets in total loans declined gradually after 1994 (BIS, 1998, p. 53); it fell more swiftly in Hungary and Poland. However, especially Bulgaria and Romania among the TE-10 have yet to sort out the financial-market problems even as they relate to banks. Concerns about financial-market stability have risen in the wake of the Asian financial-market crises and their fallout through many channels of the global economy. In this connection it is important to recall that one of the SEM's four freedoms calls for free capital movements. Recent experience has shown that such liberalization could easily be destabilizing in the event of adverse shocks hitting an unsound banking system in particular. But there are other concerns to be addressed prior to extending that component of the SEM to acceding TEs.

Since the inception of the transitions in 1989, many TEs have achieved considerable progress in establishing 'the' market economy, although one should not overlook major divergences among the TEs. Even among the original four[1] Visegrád countries (Czech Republic, Hungary, Poland, and Slovakia), which started their structural transformation earlier and with greater determination, considerable bottlenecks persist, as became evident during the Czech currency crisis in 1997. This crisis is mainly related to the lack of efficient corporate governance and the weak banking system, which in turn have slowed down the pace of structural change. Steady progress with structural change at a measured pace provides one of the crucial keys to sustaining economic growth during the transformation and thus getting over that phase of adjustment, which can be considered a prerequisite for constructive participation in the SEM. Indeed, the transformation process in the former GDR has clearly underlined the important links among structural change, economic growth, and factor rewards (Heilemann and Löbbe, 1996).

Structural change in the course of systemic transformation and economic liberalization, both in the domestic economy and toward external markets, takes the form of a high rate of intersectoral reallocation of labor so that the standard deviation of growth rates for employment measured across sectors should be rather high (see table 8.1). The intersectoral reallocation of labor can be defined as follows:

$$1 - [|\Delta E| / (|\Delta E^+| + |\Delta E^-|)] \tag{8.1}$$

where ΔE is the net employment effect, ΔE^+ is the sum of sectoral job variations in expanding sectors and thus a proxy for gross employment creation, and ΔE^- is the sum of sectoral job variations in declining sectors and thus a proxy for gross employment loss.

Likewise, the reallocation/privatization indicator can be defined as follows:

$$1 - [|\Delta E| / (|\Delta E^{pub}| + |\Delta E^{pri}|)] \tag{8.2}$$

where ΔE^{pub} is the sum of job variations in public-sector activities and ΔE^{pri} is the comparable magnitude for private-sector activities.

Tito Boeri (1997) distinguishes among nine sectors and defines an expansion-contraction reallocation index and a reallocation-privatization index covering job flows from the state sector, including SOEs, to the private sector; a rising index indicates a higher speed of reallocation. The degree of structural change in the Czech Republic, Hungary, Poland, and Slovakia was much higher than in Bulgaria and Romania (for which fully comparable data are unfortunately not available). Both countries have lagged behind in the process of privatization, in setting up functioning capital markets, and in opening up the economy. Hungary and Poland showed an increasing degree of structural change in the period 1993-1995 as compared to 1991-1993, and both countries exhibited rising intersectoral employment reallocation, which should facilitate productivity gains and real income growth. Poland indeed recorded high growth rates in the 1990s; Hungary's growth resumed after a temporary balance-of-payments crisis in the mid-1990s. Note in table 8.1 that the apparent pace of structural change in OECD countries, as measured in the same way as for the selected TEs, remained comparatively tepid, and not just because of the smaller room for privatizing state-owned assets.

Table 8.1: Structural change and jobs in TEs, 1991-1995

Country	Growth[a]	Change[b]	Privatization[c]	Labor[d]	Productivity[e]
Bulgaria					
1991-1993	13.5	0.36	0.68	1.9	+
1993-1995	10.4	0.90	0.64	3.6	
Czech Rep.					
1991-1993	21.0	0.77	0.78	14.9	++
1993-1995	6.7	0.44	0.64	9.5	
Hungary					
1991-1993	9.3	0.25	0.66	2.4	+++
1993-1995	7.0	0.53	0.88	2.6	
Poland					
1991-1993	13.4	0.49	0.73	2.5	+++
1993-1995	11.1	0.74	0.70	3.0	
Slovakia					
1991-1993	24.0	0.70	0.60	3.9	+
1993-1995	7.0	0.38	0.88	2.6	
Pro memori					
OECD[f]					
1990-1993	3.1	0.33	0.09	5.2	+

Notes:
[a] Standard deviation of growth rates.
[b] Intersectoral change as measured by formula 8.1 for nine sectors.
[c] Intensity of privatization as measured by formula 8.2 for job outflows from the state sector and job inflows into the private sector.
[d] Labor-market dynamics as measured by monthly inflows into new jobs during the period relative to the unemployment rate at the beginning of the period.
[e] Change in labor productivity over 1992-1996.
[f] Without the TE members.

Sources: Boeri, 1997; Podkaminer, 1997; UNECE, 1997.

Disregarding the employment reallocation related to privatization one finds, however, a decline in employment dynamics and structural adjustment in the Czech Republic and Slovakia—partly reflecting corporate-governance problems and the lack of strategic investors, respectively. The slowdown of economic growth in the Czech Republic and the Czech balance-of-payments crisis in 1997 therefore are not surprising. The favorable indicator for the ratio of job flow to the unemployment rate for the Czech Republic derives in part from the fact that the lack of bankruptcies and of structural adjustment kept unemployment at an artificially low level.

As regards key macroeconomic magnitudes Bulgaria, Romania, and Russia exhibited a much worse picture than the TE-5 in the 1990s. While there is some risk that the first wave of eastward expansion will transitorily accentuate the income differentials within the eastern part of Europe, one may anticipate that macroeconomic stabilization and institutional adjustment in the TE-10 that are not now on the fast track for accession negotiations will be favorably influenced by prospective EU membership. Prospects of EU membership provide adequate incentives. EU technical support within the novel APAs should also facilitate the adjustment process. A more difficult problem is economic and political geography. The second-wave TEs are strongly exposed to potentially destabilizing impulses from Russia. The latter's transformation experience has been characterized by the legacy of declining structural change and increasing overspecialization in the 1980s compounded by at best inconsistent transformation policies in the 1990s.

Catching up with the EU will require a high pace of growth sustainable over a protracted period of time. This will only be feasible if the TEs record high investment-to-GDP ratios, pursue outward-oriented economic policies in support of trade and FDI, bolster human-capital formation and R&D, and keep levels of the foreign and domestic public-sector debt within manageable proportions. As a simple extrapolation one can calculate (Richter, 1998) that TEs need the following average annual growth rates, in ascending order, to achieve 75 percent of the EU's per capita income at PPP in 2015: Czech Republic and Slovenia 3.4 percent, Slovakia 5.2 percent, Hungary 6.1 percent, Poland 6.9 percent, Romania 9.2 percent, and Bulgaria 10.1 percent. Such magnitudes are obviously unrealistic, although Poland came close to 7 percent growth in 1996-1997 and Slovakia has had a strong growth run, albeit perhaps one that cannot be sustained into the medium to long run without incisive structural change. Even for the TE-5, if they make it through the first enlargement wave, many if not all regions would qualify for so-called objective 1 structural-policy support.[2] Reforms of objective 1 supports could be achieved by lowering the threshold and/or by switching from nominal-income reference data to data measured in PPPs.

Institutional Challenges for the TEs—The EU's View

Agenda 2000 emphasizes that the challenges of eastward enlargement can be met head-on by reinforcing the pre-accession strategy—comprising the EAs, the structured-policy dialogue, and PHARE—with two new elements: (1) support for adopting the *acquis* and for extending the participation of the TE candidates to EU programs and mechanisms to apply the *acquis* by using PHARE funds to support institution building to ensure the proper functioning of the TE in the SEM; and (2) for accelerating infrastructural improvements. All this should be combined within a single framework for all the resources and forms of assistance available and provide the backdrop for the much-touted APAs.[3] There will also be pre-accession aid for agriculture and structural assistance at the regional level. According to the Commission (1997h, p. A8), the APAs will encompass "precise commitments on the part of the applicant country, relating in particular to democracy, macro-economic stabilization, nuclear safety and a national program for adopting the Community *acquis* within a precise timetable, focusing on the priority areas identified in each opinion; [and] mobilization of all the resources available in the Community for preparing the applicant countries for accession." It is unclear from this statement whether a prime requirement for accession indeed is to introduce and maintain democracy within the rule of law. The *acquis* itself consists of specific rules, above all policies regarding competition, trade, regional affairs, and monetary management (see chapter 1).

The Commission expects in its analysis of the impact of eastward enlargement, which is an integral part of *Agenda 2000*, that extending the CAP to the entering TEs will cost some €11 billion per year—an estimate that is much lower than that suggested by other studies (see, for example, Tangermann, 1997), yet quite considerable considering that the EU-15's budget in 1997 was €88 billion. No major problems are anticipated in so-called horizontal policies (as in social affairs, the environment, consumer matters, science and R&D, the information society, or culture, education, training, and youth affairs). With respect to sectoral policies the Commission also expects limited problems. The greatest hurdles will arise from the increasing heterogeneity in terms of per capita incomes in an enlarged EU, which would drop 16 percent as compared to the present EU average, and the fall of average income, to 75 when the present EU average in 1995 is considered 100 (European Commission, 1997h, p. 22), so that structural policy becomes quite important.

Average per capita GDP evaluated at PPPs for the TE-10 would come to about one-third of that for EU-15, and that average lies well below that of the weakest four EU countries (Greece, Ireland, Portugal, and Spain), which together reached 74 percent of the EU average. Among the TE-10, each of which exhibits considerable domestic regional divergences, the range extends from 18 percent for Latvia to 59 percent for Slovenia; in 1997 the poorest EU member was Greece with a level of about two-thirds the EU average. Cohesion policies in the enlarged EU would lead to sharply rising expenditures since the population eligible for structural assistance under objective 1 would rise from 94 to 200 million, and if the other objective criteria for regional policies were not changed, about 60 percent of the overall EU population would be covered (European Commission, 1997h, p. 25). One need not delve deeply into the decision making of the EU to realize that such an outcome is inconsistent with the principle of special support for the most disadvantaged regions.

The above considerations underline that urgent reform of EU structural policies is needed. As if this in itself were not formidable enough, an additional constraint proposed by the Commission is that financial funds devoted to structural and cohesion efforts will be raised from 0.41 percent to an absolute ceiling of 0.46 percent of the EU's GNP. Moreover, the Commission has proposed to restructure the regional support programs, keeping objective 1, lumping all other present programs together in objective 2, and innovating an objective 3 to focus mainly on supporting economic and social development, lifelong learning and training, and active labor-market policies. Whether support for such an objective 3 can be created remains for now rather doubtful, if only because it is not at all clear to what extent this could conceivably promote economic cohesion in a consistent manner while doing justice to the principle of subsidiarity.

While one may criticize EU structural funds, which amounted to 1.4 percent of GDP for Spain, 2.6 percent for Ireland, 2.7 percent for Portugal, and 2.8 percent for Greece in 1996-1997, it is appropriate to point out that they reflect supranational political leadership and indeed have been successful in promoting the economic catching-up process, except in the case of Greece. Note that the postwar Marshall Plan during its four-year duration was more generous than the envisaged financial support for TEs and poor regions in the EU. Together they will qualify for transfers up to 0.46 percent of EU GNP; by contrast, the share of the U.S. GNP allocated to postwar reconstruction under the Marshall Plan, including the special program for Germany, was at least twice as large in relative terms; indeed, these transfers as a percentage of GDP in the recipient countries was in some cases very high—2.4 percent in the case of Britain and 14 percent in the case of Austria (Brabant, 1990, p. 108). The EU as a less cohesive economic and political regional superpower obviously finds it more difficult to 'invest' in the transformation process than the United States did for Europe's postwar recovery. Part of the reluctance on the part of EU taxpayers to finance additional transfers to the TEs can be explained by already high marginal tax and social-security contributions throughout the EU, excepting perhaps Britain.

Integration Theory and EU Enlargement

Following neoclassical trade theory one may expect major benefits to accrue from external-sector liberalization in TEs. By 1996 the export-to-GDP ratio of the Visegrád countries had risen to 26 percent in Poland, 33 percent in Hungary, 49 percent in Slovenia, 60 percent in the Czech Republic, and 66 percent in the Slovak Republic; Bulgaria and Romania reached 32 percent and 30 percent, respectively (IMF, 1997a). Under a competitive market environment such an expansion in the degree of participation of national production and consumption in global economic activity should bolster economic efficiency, which in turn stimulates economic growth and raises consumer welfare as a result of a higher level and a different composition of consumption. In addition, modern trade theory suggests other benefits, such as those deriving from having a wider choice of goods and services available, a variety itself stimulated by the expansion of trade participation at the global level, and from easier exploitation of static and dynamic scale economies. While integration theory suggests that establishing a larger effective market will create trade, thus raising output and welfare, it may also divert trade from more efficient to preferential partners, something that may impose negative welfare effects for the integration area and former supplier firms from third countries.

While standard neoclassical trade theory implies international factor-price convergence, if perhaps not full equalization, and convergence of *per capita* income levels in a world without capital mobility, the real world looks different from the assumptions required to support the expectations based on conventional trade theory. The new trade and growth theories developed since the early 1980s have emphasized the role of R&D—with international spillovers—and of economies of scale as well as path-dependent economic development so that imperfect competition results in outcomes that are not quite compatible with the neoclassical model; indeed all these elements play a role, among others, for TEs (Welfens and Wolf, 1997).

Following basic integration theory, economic opening-up and merger into the EU can be expected to contribute via trade and FDI (EBRD, 1997; Howell, 1994; Stern, 1997) to high economic growth in TEs especially during the early years of the transformation. As a result, distributional conflicts will tend to weaken and further transition steps toward a market economy will become feasible. Rising per capita incomes in TEs tend to bolster east-west trade on the European continent and concentrate it increasingly on a class of products that is known as IIT, and less on interindustrial trade. This is useful since the latter type of structural adjustment required by external-sector opening is prone to elicit adjustment conflicts as resources in declining sectors, including especially labor, cannot be redeployed to activities receiving an impetus from the trade expansion. Note, however, that IIT can be of two types: horizontal and vertical (see chapter 7), with the latter being the less desirable kind when seen from the perspective of engineering economic catch-up—a critical ambition of TE transformation managers and a requirement without which the TEs will find it difficult to function constructively within, and successfully compete on equal terms in, the SEM.

The share of EU-15 in the TEs' trade increased markedly during the period 1989-1997 (see table 8.2). This derived in part from the collapse of the CMEA and the willful destruction of the former intragroup trade. But it also stemmed from deepening the trade involvement of the TEs as well as, in some TEs, growth in aggregate incomes leading current resource creation to levels beyond those observed on the transitions' eve. Note, however, that foreign capital has provided a substantial impetus to this trade expansion, albeit quite unequally among the

TEs. Indeed, FDI inflows have been very unevenly distributed, with the Czech Republic and Hungary recording rather high cumulative inflows (table 8.3).

Table 8.2: EU-15's share in trade[a] of TEs

Country	Direction	1989	1993	1997
Bulgaria[b]	Exports	6.0	30.0	43.3
	Imports	12.5	32.8	37.3
Czech Rep.[c]	Exports	31.9	49.4	59.9
	Imports	31.8	52.3	61.7
Estonia	Exports	n.a.	17.8	66.9
	Imports	n.a	23.3	74.9
Hungary	Exports	33.6	58.1	71.2
	Imports	39.7	54.4	62.6
Poland	Exports	39.6	69.2	64.0
	Imports	42.2	64.7	63.8
Romania[d]	Exports	27.6	41.4	56.5
	Imports	6.5	41.3	43.6
Slovakia[e]	Exports	32.2	29.5	45.0
	Imports	34.4	27.9	39.5
Slovenia[f]	Exports	58.0	63.2	63.6
	Imports	66.9	65.6	67.4

Notes:
[a] Based on custom statistics.
[b] Imports are f.o.b. until 1991 and c.i.f. thereafter.
[c] From 1993 on total trade data include Slovakia.
[d] Data are f.o.b. for both imports and exports. Latest year is 1996.
[e] From 1993 on total trade data include the Czech Republic.
[f] From 1992 total trade data include the successor states of the former Yugoslavia.

Sources: data base of the Wiener Institut für Internationale Wirtschaftsvergleiche; ESA, various issues; and CNS, 1998, pp. 628-29.

From a theoretical perspective the external-sector liberalization in TEs in combination with the prospect, and in due course realization, of EU enlargement should bring about five main growth-related effects for TEs. Three refer to the traditional arguments familiar from the standard-textbook rendition of the neoclassical theory of international trade. These are: (1) efficiency gains due to rising import competition in eastern Europe; (2) economies of scale effects related to EU market access; and (3) gains from specialization and a rise in the range of product varieties, which allow realization of a higher level of consumption and utility, respectively. In addition, recent additions to 'modern' trade theory (Baldwin, 1992; Baldwin and Seghezza, 1996) suggest two further effects: (4) growth impulses relating to imports of intermediate products and technology-intensive machinery and equipment, which might give rise to positive spillover effects; and (5) increasing FDI flows from the EU to the TEs, particularly to those with the better prospect of entry into the EU as this tends to eliminate political risk for the EU investor as well as other investors in market economies.

Table 8.3: Indicators of FDI[a] flows into TEs, 1995-1997

Country	FDI/GDP (percent)			Cumulative (million dollars)		Per capita (dollars)	
	1995	1996	1997	1996	1997	1996	1997
Albania[b]	2.9	4.5	2.0	291	330	86	97
Belarus	0.1	0.5	1.2	111	273	11	26
Bulgaria	0.7	1.4	4.3	446	884	53	105
Croatia	0.4	2.6	1.8	830	1164	184	259
Czech Rep.	5.0	2.5	2.4	7282	8582	710	838
Estonia	5.6	2.5	4.5	799	1106	602	760
Hungary	9.9	4.4	3.7	13377	15462	1331	1548
Latvia	5.5	7.5	7.3	864	1284	371	519
Lithuania	1.2	1.9	3.8	296	641	101	172
Macedonia	0.2	0.3	0.2	44	52	20	24
Moldova	4.5	2.7	2.3	152	195	34	44
Poland[b]	1.0	2.0	2.2	5492	8526	142	221
Romania	1.2	0.7	2.7	1237	2193	26	36
Russia	0.5	0.5	0.9	8092	14789	55	100
Slovakia	0.9	1.1	0.4	886	1026	166	192
Slovenia	0.9	0.9	1.6	785	1100	408	572
Ukraine	0.7	1.2	0.9	1345	1861	26	36
Total	1.6	1.3	1.6	42329	59468	127	179

Notes:
[a] Cash basis in reporting country. 1997 data are extrapolated on the basis of partial data, except for the Czech Republic and Hungary. January-November data were used for Poland, Slovakia, and Slovenia. January-September data were used for all other countries except Romania, which are official estimates for the full year.
[b] Data are net of residents' investments abroad.

Source: UNECE, 1998, pp. 162-63.

The fourth effect tends to be significant. Thus, Coe and Helpman (1993) found, in a study for OECD countries, a significant impact of trade-weighted cumulated R&D stocks of trading partners. Provided consumption goods are not dominant on the import side, one may emphasize the crucial role of rising imports for growth and transition, respectively. Also with respect to the fifth effect mentioned above, one should reckon with FDI diversion as potential U.S. investors might be crowded out by EU firms that enjoy particular advantages in investing in an enlarged home market. At the same time the overall fall in the implicit risk premium for the TEs will elicit FDI creation so that the steady state FDI flows and the respective ratio of the FDI stock to GDP levels should rise (Welfens, 1994). The long-run increase in capital intensity should, following traditional analysis, lead to higher labor productivity, hence rising real wages in eastern Europe.

In the spirit of the neoclassical trade theory one should also examine trade-induced changes in production specialization and in relative factor rewards. For the most active EU exporters to TEs one typically finds that the factor content of exports is mainly capital and skilled labor so that with the removal of trade barriers and EU enlargement, especially in a situation of rising EU net exports, the demand for skilled labor will expand in the EU, leading to a rising wage differential between skilled and unskilled labor. This conclusion, for which Smith (1997) provided empirical evidence, is not valid for all countries, however. Indeed, simulations of the impact on labor in Austria attributable to a hypothetical EU eastward enlargement paradoxically underlines that there will be declining wage dispersion (Keuschnigg and Kohler, 1998).

Conflicts and Lingering Theoretical Issues

Aiginger, Winter-Ebmer, and Zweimüller (1995) focus on the enlargement effects on the labor market for Austria and find that growing Austrian exports to the eastern part of Europe more than offset the negative employment effect of growing imports from TEs. Positive wage effects are relatively weak for blue-collar workers (in contrast to employees), older workers, and unskilled workers. Immobile unskilled workers are the relative losers of eastern enlargement. Given a high degree of wage inflexibility in the EU there is some risk that enlargement will lead to rising unemployment of unskilled immobile labor and thus to a growing share of long-term unemployment. With the exception of the fairly sophisticated analyses undertaken for Austria, on the whole there continues to be a considerable lack of well-founded investigations of the effects of eastward enlargement based on rigorous modeling.

While advanced models of trade liberalization and especially of the effects of TE entry into the EU suggest considerable economic benefits from an eastward enlargement, one should raise several issues within the context of critiquing the model setup or, putting it differently, within the context of potential extensions and refinements of the model (Ambrus-Lakatos and Schaffer, 1996; Döhrn, 1996; Gasiorek, Smith, and Venables, 1994; Holzmann and Żukowska-Gagelmann, 1997; Keuschnigg and Kohler, 1998; Winters and Wang, 1994).

First of all, one might well wish to inquire into whether and how the introduction of FDI into the trade-dominant traditional models will affect the assessment of costs and benefits of EU entry for the TEs. While there is little doubt that FDI stimulates technology transfer, thus contributing to higher growth, some TEs have obviously political reservations about high FDI inflows. This is especially so for flows originating in Germany since they heighten historical fears in TEs of dominance in some sense. Moreover, asymmetric international property rights impair the convergence process of real levels of per capita GNP, provided proper accounting of the difference between GDP and GNP is undertaken, unlike in the typical textbook neoclassical convergence model, which simply ignores FDI.

An illustrative asymmetric two-country model demonstrates this point. Let the two countries have identical production functions such that:

$$Y = K^{\beta} L^{1-\beta} \tag{8.3}$$

where Y is GDP in the source country of FDI and Y^* the level of GDP in the recipient country, and identical stocks of labor L and capital K. The result will evidently be equal GDP levels, but unequal total, hence per capita, GNP levels, taking for the sake of simplicity L to be equal to population. The difference depends on the degree to which the capital stock in one country is owned by the other country (Welfens, 1994, 1997). If the first country owns all of the second country's capital stock, the first country's GNP will be:

$$Y + \beta Y^* \tag{8.4}$$

while the second country's will evidently be:

$$Y^* - \beta Y^* \tag{8.5}$$

The ratio of per capita levels of GNP in the two countries will be in favor of the source country of FDI by a margin that entirely depends on the magnitude β. If, for example, the latter is 1/3, the margin will be 2:1. As regards economic convergence and cohesion this points to the importance of nurturing ownership-specific advantages of firms by modulating domestic policy and strengthening the market environment in the TEs so that FDI flows become a two-way avenue. This would also lessen political reservations against FDI inflows in the host country.

Second, most of the models tested so far are based on general equilibrium. In that context one may well wish to inquire into how transitory unemployment can be accounted for since it represents important individual risks and political costs. An answer could be sought along the lines of positive quadratic adjustment costs for workers shifting from declining to expanding sectors when adjustment is time consuming. Sectoral adjustment costs could be ranked by the divergence in skill intensities—factor-content differentials—of the respective sectors concerned. In other words, if declining sectors are mainly dominated by unskilled workers while expanding sectors have a high share of skilled workers, the adjustment costs will be higher than in the case of skill symmetry between declining and expanding sectors.

Third, eastward enlargement could have major real exchange-rate effects on the euro-dollar rate. If the euro should appreciate there will be two negative effects for the EU-15, but especially until the EU-11 will be widened, namely, reduced net exports to the rest of the world and falling net FDI inflows from third countries, the United States in the first instance. The latter result is a generalization of the findings by Froot and Stein (1991) to the effect that, in a model with imperfect capital markets, real appreciation of the dollar reduces the normalized FDI flows from the United States.

Fourth, depending on the type, scope, and speed of the first wave of EU enlargement there could be negative effects on other TEs, including the privileged ones that will not be included in the first round (see chapter 9). This may well require that the enlarged EU appropriate extra budgetary funds to stabilize the nonmember TEs. If trade- and investment-diversion effects should undermine the economic expansion of the outsiders, including the CIS countries, political tensions within Europe, and indeed worldwide, could grow, thus imposing immediate costs on the EU taxpayer since he would no longer benefit easily from the peace dividend accruing from low defense expenditures.

Finally, there is the issue of membership in the EU's monetary union. If poor TEs enter the euro zone too quickly, once they are EU member and have played their role in ERM II (see chapter 5), the result could be economic stagnation, high unemployment, and political conflicts in the new member. This is best avoided not only for the sake of the TEs in question but also to secure the coherence of monetary union and the advancement of EU integration.

From the perspective of structural adjustment one should highlight the problem of relative price adjustment, exchange-rate flexibility, and economic catch-up in slightly more detail. In the course of economic development and modernization via catch-up, one can anticipate a change of the real exchange rate and the relative price of nontradables (P^n) to that of tradables (P^t). The problem is compounded by the fact that price arbitrage for some tradables remains rather imperfect, even after the reduction of trade barriers in Europe.[4]

Defining q as the real exchange rate:

$$q = P^n/P^t \tag{8.6}$$

one will normally witness a rise of this ratio in the process of rising per capita incomes in part because of differential gains in productivity in the tradable sector as compared to the nontradable sector (Asea and Mendoza, 1994; Kravis and Lipsey, 1983). Indeed adjustment in relative prices is crucial for structural change and economic growth. Monetary union creates some specific problems for entering TEs as strictly fixed exchange rates are inappropriate for as long as these TEs are undergoing sizable structural change, that is, for as long as they are, in effect, in transformation. In other words, these TEs should not enter monetary union too early (see chapter 5).

Define the price level P:

$$P = (P^n)^\beta (P^t)^{(1-\beta)} \tag{8.7}$$

and assume international price arbitrage such that the domestic price of tradables:

$$P^t = eP^{t*} \tag{8.8}$$

with β, e, and P'^* representing the share of nontradables in overall consumption, the nominal exchange rate, and the world market price level of tradables, respectively. Under those conditions, one would face a major problem in a regime combining price stability and fixed exchange rates. Moving toward membership in monetary union is such a regime since we assume that the ECB is bound to observe price stability. When the TE enters the EU and pegs its exchange rate to the euro, its own monetary policy will have to target price stability as well. Indeed, the requirements of price stability and international price arbitrage imply a constant relative price of nontradables to tradables. This in turn impairs substantial structural change and growth at variance with these phenomena elsewhere in the monetary union. An alternative would be periodic appreciation of the currency so that e will fall over time and bring about the required decline of the relative price of tradables in the course of economic catch-up.

Policy Challenges and Options

There are undoubtedly risks to holding the TEs at an early stage to observing similar macroeconomic-policy constraints as under the ERM II or monetary union. These should be carefully weighed so that monetary-union membership or early pegging to the euro will be extended only after a successful minimum real-convergence process (see chapter 6), notably in terms of reducing per capita income differentials and sustaining economic growth over a sufficiently long period of time. If accession countries join ERM II upon their EU entry, policy makers should entertain the option of periodic nominal depreciations and appreciations of the exchange rates of the TEs in question as an unavoidable ingredient of the required longer-term convergence process on which ultimately nominal convergence is to a large extent predicated. Artificial exchange-rate stability should be avoided as much as strong misalignment.

Arguably the most important long-term challenge for an EU with a membership of twenty-one to twenty-seven countries (counting Malta on the accession track) is that the ratio of small and poor countries relative to the five large and wealthy EU members—France, Germany, Italy, Spain, and the United Kingdom—will rise dramatically. There is indeed a poor-country problem in an enlarged EU. Likewise there is a small-country problem in governing a policy club such as the EU's. With respect to a potential majority of poor countries in the EU, the main challenge is that with majority voting in the European Council in particular one can anticipate the emergence of policies leaning toward emphasizing income redistribution and expanding structural funds, as well as political interference even in technical matters. That would necessarily be associated with high economic opportunity costs, weaken the EU's global economic competitiveness, and undermine the prospects for regaining full employment.

With an increasing number of small countries, the decision-making power of the large countries, such as measured by the Banzhaf index from game theory, falls disproportionately, that is, by more than the rise in the number of members or the size of the EU population. As the acute last-minute difficulties with the fourth expansion[5] (see chapter 4) earlier illustrated, such an outcome could lead to weak or absent political leadership in an enlarged EU and growing frustration of large countries about majority voting; such countries could even consider exiting from the EU club. The solution to these serious problems could lie in negotiating an EU constitution that requires small countries to form EU internal clubs (for example, Belgium with Luxemburg, or even those two with the Netherlands in the context of Benelux cooperation). This rule could be anchored to the requirement of reaching a minimum population for a country to be seated independently, compelling others to form one or more interior clubs. This also has to be considered for another reason: the inability of very small countries to mobilize the necessary administrative resources, and perhaps even the political clout, for staging an effective turn in the rotating presidency in the manner increasingly required to discharge this office. It is fairly obvious that such constitutional issues must be solved prior to EU enlargement, something that poses serious problems of inefficient decision making within a political club[6] as IGC96 amply demonstrated (see chapter 4).

A more practical challenge emanates from the dilemmas about financing cohesion policies. The range of EU regions qualifying for objective 1 structural supports could be reduced by redefining the threshold in terms of PPPs and by reducing the threshold level to two-thirds or less of the average reconfigured per capita income for the EU as a whole; these cutoff points could be revised as the catch-up process in the initially economically laggard countries gets under way. Similarly, the cohesion fund set up for relatively poor euro candidates encountering difficulties in meeting the convergence criteria could usefully be redefined. Taking into account the principle of subsidiarity, EU competence and interference can be justified only for projects with positive EU-wide external effects so that cohesion funds should be allocated to certain environmental projects, to infrastructural investments, and to the promotion of a Europe-wide information society. The latter aim would be a new element among the EU's structural policies, but it clearly could be justified on the principle of positive international network effects. Moreover, it would be an active element of cohesion since, as recent empirical analysis has shown, the use of telecommunications and information technology provides a significant impetus to economic growth (Antonelli, 1998; Jungmittag and Welfens, 1998).

Successful economic catch-up is key to avoiding excessive expansion of EU structural funds. One should therefore not pursue a strategy of rigidly fixing exchange rates of newly entering countries. Even under favorable growth conditions, eastward enlargement will mean that the EU's structural funds will have to be expanded, while the relative share of especially the present EU-4 recipients will necessarily contract. If the risk of overstepping budgetary guidelines and constraints is to be avoided for an enlarged community, the present members must reform the CAP and structural-support policies in ways that basically reduce funds available to the present membership. The present four large beneficiaries, at least in per capita terms, can be expected to oppose rapid eastward enlargement, not only because they will lose subsidies in absolute and relative terms but also because they are not expected to be among the main beneficiaries of the expansion of trade and FDI that eastward enlargement is likely to generate. Those gains will accrue in the first instance to Austria and Germany, and also to Finland, France, Italy, the Netherlands, and Sweden, that is, the 'northern' and 'eastern' tiers of the present EU.

In central Europe, EU enlargement raises in some cases complex political questions. The situation on the German-Polish border is much more difficult than that on the Austrian-Hungarian border because Germany in general and the eastern part of the country in particular are characterized by high rates of structural unemployment in the late 1990s. Since xenophobic reactions and reservations against the EU's eastward enlargement can at times be observed even in Austria, it is all the more likely that such problems will crop up more and more strongly in Germany. Additionally Germany's relations with the Czech Republic and Poland are compounded by irredentist movements on the part of German nationals expelled after World War II who are now claiming, at times rather stridently, their right to, as a minimum, restitution of their property in the former German settlements or regions of eastern Europe. These and related unsettled problems could elicit political radicalization on the part of an enlarging EU, giving rise to a fragmentation of the already fragile political cohesion and willingness to cooperate so that the fifth enlargement and beyond can be seen through in a constructive manner.

Another pivotal political problem arises from the possibility that there will be increasing economic divergence between the acceding and other TEs, especially the western areas of the CIS and notably Belarus, Moldova, Russia, and Ukraine. From both a political and an economic perspective successful stabilization and sustained growth in Russia are key to long-term stability in Europe. While the Russian government's decisions have often been ambivalent in terms of the country's intentions, and indeed its actions as regards enhancing the transformation process, one should also be aware of the fact that the gradual rapprochement between some of the eastern and the western parts of Europe since the transition's inception has led to trade diversion. This may be accelerating with the effective de jure enlargement of the EU. The share of Russia's trade with the former CMEA members has plummeted considerably and the composition of the remaining trade has relegated Russia's market share essentially to fuels and raw materials.

True, the prospects for Russian exports to the former CMEA partners at this stage are not rosy. With economic recovery, however, Russian producers of manufactures would probably stand a good chance of regaining market share in the other TEs. With entry of the western TEs into the EU, however, that prospect becomes far dimmer. Only the creation of some kind of FTA between the 'new' EU and Russia, and perhaps other CIS states, would forestall such an eventuality, leaving a less skewed 'playing field' for all actors involved. Working toward such an institutional arrangement can be recommended as a useful complement of EU enlargement policies (see chapter 9). But one should not overlook that any such arrangement would compound the long-term adjustment pressures for the wider EU, which are already very considerable.

Finally, I very much doubt the assertion that the EU has only one policy choice: admission of some of the TEs as full members or leaving them on its 'borderland.' True, a country is either a member of the EU or not, and only under the first option could it conceivably enjoy all the benefits of the EU. However, a modified EEA, which could conceivably be constituted as a common market without direct political representation in Brussels and without free movement of labor, is an option worth contemplating by all concerned. I realize that the privileged TEs are not at all willing, at least overtly, to entertain such an option. But the realities of EU membership and of accession negotiations, as well as the potential of fruitful economic cooperation with former CMEA partners, once economic stability will have been regained and the prospects for economic recovery and growth improve, may well bring about a change in attitude.

Conclusions

In this chapter I have stressed several problems around structural change during the transformation process of TEs as a prerequisite for generating economic catch-up and thus facilitating entry of some of these countries into an enlarging EU.[7] In this context I have also addressed the role of trade, FDI, and institutional adjustments in both the eastern and western partners of an expanded EU. All things suitably considered, I have underlined various arguments in favor of a first round of expansion, essentially toward the TE-5, because the economic gains are considerable and the costs appear to be manageable. Likewise, the various policy dilemmas that another EU expansion necessarily entails would seem to be solvable, provided some goodwill all-around is mustered to identify accommodations and pragmatic approaches.

I have many doubts, however, when it comes to enlarging the EU beyond the TE-5. The economic and political problems that will arise in moving toward bringing the remaining five of the TE-10 into the EU, let alone other TEs, are much more daunting. Some might trigger or accelerate the effective collapse of the EU as an integration venture, such as the Rome Treaty had characterized it. The EU would be saddled with too many policy dilemmas, its governance capabilities would be hollowed out and become too inflexible and inefficient to remain attractive for the large EU members. Indeed they might, then, exit from the present EU and reconstitute their own integration area. It would not be very constructive to arrive in such a roundabout way at the conclusion that there are limits to the constructive expansion of the present EU.

While adequate constitutional reforms in the EU might cope with some of the policy issues I have raised, one should also consider alternative options for de facto eastward integration. Even without this option, the EU will be challenged to innovate a comprehensive and consistent program of assistance and cooperation to stabilize Russia economically, politically, and socially. Coming to grips with this major challenge is imperative for a stable EU, regardless of the extent to and the ways in which it will be enlarged (see chapter 9).

Notes

1. The comment can be readily extended to Slovenia, but not, of course, to Bulgaria (which formally entered in early 1999) and Romania, given their recent transformational difficulties.

2. Objective 1 regions are the countries whose per capita GDP falls below 75 percent of the EU's average. Objective 2 regions are those characterized by declining industrial employment. These are the two major categories of the EU's structural policy, claiming roughly 40 percent of the EU budget. The Commission has proposed to combine the other relatively small funds for disadvantaged regions under a new objective 3 heading.

3. As discussed in chapters 3 and 9, these were endorsed in March 1998 and are in the process of being implemented, albeit with some start-up hiccups.

4. For example, Richards and Tersman (1996) report that prices of farm products in Latvia are only one-third the Swedish level.

5. On the dimensions of the small-country problem for EU decision making at the time of the EFTA enlargement, see Hosli, 1993.

6. Much along the lines discussed in general terms by Buchanan and Tullock (1962) and Olson (1965, 1982).

7. Three interesting areas that I have not touched upon but could usefully be examined are: (1) the future of transatlantic political and economic relations with an expanded EU, (2) how best to cope with rising environmental problems in Europe (Müller and Ott, 1998) in part because expanding trade ties raise traffic congestions and emissions, and (3) shifts in the relative power of countries and regions in international organizations.

Chapter 9

The Impact of Widening on Outsiders

Jozef M. van Brabant

Almost from its inception, the EU has sought to build up an elaborate network of preferential arrangements with diverse groups of nonmember countries. Some may eventually apply for membership and be entitled in time to expect a positive response, and for that very reason the EU decided in the interim to establish a preferential trading arrangement. But the EU also maintains similar schemes with countries that for one reason or another cannot become members or, for their own economic, political, and security reasons, do not wish to aspire to that status. The latter situation may arise from the constraints on EU membership, such as when the country in question (e.g., Europe's former African dependencies) is not European by any stretch of the imagination. But third countries may also for their own foreign-policy objectives (as for Malta until it revived its application in late 1998) or out of their own calculated economic opportunism (as for Norway) decide not to join the EU even though they would otherwise be eligible for membership according to established criteria.

The EU has never attempted to be a self-contained bulwark. All the more so in the age of globalization it has come to realize that such an aspiration would be self-defeating. In any case, it has apparently come to the conclusion that it is best to be very selective about preferential arrangements for specific products in particular. That said, one must recognize that the EU's policy stances are not solely motivated by economic aspirations. Indeed, a widely diverse host of motives may argue for accommodating selective and differentiated preferential arrangements with third countries, almost regardless of their economic merits. Jacques Pelkmans (1997, pp. 307ff.) refers to them as 'anchor,' 'hegemonic,' and 'magnet' aspirations; but I do not find this terminology particularly illuminating. It does, however, usefully underline that the EU's ambitions outside its own region are not solely hegemonic, as some observers (Hart, 1997) have recently contended.

I am in this chapter especially concerned with the impact of the eventual widening of the EU toward privileged TEs for other countries. Before doing so, however, it is useful to bear in mind the kind of preferential arrangements that the EU has sought to embellish almost from its inception (European Commission, 1997a, p. 2). Then I spell out the broad implications over time and in a cross-sectional approach of the fifth widening of the EU, including for 'awkward' candidates for EU accession, notably Turkey. Thereafter I look separately at the impacts of widening for countries that in time may be credible EU candidates among the TEs and other countries, especially the TEs that will never be counted in that category or do not wish to be so considered. Next I briefly hint at the kind of implications of enlargement for EU members for they are likely to constitute the core of the conflicts weighing on accession negotiations and any transition regimes that might become necessary for orderly accession to occur at all.[1] Before concluding, I briefly point out some of the salient implications of the fifth widening and beyond for other nonmember countries that presently enjoy some type of preferential trading and/or cooperative arrangement with the EU.

The EU's Network of Preferential Arrangements

Over time the EU has elaborated a great number of reciprocal and other preferential trading and cooperation arrangements, moving the partners well beyond the commonly accepted status of most-favored nation (MFN) when it comes to ordinary commerce. With the rapid growth in membership in the GATT, now the WTO, MFN status in recent years has almost become the lowest common denominator of preferences available from trading partners. Various motivations have been at work in inducing the EU to move beyond the multilateral MFN status for third countries. But it would be too simplistic, and *in se* wrong (as in Hart, 1997, pp. 83ff.), to attribute them to the EU's ambition to create a sphere of influence erected around its *acquis*. I deem it even less illuminating to view the latter, if applicable at all, as 'an encircling' strategy. More to the point is that the EU has for its own cultural, diplomatic, economic, political, security, social, and other interests been keen on spreading its tentacles, not just *acquis*'s, or commercial interests beyond strict membership, to a range of extraregional arrangements outside the GATT/WTO framework (European Commission, 1997a).

These various categories of external relations, usually sanctioned in formal treaties, can best be discussed under nine generic rubrics that I organize here in four groups of partners: developing countries, EFTA members, Mediterranean countries, and TEs.[2] I must indicate up front, however, that in some cases further refinements within each group deserve to be heeded.[3] But this chapter does not provide the proper framework for delving deeply into the nitty-gritty variations on the nine themes I stress below. I shall therefore confine myself to briefly highlighting each of the generic types with a few words about within-group refinements when their ramifications bear on the broader discussion here.

Developing Countries

One can readily identify two different approaches. Most widely applied to developing countries is the *Generalized System of Preferences* (GSP); temporarily, pending the negotiation of special agreements, these provisions were also extended in 1989-1991 to some of the smaller eastern European TEs and since then to Albania, some of the successor states of the former Yugoslavia (such as Bosnia and Herzegovina and Macedonia), and some of the CIS members, such as Moldova. GSP provisions are maintained by most developed countries, but according to specifications and commitments set by the 'donor.' This status can therefore be treated most logically as a systemic feature, a part and parcel of the global 'trading regime,' if only because the scheme originated in an attempt to move away from the strict reciprocity rule under GATT/WTO's arrangements (Brabant, 1991, pp. 171ff.). But note that it is not part of a stable system since GSP preferences are accorded by each grantor country or group of countries, as in the EU, to a differentiated set of beneficiaries and usually only for a limited period of time, normally on an annual basis, although most often readily renewed for a similar term.

The next largest in geographical scope is now known as the *Lomé Convention.*[4] This extends trade preferences and other assistance measures, including market-access facilitation,[5] to a large number of African, Caribbean, and Pacific developing countries—hence the designation ACP program or countries—most of which are former colonies of EU members, notably of Belgium, France, Italy, the Netherlands, and the United Kingdom; however, there has been a trend in recent years to extend these preferences at least to all Asian least-developed countries (LDCs) as well. Under the present convention—known as *Lomé IV*—71 countries are included. It also encompasses aid flows and commodity-stabilization finance (McQueen, 1998; Panić, 1992; Stevens, 1992); the latter has since been extended to other LDCs as well,[6] both engendering larger exports to the EU than these countries could otherwise have reasonably counted on, given ordinary rules of access to EU markets for outsiders.[7] But the programs are also influenced by other motives, including creating 'reserved' EU export outlets, zones of political and strategic influence, and areas in which cultural and ideological precepts held usually by one EU member are to be fostered.

The present or fourth Lomé Convention is due to expire in February 2000. There is likely to be a follow-up, but one that, according to informed sources

(Collier et al., 1997; European Commission, 1997i, j and 1998c; McQueen, 1998; UNCTAD, 1998; Wolf, 1997), is likely to be very different. For one thing, a stronger political dimension will be added to the trade and aid features of the previous accords. Also benefits are due to be focused more on the LDCs, poverty alleviation, supporting the foundations of the development process "from the bottom up" by improving the enabling environment, such as for small businesses and entrepreneurship; but also by taking climatic, ecological, and economic vulnerability[8] into account in allocating financial assistance. Formal negotiations of the successor regime were initiated in September 1998. But there had for months been an intensive debate, at least at the level of the European Parliament and no doubt also at the national political level in key EU members, such as France, on how recent changes in the global scene are to be reflected therein.[9]

In the spirit of the GSP facility and the Lomé Convention, which by their very nature offer nonreciprocal concessions, essentially unilateral preferential market access, the EU has been extending such nonreciprocal preferences, as already noted, also to Albania and to some of the successor states of Yugoslavia, notably Bosnia and Herzegovina and Macedonia (European Commission, 1997a, pp. 6-7) and of the Soviet Union. In the case of the Yugoslav successor states, by the Commission's own admission, it consists of "a complex autonomous regime which is intended to replicate the concessions offered to the Former Yugoslavia under the agreement between the EC and Yugoslavia which ended in 1991" (European Commission, 1997a, p. 7). Slovenia is, of course, now engaged in fast-track accession negotiations and Croatia is too developed to qualify for such nonreciprocal advantages; relations with rump Yugoslavia and the EU remain strained over various economic and political matters.

Closing the Gap between EFTA and EU

Here there are two interrelated regimes. Arguably the most important special provisions granted by the EU, at least in terms of commodity coverage and of the magnitude of anticipated benefits, as the third category dealt with here, are the free-trading arrangements for most manufactured goods with *individual EFTA countries*. These were for all practical purposes completed by early 1984 (Dominick, 1993; Norberg, 1992) and thereafter led to negotiating the EEA agreement. These instruments were necessitated by the United Kingdom's accession to the EU in 1973 since it had to withdraw from EFTA, but it had earlier with these partners built up free trade essentially in manufactured goods. Its change of allegiance threatened that commerce if only because the application of the EU's common external tariff would otherwise have damaged the EFTA members, not just the remaining ones, economically and the EU politically.

The rationale behind the EU's treatment of EFTA members was expanded over time, and this I treat as the fourth category, in view of the fear of EFTA countries that EU 'deepening' would on balance harm them more than the magnitude of the benefits that they could expect to enjoy from trade creation (Kleppe, 1992). They therefore sought to negotiate a broader arrangement with the EU both for their own benefit as well as to forestall further requests for EU accession by EFTA members; the latter motive was arguably of even greater weight for the EU at the time of the renaissance in the integration endeavor in the latter part of the 1980s (see chapter 2). That provided the origin of the EEA, which is essentially about free trade in most manufactured goods, barring 'sensitive products' of course; agricultural and fishery products too are strictly excluded from the arrangement, as they were from EFTA provisions themselves (Kleppe, 1992).

Core EFTA members saw the EEA essentially as a stepping stone toward facilitating their integration into the EU, pending the removal of the injunction against further enlargement (see chapter 2), and other EFTA members perceived it as a means of protecting themselves against the adverse impacts of such a move. The EU, however, conceived this instrument more as a means to forestall pressure on moving forward rapidly with its response to already lodged requests for full accession, and perhaps preparing for even further enlargements, before setting decisive steps forward toward its own *finalité politique*. Following the fourth EU enlargement, the EEA now consists of three of the four remaining EFTA members (Iceland, Liechtenstein, and Norway); Switzerland has been seeking its own bilateral preferential arrangement with the EU.

Mediterranean Area

A fifth group of preferences applies to twelve *Mediterranean countries* that benefit from a rather heterogeneous arrangement, which eventually, perhaps by 2010, may lead up to something similar to the EEA for those eastern and southern Mediterranean countries that cannot hope or do not wish to join the EU (Chatelus and Petit, 1997; Lannon, 1996).[10] All agreements offer concessional access to EU markets. Most also include technical assistance and aid clauses. Only those with the more developed partners require any reciprocal market access.

Whatever optimism on mutually beneficial economic cooperation there may have been at the inception of these agreements, chiefly in the second half of the 1970s, their outcomes have been in a rather minor key, and quite disappointing to most non-EU signatories. This is to a large extent the result of the CAP, which became more protectionist over time, at least until the Uruguay Round and the reforms of the early 1990s instituted under Commissioner Ray MacSharry. But it was exacerbated by the restrictive regime for clothing and textiles, which will be removed only by the end of 2004 at the earliest, except for countries, such as the TE-10 that will have this regime abrogated before the end of the decade, depending on when the EA was signed (Brabant, 1995, p. 533).

Recall that these Mediterranean countries have a strong comparative advantage with respect to the EU, though not necessarily in comparison with some other countries, including the lesser developed TEs in particular, in the production of precisely those labor-intensive goods whose trade is managed in many developed countries. Also, the ever-increasing number of preferential arrangements negotiated by the EU, including the successive expansions of coverage of the Mediterranean agreements themselves, have reduced the effective degree of preference the original signatories had counted on enjoying in the longer run. Finally, the strategic motivations partly underlying the EU's Mediterranean policy have been sharply eroded by the transformation of the east-west environment since the late 1980s and by the EU's interest in assisting the east, even at the expense of other countries, including those with whom the EU had earlier concluded preferential arrangements (Akder, 1992); this provides one of the root causes of the recent disenchantment of Turkey with the EU, as I detail in the last section.

In some cases, the origin of these agreements reflected political factors (certainly for Algeria and Morocco) or strategic considerations (certainly in the case of Turkey). In the main, however, they came into their own because of a desire to preserve the entire Mediterranean as a European sphere of influence and market outlet, while at the same time managing this commerce and controlling migration pressures originating from the poorer regions in the southern and eastern Mediterranean, given their sizable urban unemployment and poor rural base. They also have helped to diffuse criticism over trade diversion, especially under the CAP arrangements on which the successive agreements have made some concessions (Akder, 1992), albeit to a more limited extent than these countries had coveted.

The Essen Council[11] in December 1994 proposed the formation of a Euro-Mediterranean Partnership that in time (probably by the year 2010) should lead to an FTA, at least for manufactured products, between the EU and selected Mediterranean countries, in particular those that cannot expect to become full members because they are not European. This démarche was solemnly endorsed in the so-called Barcelona Declaration of November 1995 (Lannon, 1996). Since then considerable attention has been devoted to that region, particularly by the EU's southern tier, which has few countries of direct interest among those participating in the Lomé Convention and sees potential rivals in many of the lesser developed TE-10. The details are only slowly being filled in, however (see Hoekman and Djankov, 1995). The process seems to have been started with the association agreement concluded in July 1995 with Tunisia (IMF, 1996). Since then the EU has signed similar agreements with Morocco and Lebanon, and, in late 1997, with Israel[12] and the Palestinian Authority;[13] but they have apparently not yet been ratified. Those with Egypt and Jordan are nearing the end of negotiations, whereas those for Algeria and Syria (Ghesquiere, 1998; Parfitt, 1997) are in the detailed negotiation process.

There would seem to be ground to rationalize these separate approaches as efforts to compensate the Mediterranean countries for the erosion in preferences sustained as a result of the EU's eastward 'interests' (Baldwin, 1997; Galal and Hoekman, 1997; Gautron, 1996; Velo, 1996). However, realizing the Euro-Mediterranean Partnership depends critically on progressing with settling the thorny issues that divide Israel and Palestine, a process that has been in considerable disarray for some time now.[14] And reaching the potentially substantial benefits of these agreements, especially for exporters of manufactures, hinges critically on these countries undertaking far-reaching flanking reforms (Ghesquiere, 1998).

Though Turkey forms part of the approach to and philosophy underlying the Mediterranean arrangements, its position with respect to the EU is unique in many respects. I treat it therefore as a sixth category. Not only does it have an ambivalent 'European vocation,' EU policy makers have repeatedly recognized Turkey as a potential EU member; granted the country a special association status in 1963, which came into effect in late 1964; intimated when it first applied for membership that it would in the medium run be allowed to join the 'common market' once the customs union was completed, which happened ahead of schedule in 1967 (see chapter 2). It obtained access to the common commercial policy only in 1996, after protracted difficulties, but effective implementation of this new relationship has been stalled over Greece's intransigence in particular. Especially the latter obstacle lingers in extending EU assistance. Recently Turkey's visceral reaction to its exclusion from accession negotiations as set by the Luxemburg Council in December 1997 has only exacerbated the relationship. The country's ongoing adjustment and stabilization policies as well as protracted internal ideological, political, and religious disagreements provide a bundle of reasons for this long delay and vacillation on the part of EU policy makers. But there are undoubtedly other circumstances that play more than a trivial role in sustaining this uneasiness. Anyway, with the EU decisions taken in 1997 for a while it looked reasonable to anticipate that Turkey would figure among the sixth or further wave of entrants, once the privileged TEs will have acceded. However, that has become more problematic since the Luxemburg Council.

Relationships with TEs

The last three categories of preferential arrangements refer explicitly to the place of the TEs in the EU's past and prospective ambitions. The present status of these agreements and the fact that the emerging architecture derives from the unprecedented changes in the eastern part of Europe since the late 1980s did not germinate in a vacuum, of course. Indeed the new arrangements were preceded by a fluid range of agreements worked out by the EU with these countries. And so as a seventh category one should classify the TEs with present and future EAs. The TE-10 benefit from the most far-reaching association with some of the EU's operational activities short of full membership.[15]

The EA was innovated, under prodding from Germany, to buttress and reinforce the emerging forces for democracy and for market-based resource allocation in the eastern part of Europe. Efforts to suppress national policies with respect to the so-called 'state-trading countries' had been under way for many years. It was only in early 1991, however, that some agreement was reached to harmonize EU policies within the context of its common commercial policy (Devuyst, 1992; Ham, 1993). The TEs were also viewed as having 'natural' cultural, economic, political, security, and social affinities and geographical connections with 'Europe.' For these and other reasons the then EC exercised leadership in the G-24 (Group of Twenty-four), in part through the G-7's (Group of Seven) machinery. By proceeding in this fashion, some of the EU's most powerful policy makers, in France and Germany in particular, but also Jacques Delors in the Commission, may have coveted independent foreign-policy making as well, if it had not only been quick, as it was, but also decisive and effective, which it has not been. Of course, there was also concern about stability on the EU's direct eastern borders and even beyond the then still-intact Soviet Union. Finally, there was a strongly articulated desire in the EU to succor the group's eastern neighbors and their fragile democracies, if only to forestall marked emigration from and protracted, and perhaps worsening, instability in that part of the continent.

The EA, though a fairly standard instrument, is nonetheless a very complex, voluminous exercise in commercial diplomacy with many individualized details. But there is no need to rehash them at length here (Brabant, 1995, pp. 532-36; 1996a, pp. 162-66). The key provisions reflect the EU's strong bent on securing markets and production facilities in TEs. The EAs therefore focus on managing access to the EU's markets, and avoiding serious levels of immigration. They are essentially asymmetric FTAs largely for nonsensitive manufactures: the EU first eliminates its external tariffs for TEs during a five-year period, but mainly less; and the latter reciprocate in a subsequent phase, usually five years later over a five-year stretch. Some limited concessions for agriculture and sensitive manufactures are also provided for and in the case of manufactures a more gradual loosening of nontariff barriers (NTBs) is held out. The TEs must take on the obligation to adopt the EU's competition policy over a fairly narrow time span and allow western investors market access with protection. There is furthermore some modest accommodation for westward migration of labor. And for each relationship an Association Council is set up to conduct 'a structured political dialogue.'

Since ratification of these agreements by the national parliaments of each EU member as well as by the beneficiary TE is required, and this takes years, the commercial part of the agreement, essentially an FTA, which falls within the authority of the European Commission given its mandate in fostering the common commercial policy, are activated swiftly. The remainder of the agreements can be introduced upon ratification. The eastern side from the beginning saw these agreements as the prelude to eventual full membership. The EU at first simply took note of this aspiration (notably in the agreements with Czechoslovakia, Hungary, and Poland), but later relented, officially first at the Copenhagen Council in 1993.

Much has been made of these agreements, in both the positive and negative senses. In any case, their beneficial economic nature, as distinct from the political and psychological gains they undoubtedly impart, should neither be exaggerated nor derided. With the EU's lowering of tariffs and easing or removing other barriers, the TEs obtain improved access to EU markets before similar benefits accrue to EU exporters. This is pivotal to successful transformation, particularly for the smaller TEs. But no free market access for the TEs' principal exportables—by definition the sensitive products—in the short run is provided for.

One could take the APAs negotiated with the privileged TEs as a separate category of EU preferential agreements. I consider them, however, a logical extension of the EA for TEs that are about to negotiate for membership with the EU. Because I inventory here only the agreements with nonmember countries, I discuss the APAs separately after the next section.

The EA tends to set the tone for eventual eligibility for accession on the part of the TE so honored. This raises the question whether any likelihood exists that EAs will be granted to other than the TE-10. It is well known that several countries, including Albania, Croatia, and Macedonia among the smaller eastern European TEs and Moldova and Ukraine among the successor states of the Soviet Union, have expressed more than a casual interest in obtaining such a status. Their aim is not only eventually to be allowed to request accession negotiations but also to obtain sizable benefits under the EA, including access to PHARE[16] funds for eastern Europe (now limited to the TE-10 plus Albania and Macedonia) and perhaps larger and more coherent TACIS (for technical assistance to the CIS) funds. The EU in general and the Commission in particular have thus far simply indicated that the countries expressing an interest in an EA—excepting notably Croatia in the past months—are not yet ready for such a status. I suspect that there will prospectively be very few EAs granted to other TEs, however, if only because the instrument as introduced in 1991 has not yet worked out to the mutual satisfaction of the parties involved.

The next category of relationships with TEs, or the eighth in this discussion, consists of a burgeoning number of PCAs negotiated chiefly with the CIS members (Yakemtchouk, 1997) as at present all but Tajikistan have a PCA, though most are yet to be ratified. PCAs had a dual origin. One consideration in their proliferation has been that most CIS states will never qualify for full EU membership and others are unlikely to be able to do so for several decades to come. Yet, events on the eastern flank of the 'Europe' of principal concern to the EU have been such that these states could not be left in considerable economic disarray and sociopolitical instability, if only to discourage them from reacting strategically to being 'isolated.' Also the EU feared that pressures for migration into the EU or into the privileged TEs were bound to become aggravated over time. It thus felt compelled to transcend the strict economic formats of trade and economic cooperation; hence the PCA.

As noted, the PCA is not solely about trade or broader economic relations. Indeed, specifications on human rights, on protecting the FDI at least by actors from the EU, and on safeguarding intellectual property rights at least for EU actors are also included, and these items have been playing a considerable role in molding the EU's willingness to 'assist' the TEs with their transformation.

Finally, there are various other arrangements with TEs still extant. Some are legacies of the period of communist control in the eastern part of Europe, when at best an uneasy relationship with the EU was allowed, while others reflect the EU's varying interests in these countries during the post-cold war period. First-generation trade agreements with these countries were concluded first with Romania and, after the agreement between the EC and the CMEA of 25 June 1988 was at long last signed, with several other countries. Some were turned into trade and cooperation instruments, which can be viewed as second-generation agreements. In ascending order of involvement with the EU as an alternative to EAs and PCAs are third-generation trade and cooperation agreements of somewhat wider scope than earlier formats. This applies in particular to Albania and Macedonia, the two 'other' beneficiaries of PHARE. But such an agreement will presumably in due course be extended also to Bosnia and Herzegovina, Croatia, and rump Yugoslavia (European Commission, 1996f, p. 17), and perhaps some of the western CIS states, Moldova in particular.

The Future of Preferential Arrangements

There is a recognized need to review, revise, and streamline many of these arrangements in the near term. The controversies that arose in 1995 about, on the one hand, the mid-term review of the Lomé IV Convention (Islam, 1995, p. 13) and, on the other hand, the longer-term financing of assistance to the TEs and the countries coming under the Mediterranean agreements underlined the complex political economy and weight of the many diverse issues at stake. The comparatively urgent need for reviewing these arrangements in a comprehensive fashion derives from the prospect of the eastward enlargement of the EU and from the seminal changes in the makeup of Europe after the cold war, and indeed in the rest of the world, since these agreements were first conceived. It also stems from the potential for coordinating or harmonizing more effectively the EU's global relations in cultural, economic, political, security, social, and other areas in the light of the Uruguay Round, the establishment of the WTO, the EU's more outward-looking strategy (Rydelski and Zonnekeyn, 1997) and ambitions in terms of a coherent common external policy, and other developments. Among the latter one can readily cite the formation of other regional preferential arrangements that may negatively affect the EU, such as Mercosur (Baldwin, 1997, p. 881), closer relations with Chile and Mexico, the Gulf Cooperation Council, North America (in a rapprochement billed as the 'New Transatlantic Agenda'), and the rapprochement with south and southeast Asia ('Asia-Europe Meeting').

If and when the EU will be able to solidify its other pillars, especially its common foreign policy, it *must* revise its foreign economic relations in the light of its broader interests beyond the commercial ones that were largely, but by no means exclusively, at the root of the preferential arrangements when they were first negotiated. This is especially important in the case of TEs that are unlikely to be among the first and second waves of entrants to the EU or that may never join it.

Stylized Consequences of Enlargement for Nonmembers

Bringing some TEs into the EU is bound to affect all preferential arrangements maintained by all countries involved, albeit to widely different degrees. Given the EU's discriminatory nature, the acceding TEs will gain an even more privileged status in the EU than they enjoy now. Whatever inward and outward flows result from this enlargement *may* occur at the expense of nonmember countries as their competitive position vis-à-vis the 'new' EU will, on balance, tend to deteriorate for goods and services that the two groups compete for. This determines the degree of actual or potential trade diversion[17] from nonmembers to the EU, including the new ones. I contend that these changes are not generally limited to the new EU members and third parties, and indeed that it would be shortsighted to indicate that TE entry into the EU does not directly in any way crowd out any trading group of the EU, including those with preferential arrangements (Inotai, 1998a, p. 51), if only because the TEs' real comparative advantage with EU entry will be in "highly-skilled industries" (Inotai, 1998b, p. 65). Indeed, the major impetus for adverse repercussions may come indirectly from the impact exerted by the newly acceding countries on the present EU membership, and hence their predilections or shifting sentiments regarding the EU's external arrangements. Even though this chapter addresses chiefly the repercussions of yet another EU enlargement on third parties, a brief discourse of intra-EU relations upon TE accession is required, as in the next-to-last section, to round off the picture, however sketchy and speculative it must necessarily remain at this juncture.

Even without embarking on a detailed exploration of the 'composition' of the prospective external demand and supply of the respective partners, one can speculate on the groups of countries that on balance are likely to be affected most in a broad *tour d'horizon* of the major flows and perturbations likely to materialize. One can hardly err much by asserting that EU entry of, say, the TE-5 is unlikely to affect for years to come in any substantial way the competitive position of the group's large trading partners, such as Japan or the United States; but it may well adversely impact upon, even early on, the position of some individual exporters in these countries. I abstract here from those cases, if only because these large mature market economies and most of their economic actors possess the means to adjust with minimal adversity.

On the other hand, EU entry of some TEs is bound to affect in a potentially major way overlapping segments of countries that have sought close association with the EU. This is the case in particular for preferential partners of the fast-track candidates for accession that for one reason or another cannot be included among the first group of entrants. It is bound, furthermore, to change the position of the entrants with respect to TEs that in time will lodge a credible request for opening accession negotiations and indeed to TEs that cannot or do not wish to enter.

Finally, a nontrivial effect of the entry of some TEs into the EU will be felt by a whole range of countries presently enjoying preferential arrangements with the EU. These include in particular the ACP countries and the Mediterranean partners, with Turkey as a special case. Entry will undoubtedly also affect the position of some nonmember states with substantial ties to the EU, such as Norway and Switzerland. But I shall refrain from discussing their cases if only because Switzerland for its own domestic reasons decided not to pursue entry into the EEA, and thus eventually EU membership, and the Norwegian electorate twice spurned entry after the country had concluded a draft accession treaty with the EU. One could inquire into the impact of an expansion toward the TEs on Malta, which suspended its accession request until late 1998, but I shall not do so here, except in considering the generic impact on Mediterranean countries.

In deliberating about potentially adverse repercussions of widening the EU toward the eastern part of Europe, it is important not to restrict the purview to commodity exchanges. Indeed, services and capital flows now amount to a multiple of the recorded exchanges of goods and services directly associated with merchandise commerce. Entry into the EU, perhaps after a transition phase extending possibly over ten to fifteen years, will grant the TEs full access to the EU's four freedoms (for goods, services, capital, and people), and one could consider the implications thereof for other countries. In view of the fact that the economies of the candidates for accession will continue to undergo major structural change over the next several years, perhaps even decades, and they are presently not yet on an equilibrium catch-up growth trajectory, it is not easy to conjecture about the potential pressures emanating from these countries when they join the EU. But one might speculate on what is likely to occur in the near term.

The goods for which the TEs can be expected to hold a comparative edge over the next several years range from agriculture (largely temperate products) and primary goods, to labor-intensive manufactures, and perhaps specialized parts and components for manufactures that now form, and will continue to constitute, the heart of IIT in the SEM. For the first categories that threat is real and immediate. Countries that will be harmed are those that now hold a comparative edge in EU markets for those products. TE accessions are therefore likely to affect chiefly those Mediterranean and ACP countries that have made some strides in labor-intensive manufactures. The impact of competition for the kind of IIT cited above depends critically on how fast growth momentum along the modernization path will crystallize in the TEs and be sustained, pulled largely, but by no means almost exclusively as some contend (Inotai, 1997b), by the right kind of FDI. Recall that such IIT in specialized parts and components has been the most dynamic force driving the EU's single market and effective market integration in production, consumption, and distribution. The countries affected here cover a broad range, including notably the more dynamic NIEs. These generally do not enjoy preferential access to EU markets and may thus lose market share. However, those NIEs that can adapt quickly at minimal cost will in all likelihood not be severely affected by the TEs' niche. But others will be. This is likely to apply in the first instance to the Mediterranean countries and other TEs that might be expected in time to constitute attractive sites for FDI from the point of view of substantial EU actors, given the structures and pressures of the SEM.

Services in TEs are still largely underdeveloped and for now primarily geared toward domestic-market intermediation. In time, however, one will conceivably have to reckon with an entire array of services, some of which may be internationally mobile, that the TEs can offer on a competitive basis. Initially this will apply largely to the TEs that are early candidates for EU accession. Their internationally competitive 'service products' may range from the more labor-intensive mundane services (such as credit-card transaction clearing) to technologically more sophisticated services (such as in engineering, electronics, and computer software). The countries most likely to be harmed by this expansion of the EU's sphere will be those that presently deliver such services, largely at the lower end of technological sophistication. Again, some ACP and Mediterranean countries in particular may be pulling at the short end here.

It is difficult to assess in the abstract how capital flows may be affected by another EU expansion. At the least one must distinguish among FDI, portfolio investment (equity, bonds, and bank loans), and other flows, including speculative capital flows. FDI flows will in all likelihood for years to come continue overwhelmingly in the eastward direction, rather than the other way around, even though some reverse flows have already materialized, given factor proportions in TEs as compared to present EU members. Although it is still too early to draw reliable, let alone definitive, conclusions as regards the kind of FDI flows that may be diverted, there is little doubt that of the three broad categories—for extending the export-distribution base, for production for local markets, and for integration into the investor's global corporate strategy—only a comparatively small part of the latter may compete directly with FDI that might otherwise have been allocated elsewhere. The potential for diversion depends entirely on whether TEs can become more competitive sites for FDI than non-EU countries.

As regards portfolio investment, a similarly broad comment can be made. The TEs are all offering global economic actors emerging markets that for now are far from integrated. Membership in the EU is expected to foster homogenization. It also will strengthen expectations of catch-up and economic prosperity well beyond levels that the TEs can hope to achieve outside the EU framework. If only for those reasons, even the prospect of EU membership makes the TEs more attractive as destination of investment flows. If so, hot-money flows would presumably abate, at least in relative terms, as greater economic, political, and social stability crystallizes in part because of the credibility that EU, and later ERM II and monetary union, membership is likely to impart (see chapter 5). Even the prospect of such a commitment can be expected to exert a positive impact on the 'right' kinds of investment inflows, both for portfolio and FDI reasons.

Labor competition presents one of the most worrisome, as well as thorniest, aspects of engineering yet another EU enlargement. Chronic levels of unemployment and considerable popular resentment with political repercussions about migrants in several of the present EU members cannot but further complicate this conundrum (see chapter 8). This manifests itself not only for migrants from outside the EU moving into EU markets, but even for those already residing there. Clearly, for the time being, the TEs offer human capital comparatively cheaply and thus cannot but present a competitive challenge to labor in the EU, regardless of origin. On the other hand, it is unclear how many people from newly entering TEs would be prepared to move into the 'other' EU markets. Estimates vary.[18] Also, if catch-up to average EU levels of productivity, income, wealth, and so on can get well under way prior to effective enlargement and full application of the four freedoms to new entrants, presumably the competitive edge for skilled labor in effective-wage terms in particular might already be severely eroded. For unskilled labor, however, substantial problems might arise in competing for low-skill jobs, not just for those residing in the EU but also for migrants from outside the EU, including for those that are physically within EU borders but currently enjoy less than assured employment (see chapter 7).

Presumably by the time the TEs will accede to the EU, perhaps toward the end of the next decade (see chapter 10), the financial and other official development assistance (ODA) from which these countries have been benefiting will have shrunk markedly. This should ease the strains on the availability of ODA for other TEs and indeed for the conventional developing countries, of course after allowing for the considerable aid fatigue that has been besetting the international donor community. But one should also take another element into account: with more prosperous TEs in the EU, these countries might be expected to begin again to contribute to ODA either through the EU's common programs or by formulating their own bilateral development-assistance policy. The international community should prospectively be able to count on this broader burden sharing, at whatever level of aggregate support mustered, even though that issue has all-but-completely vanished from the policy agenda with the emergence of transition as a policy topic in national, regional, and international debates. Some attention deserves to be devoted to the *full* integration of the TEs into the global community of nations, with all the advantages, obligations, and responsibilities entailed.

Implications of Enlargement for TEs with Preferences

There are at least three groups of TEs that deserve to be considered separately in analyzing the actual and potential impacts of an eastward enlargement of the EU.

First come the TEs that are currently negotiating their fast-track accession and are hence likely to be among the first entrants. These are the TE-5, but other countries with an EA, especially Slovakia, may be added by year-end 1999. These countries upon entry will have to adopt the common EU external tariff and eliminate reciprocal tariffs, as well as gradually submit to the EU's common commercial policy in other respects. Shifts in protection-induced comparative advantages are bound to be provoked, not only for these countries but also for other partners, including other TEs for reasons discussed below.

The TE-5 either have no (Estonia) or fairly low tariffs or are CEFTA members, and presumably will have substantially abolished their reciprocal tariffs by the time they join the EU. If CEFTA succeeds in its endeavor, reciprocal tariffs also of other CEFTA members—notably Bulgaria, Romania, and Slovakia) as well as other BFTA members—Latvia and Lithuania—will become very low. Similarly for relations with other countries with which the TEs have concluded FTAs. The EU's external tariff would not apply to these other TE-10 countries inasmuch as by then they will have free access to the SEM thanks to their EAs. However, the EU's less formal trade barriers as well as the CAP could disadvantage these countries unless some ad hoc accommodation for them is introduced upon accession of the fast-track TEs (see chapter 3).

Reciprocal adjustments for the early entrants because of these shifts in tariff regime are likely to be small, however. But NTBs continue to be very substantial (Messerlin, 1996). So is sectoral protectionism, notably in agriculture but also in the automobile sector. However, the impacts of adjusting to the present EU economy can be reckoned to be substantially larger than those likely to be felt in reciprocal ties among the entering TEs. Even in the case of sectoral protectionism, adjustments on average, though not necessarily in individual sectors (say, Estonian agriculture), can be expected to be minor to negligible.

The second category of TEs to consider are the TE-10 that are not engaged in fast-track negotiations. Adjustments in these economies (Latvia and Lithuania in the BFTA and Bulgaria, Romania, and Slovakia in CEFTA) will be twofold, unless the EU makes special arrangements for these preferential arrangements, as it did during previous enlargements to accommodate EFTA or Commonwealth trade. Much depends on the degree to which these agreements will have resulted in substantially free trade among the members of BFTA and CEFTA, and indeed several extensions in bilateral FTAs. By virtue of their EA and if trade liberalization in the two cited schemes will remain no more generous than in the EA (Brabant, 1997; 1998b), the major adjustments will arise from several sources. One is that the external tariff of the acceding TEs will become the EU's, thus changing the calculus of trade-deflection tactics. Another is that protectionist barriers will remain in TEs that do not join as compared to those that do. This may be important for sectoral protectionism, the CAP in particular and especially if the future CAP[19] will be more restrictive than the presently apparently more liberal provisions, notably in the case of CEFTA.

Harriet Matejka (1998) feels that the damage would be minimal if the EU were not to make special accommodations for the preexisting FTAs. However, the drawback might be quite considerable for the so-called sensitive manufactures (Brenton and Mauro, 1998) and, of course, for agriculture even though for now agricultural trade within the BFTA and CEFTA is not substantial, in part because these two arrangements do not aim at free trade in agriculture. But the share of sensitive manufactures is particularly pronounced in the EU's trade of these other TEs with preferences. The TE-5 would, of course, see the actual and potential discrimination against their sensitive products vanish upon entry (but possibly only during the completion of the post-accession transition period), whereas it would remain in force against other TEs and indeed other third countries.

Finally, there are the seventeen TEs that do not presently enjoy an EA or a formal regional free-trade format, although some countries do have bilateral FTAs with the EU and/or some of the TE-10. The impacts of enlargement on these economies depend on how the EU will accommodate existing FTAs of the entering TEs with outside partners. Nothing is as yet known about the EU's stance on accommodation. Judging by past performance, however, there is considerable likelihood that the accession negotiations will deal magnanimously with these issues. The economic costs to the EU would be negligible as compared to the substantial benefits to the TEs under discussion. And the political good will earned in the process could be substantial.

The Luxemburg Council recommendation in December 1997, as far as TE accessions are concerned, acting on elaborations of the European Commission (1997h), contained several suggestions on differentiating among the TEs while at the same time preserving the substantial negotiations with the TE-5. All candidates presently considered as such are united in the twice-a-year European Conference, of which the first was held on 12 March 1998; but it is uncertain what its future role will be; Turkey too was invited to the conference but spurned the offer for reasons examined in the final section. Next all candidates anointed for accession—Cyprus and the ten TEs with an EA—were convoked to the opening conference on 30 March 1998 for accession negotiations, which were inaugurated for the fast-track candidates on 31 March in bilateral intergovernmental negotiations. As detailed in chapter 10, these negotiations are structured over a protracted period of time into several phases. One involves "screening," in the first instance the thirty-one chapters of the *acquis*, between the European Commission and each of the candidates, but in the first instance, those on fast-track accession negotiations. The other involves "actual negotiations." These are conducted bilaterally at the intergovernmental level between those acting on behalf of the European Council and each of the fast-track accession candidates at the end of which, if the negotiations are successful, a draft accession treaty will be signed. The Commission as such is involved in these negotiations only as facilitator and honest broker.

All anointed candidates have been working out an APA, which sets forth in detail and in a dovetailed manner reciprocal commitments, including on financing from the EU, possibly together with pledged TE resources, between the Commission and each TE. For the fast-track TEs, these agreements focus on what the Commission considers to be required for these countries to fulfill at the earliest opportunity key preconditions for holding productive negotiations and what the candidate intends to implement with EU assistance. For other TEs, these agreements revolve essentially around meeting soonest the conditions that will permit the Commission to adjudicate positively the application for inaugurating accession negotiations.[20] Annual 'reviews' on progress for the end-year European Council will be drawn up. In the case of the second group of anointed candidates, if the Commission confirms that sufficient progress in the TE in question has been made, the country may be invited for fast-track negotiations too by the subsequent European Council. Especially Latvia, Lithuania, and in late 1998 also Slovakia had been hoping to be so designated, but in vain (European Commission, 1998i).

The recognition that the EU needs a strategy in dealing with the privileged TEs and the fact that the EU institutions are doing something concrete about it at the political level as well as in reshaping their assistance programs for selected TEs constitute considerable progress over the rather bland 'pre-accession strategy' put in place since the Essen Council of December 1994 (Brabant, 1996a, pp. 168ff.). In fact, this was at best a euphemism for the various types of EU involvement with the TEs in question—anything but a coherent, bold, and effective strategy designed to facilitate accession in the shortest period of time while buttressing policy efforts to climb onto the coveted catch-up growth path within each TE. Presumably such a more pragmatic, result-seeking strategy will now materialize in particular for the TE-5. It is as yet unclear what the EU will, in fact, undertake for other TEs with an EA, which have now a less privileged status. And not a word has as yet been said about its strategy regarding the seventeen other TEs.

The Impact of Enlargement on Other TEs

Abstracting from the daunting array of the cited unresolved matters, I deem it important to consider in addition to the TEs with an EA countries farther east of strategic significance to the EU as a regional organization bent on having an own CFSP. It is even more germane to members on the EU's present eastern borders (Austria and Germany in particular). It is, however, crucial to allocate these non-acceding TEs in two or three separate groups: those that in time may gain a credible accession status and other TEs, with the former group further divided into those that are likely to be credible candidates earlier than the rest. Among the former I include Albania and the other successor states of Yugoslavia (Bosnia and Herzegovina, Croatia, Macedonia, and rump Yugoslavia) and the western CIS members (possibly Belarus if it were to change its policies, Moldova, and Ukraine, but perhaps also Armenia and Georgia given their western Christian heritage).

It seems reasonable to assert that countries like Croatia and rump Yugoslavia are more likely to be of interest sooner to the EU as credible candidates for accession than the more remote and even less-settled successor states of the Soviet Union that may in a distant future wish to seek accession and be welcomed as such in Brussels (compare, for example, Moldova and Ukraine, both having already expressed their interest in eventually joining[21]). Albania and the successor states of Yugoslavia other than Slovenia—pending suitable socioeconomic restructuring, leading to a solid growth performance with a vibrant market economy and functioning democratic institutions, and the normalization of relations in the Balkans—presumably will wish to seek entry into the EU, and be allowed to do so after completion of the next wave(s) of enlargement. Whereas accession issues for these other TEs are moot at this stage, the EU will need to refashion its foreign-policy strategy in general and its preferential arrangements in particular as part and parcel of a much broader overhaul of its pillar 2, the foreign-policy component in particular. Accession of some TEs will elevate this into an even greater priority.

The obstacles to recovery and sustainable growth that the above-cited TEs face are quite different from those prevailing in the present candidates for EU entry (Brabant, 1998a) and they affect the debate on how to proceed with deepening and widening in the EU at best only on the margin, at least for now. To the extent that this mirrors the EU's stance, this approach might well be in error. Albania and the successor states of Yugoslavia (except Slovenia and perhaps Croatia) have an immediate need for reconstruction and basic development before they can hope to jump onto a desirable catch-up growth path, as well as for making headway with the rudiments of a coherent transformation agenda (notably stabilization, privatization, fiscal reform, governance issues, financial markets, and restructuring), albeit to greatly varying degrees. Their potential for being brought under the EU's umbrella as full partners is therefore more latent than in the case of the TEs with an EA. There is little doubt, however, that at some future point these countries too will, on present policy stances, hope to become credible candidates for entry, something that Brussels will find it hard to ignore. If only for that reason, the present and prospective concerns of these TEs as regards their EU relations deserve to be addressed not only by the TEs themselves but also by the EU, at least in refashioning its external-policy framework.

Indeed, EU enlargement toward the eastern part of Europe should form part and parcel of the broader remaking of Europe for which the political opening of 1989-1991 has offered an unprecedented opportunity, but confronted the western European leadership in particular also with an obligation. I am referring here to all TEs without exception. Yet, pursuing eastern enlargement only toward the first wave of TEs (essentially the present favored five) will not do, however much economic and organizational logic there may for this stance (see chapter 8). Even if the EU will eventually proceed with taking in the TE-10, it will still be in need of a home-grown strategy on how best to remake Europe and govern that space, including in reflecting upon how best to cater to its foreign-policy precepts. The

TEs farther east and south should figure prominently in that new conceptualization of the ultimate purposes of EU integration—the famously ill-defined *finalité politique*. It would be best to remain concerned about the process whereby the relationship between the EU and these other TEs can be streamlined into a constructive partnership for years to come. At least in commercial, environmental, human rights, transportation, security, social, and related matters the EU has fundamental interests at stake that cannot be ignored.[22]

In that perspective, it might be useful for the EU to think strategically about how best it can earmark available funds, even if only from within existing assistance budgets, to service the framework that it deems to be in its own long-term interest. I do not know what these goals precisely entail, of course. But I would conjecture that targeting assistance funds at expediting economic recovery in the area; establishing a democratic political culture with at least minimal respect for human rights; accelerating the sociopolitical and economic transformation processes, including the role of the state and of the public sector in economic affairs, in such a way that the countries will be able to deal constructively with the prospect of eventually dovetailing with the EU; and regaining sustainable economic growth with substantial structural change over the next several years must be integral components of any coherent foreign-policy strategy toward the TEs. In terms of economic development, these TEs are now even less capable than the present candidates for EU membership of engaging in open competition in the SEM, and of integrating themselves into the virtuous growth circle around vibrant IIT. That anchor is still largely absent. A priority therefore is to assemble programs that reduce the risk of peripheralization, which would be undesirable in itself and counterproductive for EU integration, let alone the obligation to remake Europe (see Brabant, 1996a, pp. 174ff.).

In rethinking its approach to Europe, reflecting its own long-term foreign-policy and commercial interests, the EU needs also to place the other TEs, certainly the larger and strategically located CIS states, including others than those that can be expected eventually to be credible candidates for EU accession. These countries are potentially of great importance for shaping the future relationship of the EU with Europe as a whole, given their economic and/or strategic importance. Whether or not they will eventually seek membership and be considered 'European' for EU purposes, while important, should not detract from configuring them integrally within the EU's broader foreign-policy strategy.[23] Some of these TEs, such as Russia and Ukraine, are large and potentially significant trading partners for the EU. Without exception, all have been benefiting from some types of EU assistance, notably via TACIS, a program that itself could usefully be overhauled and thoroughly streamlined.

Such a compact would, of course, be different in nature from the one that could usefully be entertained with respect to TEs farther east, just as it would be quite distinct from the pre-accession strategy I have advocated for the TE-10 (Brabant, 1996a, pp. 212ff.), which is only now being realized via the APAs. If there were to be any likelihood that some of the western successor states of the Soviet Union would eventually be chosen for accession negotiations, those countries could be dealt with separately from the other successor states that will not be so treated because they are not European or will not wish to seek membership for their own political reasons. Comprehensive trade and cooperation agreements are probably the most useful way of dealing with the core issues at stake in a first revamping of relations of these TEs with the EU. They would also seem to offer the preferred channel for assisting the most western members of the CIS over the next several years. Eventually, however, more substantial assistance, but not necessarily major financial transfers over and above present levels, may be required to check the decline in support for economic transformation. The latter could not but have repercussions on other reforms, notably in the political and strategic arenas.

Comprehensive, well-targeted assistance might well be warranted to ensure that the lukewarm transformations that have kept these countries on a trajectory of socioeconomic decline for all too long now will not further deteriorate and hollow out whatever penchant for pluralistic political democracy and market-based resource allocation might still be rescued and strengthened. At the very least, strenuous efforts are needed to overcome the prevailing state of indecisiveness, and in some TEs egregious amassing of property rights by borderline legal means, when not formally altogether illegal. Once such a recovery will be within reach, the scenario of moving toward the kinds of support programs just outlined for the Balkan countries, suitably interpreted, of course, could again be seriously contemplated.

In one way or another, then, all of these arrangements will involve working out to mutual satisfaction some degree of preferential access to the EU's market and to its financial resources, possibly at the explicit expense of other beneficiaries of preferential arrangements with the EU. Their impacts on EU members and present beneficiaries of the various preferential arrangements will need to be reconciled with the EU's cultural, economic, environmental, health, political, security, social, and other interests in formalizing relations with both TE groups. For those remaining outside the EU framework altogether or seeking entry only in a very remote future, the consequences for the present arrangements of the EU will naturally be less severe and daunting than those that may arise in fusing the other TEs into the EU framework as full members. Just the same, the EU can hardly afford to ignore the TEs, if only because it must safeguard its own manifold and diverse interests.

Enlargement, Third Countries, and the Fifteen

As pointed out on several occasions, the EU's eastward enlargement cannot but affect the competitive position also of the present EU members and indirectly that of other nonmember countries. Among the many effects that are likely to ensue in the short to medium run, four are pertinent in the present context. First of all, the new entrants will gain access to markets that up to now have been circumscribed for them as a result of open or more subtle forms of discrimination. The EU's common policies for agriculture and fisheries in particular, but also for transportation, offer examples. Some of the likely entrants, notably Hungary and Poland, are expected to become important competitors for a range of temperate agricultural products and for Poland also for some fishery products. This competitive strength is more likely to affect the sustainable market share for northern EU members as well as for outside competitors than for that of the countries with a more Mediterranean climate. Hungarian and Slovenian wines would, of course, enter too. But their quantities are not expected to exceed more than a marginal percentage of the vast EU wine market.

Second, new entrants will gain free access to markets of manufactures whose imports the EU has managed, including through contingent protectionism. This holds for a wide range of rather labor-intensive products such as footwear and clothing and textiles. But it applies equally to resource-intensive products, such as chemicals and products of the iron and steel industries. The first range of products is expected to compete directly with southern-tier exports, affecting the competitive position of the NIEs in particular. The other type of manufactures are more likely to aggravate chronic adjustment problems in heavy industry in the more northern EU members. Hence the EU's interest in encouraging through PHARE as an integral part of the APA approach 'appropriate' transformation of the TEs' iron and steel sectors already at this early stage of the accession negotiations.

As regards services, given the proximity of the favored TEs to core EU markets and their competitive edge in labor-intensive products, market shares are likely to be extended especially if prior to accession catch-up will have been under way for some time and thus the competitive edge of these TEs will have been further honed, moving it well beyond the advantage of low-cost labor. Some services now provided from within the EU can be expected to migrate toward TEs. Likewise, as mentioned earlier, the TEs are likely to gain from providing low-cost services in a range of labor-intensive transactions for some time to come. But the main loser is likely to be some ACP or Mediterranean partner.

Third, the core of financial markets in the EU is not very likely to shift measurably from where it is presently located and where it is likely to gravitate as monetary union takes hold after 1998: Frankfurt, London, and Paris. TE accession is not expected to make a dent in this development. But it might have effects on the margin, such as the relocation of financial services to the TEs rather than having them executed from headquarters or a regional head office. With catch-up growth crystallizing in the TEs, inward FDI will increasingly gravitate toward including acquired TE firms in the global corporate strategy of the parent company as a whole, rather than consist chiefly of setting up establishments in support of exports or for catering to the local market. That is likely to exert a negative impact on agglomerations of capital within the present EU, particularly if growth in the TEs were to remain strong for a protracted period of time. Whether it will have indirect effects on other competitors is unclear.

Finally, as noted earlier, the potential for competition in providing labor services in the broad sense is likely to emerge as the most central, sensitive as well as corrosive, source of disharmony between TE entrants and present EU members, and indeed exert significant repercussions for access to EU labor markets by residents of other nonmember countries. For the foreseeable future potential EU entrants will continue to offer fairly low-cost labor, even when adjusted for productivity differentials. These TEs have recently made significant gains in market shares with the EU on account of this advantage (Brabant, 1997; 1998b). With entry, and even the prospect thereof, they are likely to build further thereupon for it is bound to bolster the confidence of economic agents, both of the entrants and of outside investors. Given the already appalling levels of unemployment in the EU as well as resentment against non-EU nationals prospecting for jobs in the EU, the arena for disagreement is considerable. The problem can be expected to be exacerbated by labor embodied in products coming from TEs, though considerable migrant flows into the present EU are estimated to materialize and put pressure on some EU labor markets (Bauer and Zimmermann, 1997).

In this connection, it is important to bear in mind as objectively as possible what motivates foreign investors, for example. Although some surveys of foreign-investor motivation (see Meyer, 1995) suggest that low labor costs are not a critical determinant of global investment strategies for major TNCs desirous of expanding their activities into the eastern part of Europe, that assertion is not plausible at face value. After all, foreign investors in general and the TNCs in particular are motivated by profit and market shares, with the latter eventually being overtaken by long-term returns on assets, that is, sustainable profit levels. Since long-term returns to assets by definition depend on expectations with regard to the difference between the revenue and cost streams associated with the assets under consideration, and the effective cost of labor remains an important consideration especially for labor-intensive products, unit labor costs in new entrants must compete eventually with labor in EU-based producers that presently enjoy comparatively low unit labor costs. That is likely to be the case more for the southern tier than for the rest of the EU.

Furthermore, it should be clear that enlargement toward countries with low unit labor costs affects the entire scale of labor considerations in investment decisions and, thus in time, a rearrangement of operations is bound to occur. That cannot but exert pressure on high-cost labor, usually of the less skill-intensive kind, in the more developed EU members. Given the already high rate of unemployment for unskilled labor in particular, and the serious preoccupations of policy makers about the state of EU labor markets in recent years (see chapter 4), increased disharmony between new entrants and the 'core' EU members cannot be ruled out. The need for managing the changes that will eventually become associated with this portion of 'creative destruction' is obvious. Governing real economic processes in the EU is therefore even more urgent and complex. Finding pragmatic solutions to deepening EU integration as a result assumes new dimensions in structuring priorities among the problems to be tackled.

As pointed out earlier, the scope of the changes required in new entrants can be expected to vastly exceed what the present EU members should prepare themselves for. Nevertheless, changes on the margin rather than in relation to the overall economic setup tend to determine the intensity of and scope for disagreement if for some reason such change cannot be managed in an orderly manner. Resolving discords in the regional-governance compact of the EU, and indeed forestalling their emergence, should therefore command even more attention, and indeed preferably on a priority basis at this juncture, than has been the case since the clashes over the scope and intentions of the Maastricht Treaty erupted in the early 1990s (see chapter 2). In short, managing the new accessions cannot possibly be a trivial matter.

Enlargement and Other Partners—The Case of Turkey

One could, of course, speculate on implications of EU enlargement toward the TEs for countries not yet identified. I shall refrain from doing so and concentrate instead on the peculiar case of Turkey as an exemplar of that broader range of countries. I do realize that Turkey presents unique features of culture, history, ideology, and politics, as well as economics and social matters. Yet by singling it out for a more in-depth focus, I do not particularly want to draw attention to this anomaly in the EU's specific stance on this candidate or the bungling foreign-policy approach adopted most egregiously since the Luxemburg Council in December 1997 (Akagül, 1998). Rather, I consider Turkey's contorted EU relationship as symptomatic of what *may* happen when other TEs, especially those not presently included among the TE-10, in due course will knock at the EU's doors.

Turkey lodged its formal application for accession in 1987. But its intentions and designs on EU membership date back to 1963, when it tried to join the customs union but was rebuffed. At least, this earlier attempt to formally request accession was diplomatically shoved aside in exchange for associate status granted in 1963, which took effect in 1964 (Temprano-Arroyo and Feldman, 1998). Turkey obtained a commitment to working toward full membership in the then EEC customs union within two decades, but this got delayed several times, and a promise that a new request for full accession would be duly received with an appropriate response at a later date, so that the country would eventually be able to participate more fully in broader EU integration efforts.

In spite of this experience, Turkey was not even considered for inclusion in the fourth round of enlargement, which the EU-12 at the time sought assiduously to limit to the four EFTA applicants. Neither is Turkey included in the Council's list of those eligible for either fast- or slow-track accession negotiations at this juncture. The Luxemburg Council invited it to the European Conference and some EU members continue to stress Turkey's 'European vocation.' However, all these diplomatic contortions failed to assuage the feelings of Turkey's leadership. Instead, they only elicited a very vocal, angry as well as defiant, response from Ankara (Akagül, 1998).

Turkey has also pointedly been omitted in recent visions of the EU's future advanced by key policy makers in Europe, even though especially the French continue to emphasize the importance of Turkey's European vocation, hence its eventual eligibility for accession (France, 1998). This has constituted a change of heart, at least for some keen EU participants. For example, Jacques Chirac (1995) in his concept of Europe's future simply ignored Turkey. It was also glaringly, and quite noticeably, omitted from any potential list of EU members in the discussions around the preparation of IGC96 (Brabant, 1996a, pp. 49ff.). This is all the more curious in a sense, given that the EU and Turkey inaugurated their customs union in early 1996,[24] but with some transitional allowances for Turkey until 2001, after the protracted delays noted above. Yet, EU widening toward Cyprus cannot conceivably move forward without the collaboration of Turkey to defuse the tense situation on the island, to bring Greece and Turkey closer together, and to remove lingering tensions in the Aegean.

Instead of inviting Turkey to the negotiating table, the EU in its Luxemburg Council deliberations confined itself to recommending the elaboration of what it called a new "European strategy for Turkey." The proposal aims at strengthening Ankara's ties with Brussels by broadening its customs union with the EU, which has not yet been fully implemented, and increasing cooperation in industry, services, and agriculture. An integral part of this intention has been unlocking Greece's grip on the release of assistance money earlier agreed upon in the context of the customs union. In fact, the so-called European Conference, first convened on 12 March 1998, was a French invention essentially to accommodate Turkey diplomatically into the EU's European framework without bringing it up to par with even the lowest eligible TE candidate.

Turkey's reaction to this apparent snub has been very vocal, angry as well as defiant (Akagül, 1998), with full-scale designs on elaborating a coherent foreign policy that pointedly does not rely on the EU (RFE, 1998a). The heart of the matter revolves, from the EU's perspective, around human rights, democratization, market-economy building, and pluralistic political democracy. From Turkey's perspective, the major objection is that the EU wants to be a 'Christian club.' Quite apart from culture, ideology, foreign policy, religion, and so on, one cannot deny that there are very considerable economic, political, and social problems in fusing Turkey into the EU.

For starters, Turkey is a large as well as fairly poor, agricultural, and populous country. Assistance to bring it up to reasonable par with EU members would lay claim to considerable financial resources. Not only that, the country possesses a comparative advantage in a range of products that compete directly with Mediterranean products and low labor-cost manufactures of the EU's southern tier in particular, but also from the TEs. Furthermore, very sizable contingents of Turkish nationals live in EU countries, Germany in particular. Any loosening of migration restrictions would almost certainly unleash a substantial influx of unskilled labor from Turkey and a reunification of extended families for Turkish nationals residing in the EU. Turkey's progress toward a functioning market economy, while remarkable at some stages of its more recent development, has in the past few years been sluggish at best. The economy is neither stable nor prospering. It could hardly qualify for inclusion in anything like the ERM II for years to come. That said, however, I find it equally difficult to gather sympathy for the EU's implicit position, such as maintaining that, on truly objective grounds, the second-tier TEs are more ready for accession than Turkey.

The point I am trying to make here is that many of the problems burdening the EU-Turkish relationship are comparable to those weighing in heavily on arguing the case for or against the EU's eastward expansion. The only difference perhaps is that several core EU members, with Germany in the lead, were for some time keen on extending the EU formally toward that part of eastern Europe of particular interest to them; central Europe, of course, figures most prominently here.[25] More recently, however, under domestic electoral pressures, there has been a marked cooling in the ardor with which the "front states"—Austria and Germany in the first place—but also France have been advocating enlargement. I doubt that the same interest and commitment exist with respect to the other TEs, especially those that are presently bent on joining the EU or have already expressed an interest in doing so in the foreseeable future. If so, Turkey's experiences in EU matters may be helpful in coming to terms with the EU's relationship with these other TEs. It would be a pity, however, if the EU's response were simply to extend its contorted relationship with Turkey to those countries. Instead of letting evaporate the unique chance for remaking Europe, the EU would do better in actively propping up the elaboration, implementation, regular assessment, and fine-tuning of a coherent strategy with respect to these TEs, and to configure all this with as much magnanimity and foresight as possible. A genuine new, strategic approach toward Turkey might also be desirable. But that matter falls outside this chapter's compass.

Conclusions

This political-economy excursion has underlined that eventual accession of TEs to the EU presents a number of economic challenges as well as a host of other problems. This holds not only for the present EU members and the favored TEs, for whom daunting questions of distributing the costs and benefits over the membership and entrants, as well as over time, remain to be resolved. Possibly even larger problems may be entailed by the accession of the fast-track negotiators for other TEs, regardless of their preferential status in the EU. These issues are especially cumbersome for those bent on the sixth enlargement or beyond; the other countries with preferential arrangements in the EU that will see their preferences erode, notably the ACP and Mediterranean countries, and a range of other countries, including the NIEs that find adjustment to foreign competition not all that easy to engineer for institutional, policy, and other reasons.

In other words, it might be useful for the EU to contemplate these issues with a much more open mind than it has displayed to date, but within the context of a thorough reconceptualization of its various preferential arrangements in the years to come. That in itself should be fully cast within the remit of the EU's new foreign-policy framework, which must therefore be more solidly anchored than has been the case to date. A strategic approach modulating the EU's varying interests in these countries might be preferred. Except for a commitment to developing accession strategies for the fast-track TEs, and perhaps for the other privileged TEs, though matters are certainly not as clear here, and Cyprus, no such coherent revamping of the EU's external architecture seems as yet to be on the drawing boards. This is a pity. The governance issues at stake are perhaps less daunting than those in need of urgent resolution in order to reconcile widening with deepening, and blend the two needed approaches to European integration in an orderly manner. They are no less acute, however.

Notes

This chapter is a much expanded and updated redraft of Brabant, 1998d.

1. Of course, the main implications of another EU enlargement for present members are likely to be far more important in clarifying the actual and potential conflicts that are bound to weigh on accession negotiations and any transition regimes that might become necessary for orderly accession to occur at all. These matters fall outside the scope of the present contribution, however (see chapter 8).

2. Many alternative 'views' exist on how best to classify these various regional trading agreements. For a recent overview in different categories, see Sapir, 1998.

3. Thus one could legitimately specify a separate southeast European approach, with reference to the Balkan countries other than Turkey that are not in the process of negotiating accession (such as Slovenia), do not have an EA (such as Bulgaria and Romania), or are already an EU member (Greece). I shall not do so if only because that approach focuses more specifically on settling the affairs of the former Yugoslavia, other than Slovenia. For a useful roundup, see Lopandic, 1998.

4. This was earlier known as the Yaoundé Convention for the city where the premier agreement between the then EEC and some forty-six ACP countries was first signed in 1963 and renewed in 1969, after which the Lomé Conventions came into existence

(European Commission, 1998c).

5. For details with an historic overview, see McQueen, 1998; Wolf, 1997.

6. There are presently eight such countries: Afghanistan, Bangladesh, Bhutan, Cambodia, Laos, Maldives, Nepal, and Yemen; Myanmar would have benefited from the same arrangement as well, but it has not been included because of its unacceptable human-rights record. For details, see McQueen, 1998, pp. 427ff.

7. Views on the merits of Lomé IV, hence on what should be done with any successor regime, vary widely (see Pangeti, 1997).

8. This has been invoked especially in the context of upgrading the development chances of small-island developing countries. However, the notion is by no means confined to disaster alleviation. But other connotations, such as operationally measuring economic, ecological, and natural vulnerability, have remained ill-defined in remolding development-assistance programs.

9. Michel Rocard, former French prime minister and chairman of the committee dealing with development cooperation in the European Parliament, has recently made this abundantly clear (UNCTAD, 1998).

10. Morocco suddenly applied for full accession in 1988, but was turned down on the ground that it was not a European country (art. 237 of the Rome Treaty).

11. Recall from chapter 2 that the EU at that meeting also endorsed the formulation of a pre-accession strategy for TEs, thus underlining the importance of maintaining balance between 'southern' and 'eastern' interests (see Gautron, 1996, p. 315; Velo, 1996) among the then twelve members.

12. But this was termed a 'modernization' of an already existing agreement.

13. Conflicts over implementation of these two agreements continue because of Israel's insistence that products from the occupied territories be labeled 'Israeli' and its reluctance to recognize the agreement with the Palestinian Authority (see *Foreign Report*, 15 October 1998).

14. That conflict continues to burden dialogue between the EU and the Partnership members (Algeria, Egypt, Israel, Jordan, Lebanon, Morocco, Palestinian Authority, Syria, Tunisia, and Turkey) as well as some of the successor states of Yugoslavia other than Slovenia (Nsouli, Bisat, and Kanaan, 1996); Cyprus and Malta were the other two members of the group included in the Barcelona Declaration, but because of their request for EU accession they were treated separately. For anecdotal evidence, see *Financial Times*, 15 December 1997, p. 5.

15. Apparently negotiations between the EU and Croatia for its EA are well along in technical matters. Croatia confidently claimed that the EA would be signed before the end of 1998 (*Croatia Weekly*, 17 July 1998, p. 5), but this did not occur.

16. As noted in chapter 3, this label referred explicitly to Hungary and Poland because this program was originally conceived solely in support of the transitions in those TEs in 1989. It was subsequently extended to the cited twelve TEs.

17. In both the static and dynamic versions, of course. The first refers to actual substitution of low-cost non-EU supplier for EU supplier; the latter to growing trade with EU partners although the lowest-cost supplier is a non-EU partner.

18. For a review of the literature with estimates applicable mainly to Germany, see Bauer and Zimmermann, 1997.

19. Reform of the CAP is imminent over the next several years for two reasons. One is budgetary pressures within the EU itself. The other is commitments made during the

Uruguay Round to revisit agricultural protectionism as well as other matters in the context of the WTO and to initiate concrete negotiations before the end of 1999.

20. Recall that the European Commission (1997h, part II) in mid-1997 tabled its so-called *avis* to the Council on suitability of the candidates for eventually acceding to the EU. In its report on each candidate the Commission set forth various shortcomings that prevented a candidate from being endorsed for accession negotiations or, for those invited, matters that deserve priority attention in order to expedite accession negotiations and successfully conclude them in the foreseeable future (see chapter 3).

21. Whereas both have expressed their general interest on several occasions, Ukraine on 9 June 1998 reportedly requested associate status in order to pave the way for full-fledged accession negotiations (*RFE/RL Newsline*, Vol. 2, No. 110, part II, 10 June 1998, p. 2). Not surprisingly, Commissioner Hans van den Broek, who is entrusted with ironing out relations with TEs, is quoted to have replied that "in the medium term Ukraine will arrive at that point which in our view, at the present time, it has not arrived at yet." While the EU may try to defuse these claims in such a cavalier, and awkwardly phrased, manner, it cannot continue to ignore the need for formulating its own strategic approach to countries such as Ukraine.

22. In fact, in certain positions taken by leading political parties, such as the CDU/CSU in Germany, extension toward the eastern part of Europe and avoiding the emergence of a vacuum in the area by maintaining a constructive relationship with other TEs, notably the other successor states of the Soviet Union, figure among the core tasks of shaping the EU's future (see, for example, Biedenkopf, 1995; Lamers and Schäuble,1995; Mayer, 1997).

23. Most CIS states will never qualify for membership because they are not European or for their own economic, political, and security reasons do not contemplate pursuing such a démarche. Note that just about all of these countries benefit from preferential arrangements with the EU, or soon will upon ratification of their PCAs or trade and cooperation agreements, or activation of their trade part.

24. On the potential benefits of the customs union, see Harrison, Rutherford, and Tarr, 1997; Mercenier and Yeldan, 1997.

25. With the change in government in October 1998, the ardor with which eastward enlargement is being sought in Germany appears to have markedly shrunk. Some observers (as reported in RFE, 1998b) even associate the new government with the Belgian, French, and Italian position on enlargement (see chapter 4).

Chapter 10

Conclusion: Toward Membership

Jozef M. van Brabant

It is by now all but crystal clear that some TEs will at some point in the future become full EU members. This will in all likelihood occur after a protracted transition period following formal entry to enable the new members to comply in full with the obligations of the *acquis* that they cannot meet immediately or even in the medium run. The transitional arrangements will set firm deadlines, perhaps spread over several phases, to ensure that the entrants will in time abide fully, not only in law but in actual practice, with major stipulations, such as on the environment, health, and labor, of the *acquis* for which they are deficient at this stage of their structural transformation. Without such derogations membership could occur only far into the future.

Formal entry will be preceded by accession negotiations that are proving to be protracted, difficult, and complex. Also other reforms, such as with regard to the institutions, to deepening, to budgetary priorities, and to the CAP, in the EU will be required before the TEs can realistically envision formal entry. Finally, all of these draft agreements need to be vetted through the EU institutions and the political processes of the member states. Only then emerge agreements that can be approved. Once the latter are signed, they need to be submitted for ratification to the parliamentary, and in some cases the political (such as through referenda), procedures in place in each member state. Also the potential entrant will have to ratify the accession treaty in accordance with its own parliamentary or related administrative and political procedures.

When accession will be consummated; which TEs will enter first and which next, perhaps spread over several waves; the concrete path for negotiations ahead; and under which modalities transition phases will be granted are all outstanding questions. For now answers can be formulated only by postulating various political scenarios and conjecturing about alternative outcomes. In proceeding thus the analyst must hedge pronouncements against all too many contingencies, no matter the rather high degree of discomfort this implies, including for the reader. In fact, only on the negotiation path is there some clarity.

By way of conclusion I set forth below the details about what is likely to happen over the next twelve months or so, say, until mid-2000, and spell out conjectures on what *may* crystallize thereafter. But on the latter issues I must speculate with considerable trepidation, if only because I can at best air my feelings and views, perhaps even prejudices, regarding the nature of the answers to be provided to the other accession questions enumerated above.

Prelude to Opening Accession Negotiations

In several of the preceding chapters, 2 and 9 in particular, I set forth some of the details as regards the cumbersome path traced from the moment the transitions broke in the eastern part of Europe, and the "return to Europe" wish was etched, until the Luxemburg Council in December 1997 acted upon the Commission's recommendation to open up accession negotiations with only five of the TE candidates—the TE-5—and Cyprus, but the latter I shall mostly disregard in what follows. As it turned out, for political reasons the Council, in fact, decided to open up 'negotiations' with the TE-10 but to divide the group into two with the TE-5 candidates being placed on fast-track accession negotiations and the other five being requested to persevere with their economic transformation and, especially in the case of Slovakia, to improve also their political record; in many instances, these matters should be taken care of on an accelerated basis.

Once a year, the Commission prepares the so-called *regular reports*. These are sort of updates of the *avis* tabled in mid-1997, in which the Commission gave its views on the suitability of each candidate for initiating accession negotiations and ability to comply in the medium run with the economic and political conditions for entry into the EU. There is a major exception, however: in the reports the Commission evaluates each candidate's performance in terms of its recommendations for further economic and political changes that it deems necessary in order for the candidate to move eventually to accession and entry in a credible manner (see chapter 3). These may be formulated against the backdrop of the assessments first made in the *avis*. But new issues can be taken up as well if circumstances warrant it. If any of the slow-track countries is adjudicated to have made sufficient progress with its economic and/or political adjustments, the Commission may recommend to the next Council that the country in question be graduated to fast-track negotiation status.

In its reports for 1998 (European Commission, 1998i), the Commission aired favorable assessments of the economic progress achieved by Latvia and Lithuania, and of the economic and especially the political changes, following elections in fall 1998, sustained by Slovakia. It suggested, however, that none be elevated for fast-track negotiations but that Latvia could possibly be upgraded in late 1999, provided it booked further progress with its economic transformation. If this were to materialize and the Council in late 1999 were to approve the Commission's recommendation, fast-track negotiations could then commence in 2000 at the earliest. Nothing was said about a date for graduating Lithuania and Slovakia, however. Nonetheless, EU policy makers are feeling the political pressures militating for ushering also these countries onto the fast-track negotiation path in the near term, all the more so since Malta will now (European Commission, 1999d) in all likelihood be elevated to fast-track status before the end of 1999. This would leave only Bulgaria and Romania on slow-track negotiations, with Bulgaria having a better chance of passing the hurdles in the medium term.

The difference between fast- and slow-track negotiations is considerable. All TE-10 are included in the review of the *acquis* and coaxed into accepting the Commission's recommendations for applying appropriate institutional, legal, and other adjustments. These 'negotiations' of a sort were inaugurated simultaneously on 27 April 1998. However, this screening process is done in much greater detail for the TE-5 than for the other candidates. The outcomes are accordingly expected by all TE-5 involved to be binding in a sense and thus soon to lead to negotiations about a draft accession treaty. The broad multilateral overview of the *acquis* for all candidates, including those on slow track, was apparently concluded before the end of 1998 (European Commission, 1999c); bilateral negotiations are set to start on 1 March 1999 (O'Rourke, 1999b). In what follows I focus primarily on the situation for the TE-5.

Accession Negotiations—Screening

Organizationally, accession negotiations consist of "screening" and actual "negotiations" at the political level. Note that these activities differ from "preparing" the TEs for accession such as through the various assistance programs, the pre-accession strategy, and notably the APAs first worked out and approved in March 1998. These preparations are solely between the Commission and the candidates, with overall steering by the Council of Ministers, of course.

Recall from chapter 9 that the Luxemburg Council's decision to open up accession negotiations in 1999 actually had several facets. One was the institution of the European Conference, largely to accommodate Turkey, but it declined the invitation (see chapter 9), held for the first time on 12 March 1998. The other was the simultaneous opening of accession negotiations with eleven candidates (TE-10 plus Cyprus) on 30 March 1998 and the inception of fast-track negotiations with TE-5 and Cyprus on 31 March 1998 in bilateral intergovernmental fora.

Though the process of preparing for accession was formally started with "negotiations" at the political level, the original idea was first to pass through the long process of screening the entire *acquis* to be followed thereafter by negotiations about derogations. The latter are conducted at the bilateral political level and hence aim at working out the real nitty-gritty of the accession instruments. But because screening would take a long time, perhaps until late 1999, the candidates were pining for 'good faith' signs from Brussels. Because of the resulting pressures brought to bear on EU members to actually show results and progress with these politically and diplomatically sensitive negotiations, it was soon decided to slice up the various chapters of the *acquis* into several groups. For each, first screening is conducted and soon thereafter actual political negotiations follow. The latter's purview may well be cumulative in the sense that if the items screened cannot be finalized in the subsequent negotiation session, possibly only for some candidates, the leftover matter(s) will be carried into the next or, if more time for compliance is required, into a later round for that particular candidate.

Screening is an exercise between the European Commission and each of the candidates. It consists of explaining to all candidates on a multilateral basis the details of each of the thirty-one chapters of the *acquis*, which is then followed by bilateral sessions in which each candidate furnishes the Commission with evidence that it can comply with that part of the *acquis* or that it will apply for a derogation. But the latter becomes solely the subject of the real negotiations. Screening means literally that the Commission staff assesses the degree to which each candidate can abide by each part of the *acquis* or will need, and in the Commission's approach may deserve, a derogation. If so, it will accordingly formulate its recommendations to the Council for political negotiations at the intergovernmental level.

It is estimated that for each chapter of the *acquis* screening will take on average seven working days: one for the multilateral presentation and one day each for bilateral sessions with each candidate (including Cyprus). During the multilateral session the Commission sets forth its views on that part of the *acquis*. The bilateral sessions focus, then, on how the candidate lives up to or expects to be able to live up to these aspects of the *acquis* prior to entry, and whether it requests derogations, which the Commission may or may not take to heart (European Commission, 1998j). The bilateral sessions are held sequentially so that one should count with the need of some 217 working days, or nearly forty-four weeks in full, for screening. This means essentially well over a year of work, taking into account holidays, especially the summer pause typical of European institutions, and the other processes of integration, including preparing recommendations for and acting upon feedback from the Council.

Well in advance of the screening, the candidates are expected to table their views on the extent to which they can comply with the obligations of the *acquis*, the credible commitment they can make by way of complying in time with these regulations, or components for which they believe they need and deserve a derogation. To the degree that, in the Commission's view, a candidate cannot live up to the obligations of the *acquis*, derogations may have to be negotiated or the candidate will be urged to comply soonest with the regulations in place by making further progress with its structural transformation. As a rule, there can be no permanent derogations from the *acquis*, so the negotiations involve haggling over the precise character of the deviations, remedial policies to be adopted individually or with support from Brussels, and time frames for assuming the full *acquis*.

Because of the political pressure exerted by the TE-5 in particular, especially once it became clear how cumbersome and time consuming screening would be, in the fall of 1998 it was decided to conclude a first round of screening, which had then been completed for seven areas (science and research, telecommunications and information technologies, education and training, culture and audiovisual policy, industrial policy, small- and medium-size enterprises, and the common foreign and security policy) and to move to negotiations (as detailed next).

At the same time, a second round of screening was initiated or continued for chapters on which deliberations had already earlier commenced. These chapters are in particular: company law, consumer protection, fisheries, statistics, free movement of goods, external relations, customs union, and competition policy (European Commission, 1999b).

By late 1998, about one-fourth of the thirty-one chapters of the *acquis* had been 'screened' for the fast-track accession candidates. Since political negotiations in mid-1999 focus on less than half of the chapters, there will in all likelihood be several, at least two, more rounds before the process will be concluded. Although it had been hoped originally to terminate screening sometime in mid-1999, that calendar has been slipping and will need to be stretched out until the end of 1999, with negotiations about the final chapters of the screened *acquis* sometime in 2000, or even later, for a round of negotiations does not mean that agreement will be reached, as detailed in the next section.

Accession Negotiations—Derogations

As indicated, political negotiations are conducted by a group of negotiators acting on behalf of the European Council with the candidates at the bilateral intergovernmental level. This is so because enlargement is one of the decisions falling within the prerogatives of intergovernmentalism for two reasons. One is that pillar 2 and 3 matters can be decided only at that level. Furthermore, although the European Commission is responsible for pillar 1 and its extensions, enlarging the EU involves a host of political deals that can be approved only while maintaining the veto as a sovereign right of the member states. The Council's negotiating position must therefore be endorsed unanimously. It will then provide the negotiating mandate to which its negotiating team, which is drawn from its General Secretariat, needs to adhere. Several rounds may be required to provide a platform around which agreement can be hammered out. In all this, the Commission proposes solutions to the Council on matters for which it is responsible and otherwise it acts only as honest broker in these deliberations (Preston, 1997).

In fact, the Commission's role is essentially to propose common negotiating positions for the EU for each chapter relating to matters fully within its constitutional competence, including the items that the Amsterdam Treaty entrusted to the Commission (which are not yet part of pillar 1 because the new TEU has not yet been endorsed by all EU members, as noted below). The Council Presidency, in close liaison with member states and the Commission, makes proposals for such positions on the chapters concerning pillars 2 and 3 on which all members have to agree in full for negotiations to proceed with any chance of success. Negotiations are actually coordinated by the General Secretariat of the Council of Ministers and each of the applicants. Once the screening process has been concluded for all candidates on some components of the *acquis*, bilateral negotiations at the political level are conducted to examine the need and justification for derogations or to ensure that further work be done by the Commission or that the candidate engages in supplementary upgrading for the contested items.

The negotiations focus on the terms under which the applicants will adopt, implement, and enforce the *acquis*. In principle all regulations on the books have to be adopted in their entirety. Since this is not always feasible, for pragmatic reasons, therefore, the negotiations are essentially about granting possible transitional arrangements, which "must be limited in scope and duration" (European Commission, 1999a).

As explained earlier under the heading of screening, the originally envisaged mode of conducting the negotiations had to be revamped under pressure from the TE-5 in particular. Politics dictated that some matters be 'concluded' earlier than finalization of 'screening' would have permitted. Following the change in the original modus of procedure in mid-1998, when it became clear that screening would take more time than had originally been anticipated, the first negotiations were held on 10 November 1998. In truth, these involved political negotiations of a sort (see below) on some of the 'easiest' chapters of the *acquis* (OA, 1998), which were 'concluded' for most candidates without too many problems as regards embedding the rules in national laws. But major obstacles are nonetheless deemed to reside in implementation, including enforcement, in spite of otherwise thoroughly optimistic assessments (European Commission, 1999c).

Note that a host of terms used in the relations between the EU and the candidates for accession are heavily loaded, and thus carry rather unusual meanings. The negotiations of 10 November 1998 essentially consisted of ninety-minute sessions—nine hours in all!—for each candidate during which the Council of Ministers, acting on the recommendations of its negotiators, essentially instructed the fast-track candidates on what they must do in order to comply with the chapters under discussion. Apparently no derogations were granted.

Though the 10 November 'negotiations' covered seven chapters of the *acquis*, agreement was reached with each applicant only on at least three chapters, dealing with generally noncontroversial issues such as education and training policies, science and research policies, and small and medium-size enterprises. Agreement was not reached on telecommunications and information technologies, culture and audiovisual policy, industrial policy, and the common foreign and security policy. In some cases, matters were deferred until future negotiations. In others the Commission was urged to reexamine its recommended positions. And for a third group one or more TEs were requested to implement further changes on their own strength, but possibly with PHARE and/or other APA assistance.

The next round of negotiations is slated for the second quarter of 1999 (19 April and 19 May) to be followed by a full ministerial on 22 June 1999, just prior to the regular mid-year European Council. These sessions will address slightly more difficult stipulations of the *acquis*, but do not yet engage the chapters that can be expected to be really troublesome. These include agriculture, regional assistance, and social spending (O'Rourke, 1999a). The topics slated for June 1999 are, in addition to those left over from November 1998, company law, consumer protection, fisheries, statistics, free movement of goods, external relations, customs union, and competition policy (European Commission, 1999b). It is already evident that several of those domains, such as free movement of goods, consumer protection, and fisheries, are likely to pose problems.

Perhaps a third series will be held before the end of the year on topics yet to be decided, pending the evolution of the screening exercises. At that point, the European Council has committed itself to perhaps becoming more concrete about the likely entry date of the fast-track negotiating candidates.

Possibly only toward the end of 1999 or perhaps even in the year 2000, the 'screening' of all chapters will be concluded and so the really difficult chapters of the *acquis* will be ready for the hard-core accession negotiations to be embarked upon soon thereafter. Nobody knows at this stage how long these exchanges will take as everything depends on the degree to which time-limited exemptions from the *acquis* will have to be allowed for and the transition phases for catch-up. Current expectations (or is it just plain political hope?) are that around the end of 1999 it will be possible for the EU to set a tentative entry date for the fast-track accession candidates.

Once the member states agree on a common negotiating platform and a reasonable arrangement is worked out with the applicant, the results of the negotiations are incorporated in a draft accession treaty. This is submitted to the European Council for approval and to the European Parliament for assent. Once signed by all concerned, the accession treaty is submitted to the member states and to the applicant country for ratification involving, in some cases, referenda. It takes effect, and the applicant becomes a member state, on the date of accession (European Commission, 1999a).

The First Entrants

Since negotiations were first started on the fast track with the TE-5 and Cyprus, it would be entirely natural to hazard the guess that the first entrants should come from among those six countries. But this logic does not necessarily hold for several reasons. Perhaps most compelling has been the agitation on the part of policy makers in TEs and in the EU, which has received added impetus since late 1998, to upgrade the other five TEs to fast-track negotiation status at the earliest opportunity.

Coming in late for actual screening might by its very nature seem to be a veritable handicap. But the Commission maintains that the modi operandi in place, including the simultaneous screening of the TE candidates that are not among the TE-5, albeit at the multilateral level, will actually permit rapid catch-up. Indeed, for these countries the *avis* of 1997 still stand, the annual reports specify areas in which progress has been made as distinct from others where there has been backtracking or slow progress, and they have all become more familiar with the obligations of the *acquis*.

While all this sounds eminently sensible, there are at least two reasons for concern. One is that the pre-accession assistance for the TE-5 is palpably larger than for the other TEs. The other is that the real nitty-gritty of the *acquis*, hence the formulation of negotiation strategies on the part of these TEs, has to date been much more superficial than for the TE-5. That is, while rapid catch-up cannot be precluded, it would be miraculous if enlarging the range of fast-track candidates were not to slow down the accession process for the TE-5 or those deemed to be most advanced in their quest for complying with the EU's regulations.

The expectation is that by late 1999 at least Latvia, in view of its very positive appraisal in the 1998 review exercise (European Commission, 1998i), will be graduated to fast-track status. It stands to reason that at that point, or soon thereafter, Lithuania and Slovakia will be brought on board as well, if only to circumvent the problems of the BFTA and of the Czech-Slovak customs union that would arise otherwise; but Bulgaria and Romania in the CEFTA, if left out, will continue to pose problems for all concerned.

I have the feeling that those two TEs will probably also be brought to fast-track status, if not in 1999 then soon thereafter provided they can book progress with their economic restructuring and Romania can in addition reach once again, and prop it up, a minimum degree of political stability in a more predictable, anchored manner than it has succeeded in doing these past years. If this forecast were to be borne out, one would be back to the position advocated by several EU partners in the earlier drawn-out debate on which TEs to invite for fast-track accession. In the end, all ten TEs will be involved and they will probably be brought into the EU at approximately the same time.

The Likely Date of Entry

When effective entry will come to pass is anybody's guess at this stage for it depends not only on satisfactorily concluding the accession negotiations, but also on whether and when the present EU can iron out its own differences, including with respect to other candidates—Cyprus, Malta, and Turkey in the first instance. There are presently many. As a leftover from IGC96, institutional reform will have to be worked out before new entrants can be admitted, as per the explicit stance taken by Belgium, France, and Italy; but other EU members probably share their view. Likewise a thorough overhaul of the EU's budget procedures will be required, not only as concerns expenditures to accommodate new members but also with regard to receipts, given the stance taken notably by the new German government under Gerhard Schröder (James, 1999).

But several procedural steps need to be completed before formal entry of the candidates can occur. These include conclusion of draft accession treaties, the latter's vetting through the institutions and by the policy makers in place to transform them into accession treaties that can be signed, and ratification of the signed treaties by the present EU member states and the candidates according to their own national legislative or parliamentary procedures.

This is not the end of the environment within which enlargement toward the TE will have to proceed, however. Greece for one has been adamant that no further enlargement can be contemplated without Cyprus being admitted as well. That, in fact, requires first thrashing out a political solution for the division of Cyprus, something that has eluded international diplomatic efforts for a quarter century. A satisfactory compromise can be attained only by accommodating Turkey, at least as far as Cyprus is concerned. But in all likelihood it will require bringing Turkey back to the stage where "its European vocation" means it will be anointed as a credible candidate for accession.

Most of the above hindrances suggest that arguably the most important ingredient in engineering yet another EU enlargement will be mobilizing political will, indeed goodwill, notably on the part of the present EU members. Whereas the EU's further enlargement must necessarily remain a matter of high politics, indeed a highly politicized decision, the latter does not solely depend on simply mustering sufficient political will. Similarly, the candidates must display a good deal of political will to engage themselves fully for this venture. And this includes sufficient commitment to bear sizable costs up front with a payoff forthcoming at best much later. They must also assiduously work toward mastering the technical competence to work constructively within the framework of the EU as a highly developed policy club and to do so in quite a short period of time.

In other words, while there are no strict bans on TE accession to the EU, there are serious reservations, especially on the part of the EU policy makers, on enlarging the EU early in the next century. These should be of serious concerns also on the part of TE policy makers so that they engage themselves fully in the accession exercise, eventually permitting a blissful marriage.

It has become abundantly clear, however, that bandying 2000 as the magical year for entry by French (such as Jacques Chirac) and German (such as Helmut Kohl) politicians in a not-so-distant past was shamelessly politically motivated. The European Commission in its budget proposals has set the end of 2002 as the magic mark. But that deadline too has been slipping very rapidly. More realistic targets now being whispered about in the Commission focus on 2005 or even later.

The later date now appears increasingly to be the more likely one. Realistically one should reckon with at least two more years of screening and negotiating, and at least double that if the other TEs are brought on board for fast-track negotiations—one year for ushering the drafts through the EU's institutional organs and two years and perhaps longer for ratification, especially by the present EU members. In other words, at least another five years until formal entry can realistically occur. But even that deadline hinges on whether the EU can book real progress with the other 'urgent' matters on its policy agenda. Even under favorable circumstances, that will probably delay the accession process by another two to three years.

Recall in this connection that any further change to the Amsterdam version of the TEU (such as the institutional modifications that will ensue from any new IGC) will require ratification by each EU member according to its habitual procedures; in some cases that may be possible only after appropriate popular consultations have been successfully concluded—a time-consuming process in and of itself. And it might be worth reminding ourselves that at this stage, nearly two years after it was first agreed upon, that treaty has not yet been ratified by all EU members, and is thus not yet in force.

So entry would seem to be feasible only later in the first decade of the next century. If this were to be borne out, it would only confirm the assessment I made in 1996 (Brabant, 1996, pp. 203-9) to the effect that entry of even the best prepared TE, that is the wealthiest and most advanced with its transformation policies, is more likely to occur toward the second half of the first decade of the twenty-first century than around the turn of the millennium. Given present deliberations, that now seems perhaps an optimistic scenario. One might possibly have to begin to reckon with 2010 and later, and even then there will have to be a transition period if only because 'person mobility' for TEs may strain the social fabric in core EU 'front states.'

Bibliography

Abd-el-Rahman, Kamal (1991), "Firms' competitive and national comparative advantages as joint determinants of trade composition," *Weltwirtschaftliches Archiv*, Vol. 127, No. 1, 83-97.

Abraham, Filip (1994), "Social protection and regional convergence in a European monetary union," *Open Economies Review*, Vol. 4, No. 1, 89-114.

Addison, John T. and W. Stanley Siebert (1993), "The EC social charter: the nature of the beast," *National Westminster Quarterly Review*, No. 1, 13-28.

Aiginger, Karl, Rudolf Winter-Ebmer, and Josef Zweimüller (1995), "Der Einfluß der Ostöffnung auf Industrielöhne und Beschäftigung," *Wirtschaftspolitische Blätter*, Vol. 42, No. 2, 399-408.

Akagül, Deniz (1998), "Le cinquième élargissement de l'Union européenne et la question de la candidature turque," *Revue du Marché Commun et de l'Union Européenne*, No. 419, 359-69.

Akder, A. Halis (1992), "The single market and commercial relations for non-member countries: views from developing countries with preferential arrangements with the EC—the Mediterranean countries," *Journal of Development Planning*, No. 21, 179-93.

Altmann, Franz-Lothar, Wladimir Andreff, and Gerhard Fink (1995), "Die zukünftige Erweiterung der Europäischen Union in Mittelosteuropa," *Südost-Europa*, Vol. 44, No. 5, 235-58.

Ambrus-Lakatos, Lorand and Mark E. Schaffer, eds. (1996), *Coming to terms with accession*. London: CEPR.

Amin, Ash and John Tomaney, eds. (1995), *Behind the myth of European Union —prospects for cohesion*. London and New York: Routledge.

Andreff, Madeleine and Wladimir Andreff (1997), "L'investissement direct étranger en Russie et dans les pays de la Communauté des états indépendants: emploi et attractivité," in *Commerce nord-sud, migration et délocalisation: conséquences pour les salaires et l'emploi*, edited by Jaime de Melo and Patrick Guillaumont. Paris:

221

Economica, pp. 363-92.

Andreff, Madeleine and Wladimir Andreff (1998), "Some macroeconomic determinants of foreign direct investment facing Russia and CIS countries' attractiveness," in *Foreign direct investment in transforming economies*, edited by Wladimir Andreff and Xavier Richet. Cheltenham: Edward Elgar. Forthcoming.

Andreff, Wadimir (1992), "Convergence or congruence between eastern and western economic systems," in *Convergence and system change—the convergence hypothesis in the light of transition in eastern Europe*, edited by Bruno Dallago, Horst Brezinski, and Wladimir Andreff. Dartmouth, VT and Aldershot: Edward Elgar, pp. 47-85.

Andreff, Wladimir (1994a), "Quand la stabilisation dure...—l'hypothèse d'une inflation inertielle en Europe centrale et orientale," *Revue Économique*, Vol. 45, No. 3, 819-31.

Andreff, Wladimir (1994b), "East European privatization assessed from west European experience," *Emergo: Journal of Transforming Economies and Societies*, Vol. 1, No. 1, 21-33.

Andreff, Wladimir, ed. (1995), *Le secteur public à l'est—restructuration industrielle et financière*. Paris: L'Harmattan.

Andreff, Wladimir (1996), "Corporate governance of privatized enterprises in transforming economies: a theoretical approach," *MOCT-MOST*, Vol. 6, No. 2, 59-80.

Andreff, Wladimir (1997a), "Pays de l'est et Union européenne: convergence ou congruence?" in *Convergence et diversité—l'heure de la mondialisation*, edited by Jean-Pierre Faugère et al. Paris: Economica, pp. 229-40.

Andreff, Wladimir (1997b), "Science and technology and the future of economies in transition: an economic perspective," in *Transforming science and technology systems— the endless transition?*, edited by Werner Meske, Judith Mosoni-Fried, Henry Etzkowitz, and Gennady Nesvetailov. Amsterdam: IOS Press, pp. 346-60.

Andreff, Wladimir (1998a), "Privatization and corporate governance in transition countries," in *Privatization, corporate governance and the emergence of markets in central-eastern Europe*, edited by Hans-Jürgen Wagener. London: Macmillan. Forthcoming.

Andreff, Wladimir (1998b), "Évaluation des programmes d'ajustement et des performances macro-économiques des économies en transition, *Cahiers du Centre Interuniversitaire d'Études Hongroises*, forthcoming.

Andreff, Wladimir (1998c), "Some thoughts on the possible contribution of the economies in transition to the rehabilitation of demand," in *Restoring demand in the world economy: finance, trade and technology*, edited by Jean-Marc Fontaine and Joseph Halevi. Cheltenham: Edward Elgar. Forthcoming.

Andreff, Wladimir (1998d), "Les aspects inertiels de l'inflation," *Cahier de la Recherche*, forthcoming.

Andreff, Wladimir (1998e), "The global strategy of multinational corporations and their assessment of eastern European and CIS countries." Paper prepared for "International Conference: Communist and Post-communist Societies," held at the University of Melbourne, Melbourne, Australia, 7-10 July.

Antonelli, Christiano (1998), "Localized technological change, new information technology and the knowledge-based economy: the European evidence," *Journal of Evolutionary Economics*, Vol. 8, No. 2, 177-98.

Asea, Patrick K. and Enrique G. Mendoza (1994), "Do long-run productivity differentials explain long-run real exchange rates." Washington, DC: IMF Working Paper No.

WP/94/60.

Balassa, Béla (1964), "The purchasing power parity doctrine: a reappraisal," *Journal of Political Economy*, Vol. 72, No. 6, 586-96.

Balázs, Katalin (1995), "Transition crisis in the Hungarian R&D sector," *Economic Systems*, Vol. 18, No. 3, 281-306.

Baldwin, Richard E. (1992), "Measurable dynamic gains from trade," *Journal of Political Economy*, Vol. 100, No. 1, 162-74.

Baldwin, Richard E. (1997), "The causes of regionalism," *The World Economy*, Vol. 20, No. 7, 865-88.

Baldwin, Richard E. and Eli Seghezza (1996), "Trade-induced investment-led growth." Cambridge, MA: NBER Working Paper No. 5582.

Baldwin, Richard E., Joseph F. Francois, and Richard Portes (1997), "The costs and benefits of eastern enlargement: the impact on the EU and central Europe," *Economic Policy*, No. 24, 125-70.

Barro, Robert J. and Xavier Sala-i-Martin (1991), "Convergence across states and regions," *Brookings Papers on Economic Activity*, No 1, 107-82.

Barro, Robert J. and Xavier Sala-i-Martin (1992), "Convergence," *Journal of Political Economy*, Vol. 100, No. 2, 223-51.

Barro, Robert J. and Xavier Sala-i-Martin (1995), *Economic Growth*. New York: McGraw-Hill.

Barysch, Katinka (1997), "Eastern European exchange rate policy in the pre-accession phase: politics vs. markets?" Brussels: European Commission, Directorate General II, Economic and Finance Affairs, Doc. II/623/97, 31July.

Bauer, Patricia (1998), "Eastward expansion—benefits and costs of EU entry for the transition economies," *Intereconomics*, Vol. 33, No. 1, 11-19.

Bauer, Thomas and Klaus F. Zimmermann (1997), "Integrating the east: the labor market effects of immigration," in *Europe's economy looks east—implications for Germany and the European Union*, edited by Stanley W. Black. Cambridge and New York: Cambridge University Press, pp. 269-306.

Bean, Charles R. (1992), "Economic and Monetary Union in Europe," *Journal of Economic Perspectives*, Vol. 6, No. 4, 31-52.

Becker, Peter (1997), "Das Joint-Venture zwischen Volkswagen und Skoda—eine erste Bilanz," *Osteuropa-Wirtschaft*, Vol. 42, No. 4, 388-418.

Begg, David K. H. (1996), "Monetary policy in central and eastern Europe: lessons after half a decade of transition." Washington, DC: International Monetary Fund, Working Paper No. 108.

Bernanke, Ben S. and Frederic S. Mishkin (1997), "Inflation targeting: a new framework for monetary policy?" Cambridge, MA: National Bureau for Economic Research, Working Paper No. 5893.

Bernard, Luc D. (1997), "Exchange rate policy in the euro area and the CEEC candidates." Paper presented to the Conference "EU Adjustment to Eastern Enlargement: Polish and European Perspectives," held at the University of Gdańsk, Gdańsk, Poland, 23-26 October.

Besnainou, Denis (1995), "Les fonds structurels: quelle application aux PECO," *Économie Internationale*, No. 62, 215-31.

Bhaduri, Amit (1994), "Patterns of economic transition and structural adjustment." Vienna: Wiener Institut für Internationale Wirtschaftsvergleiche, Working Papers, No. 2.

Biedenkopf, Kurt (1995), "Rethinking the European Union I—a German perspective," *The World Today*, July, 130-33.

BIS (1998), *68th annual report*. Basle: Bank for International Settlements.

Boeri, Tito (1994), "'Transitional' unemployment," *Economics of Transition*, Vol. 2, No. 1, 1-25.

Boeri, Tito (1997), "Heterogeneous workers, economic transformation and the stagnancy of transitional unemployment," *European Economic Review*, Vol. 41, No. 4, 905-14.

Boone, Laurence and Mathilde Maurel (1998), "Convergence of CEECs towards the EU and implications for the monetary policy." Paper prepared for "XVe Journées Internationales d'Économie Monétaire et Bancaire," held at the Université de Toulouse, Toulouse, France, 1 June.

Boulouis, Jean (1992), "À propos des dispositions institutionnelles du traité sur l'Union européenne," *Revue des Affaires Européennes*, No. 4, 5-8.

Brabant, Jozef M. van (1991), *Centrally planned economies and international economic organizations*. Cambridge and New York: Cambridge University Press.

Brabant, Jozef M. van (1992), *Privatizing eastern Europe—the role of markets and ownership in the transition*. Dordrecht, Boston, MA, and London: Kluwer Academic Publishers.

Brabant, Jozef M. van (1993), *Industrial policy in eastern Europe—governing the transition*. Dordrecht, Boston, MA, and London: Kluwer Academic Publishers.

Brabant, Jozef M. van (1995), *The transformation of eastern Europe—joining the European integration movement*. Commack, NY: Nova Science Publishers.

Brabant, Jozef M. van (1996a), *Integrating Europe—the transition economies at stake*. Dordrecht, Boston, MA, and London: Kluwer Academic Publishers.

Brabant, Jozef M. van (1996b), "Bonding the EU and the transition economies," *MOCT-MOST*, Vol. 6, No. 4, 31-53.

Brabant, Jozef M. van (1997), "The morning after: regional cooperation—challenges and possibilities" Paper presented to the conference on "Eastern Europe's Foreign Insertion," organized by the Universidad Complutense de Madrid, Madrid, Spain, 26-27 May 1997.

Brabant, Jozef M. van (1998a), *The political economy of transition—coming to grips with history and methodology*. London and New York: Routledge.

Brabant, Jozef M. van (1998b), "Is regionalism compatible with global integration?—the transition economies," *Comparative Economic Studies*, Vol. 40, No. 4, 33-58.

Brabant, Jozef M. van (1998c), "On the relationship between the east's transitions and European integration," *Comparative Economic Studies*, Vol. 40, No. 3, 6-37.

Brabant, Jozef M. van (1998d), "The implications of widening for third countries," *Comparative Economic Studies*, Vol. 40, No. 3, 104-32.

Brenton, Paul and Francesca Di Mauro (1998), "Is there any potential in trade in sensitive industrial products between the CEECs and the EU?" *The World Economy*, Vol. 21, No. 3, 285-304.

Brenton, Paul, Daniel Gross, and Guy Vandille (1997), "Output decline and recovery in the transition economies: causes and social consequences," *Economics of Transition*, Vol. 5, No. 1, 113-30.

Bruno, Michael (1992), "Stabilization and reform in eastern Europe: a preliminary evaluation," *IMF Staff Papers*, Vol. 39, No. 4, 741-77.

Buchanan, James and Gordon Tullock (1962), *The calculus of consent: logical foundations of constitutional democracy.* Ann Arbor, MI: University of Michigan Press.

Busson, Frédéric and Pierre Villa (1996), "L'effet Balassa: un effet robuste et de longue période," *Économie internationale*, No. 66, 43-53.

Cacheux, Jacques Le (1996a), *Europe, la nouvelle vague—perspectives économiques de l'élargissement.* Paris: Presses de la Fondation Nationale des Sciences Politiques.

Cacheux, Jacques Le (1996b), "Scénarios d'intégration des PÉCO à l'UE: la politique agricole commune," in *L'élargissement de l'Union européenne aux pays d'Europe centrale et orientale: une analyse prospective des conséquences économiques et budgétaires.* Paris: Les Rapports du Sénat, 1995-96, No. 228, annex, pp. 55-68.

Calleo, David (1997), "An American skeptic in Europe," *Foreign Affairs*, Vol. 76, No. 6, 146-50.

CDC (1998), Caisse des Dépôts et Consignations, Service recherche risque pays marchés émergents, "Dix pays, deux cercles." Paper prepared for "Colloque International—L'Intégration des Pays d'Europe Centrale dans l'Union Européenne," organized by Centre d'Économie et de Finances Internationales, Centre d'Études Prospectives et d'Informations Internationales, Caisse des Dépôts et Consignations, and *Revue Économique*, Prague, Czech Republic, 15-16 September.

Chatelus, Michel and Pascal Petit, eds. (1997), *Le partenariat euro-méditerranéen: un projet régional en quête de cohérence.* Paris: La Documentation Française. Special issue of *Monde Arabe: Maghreb-Machrek*, December.

Chesnais, Jean-Claude (1997), "La mondialisation des migrations," in *RAMSES '98*, edited by Thierry de Montbrial and Pierre Jacquet. Paris: IFRI, pp. 247-65.

Chirac, Jacques (1995), "Pour une Europe forte," *Revue des Affaires Européennes*, No. 1, 27-32.

CNS (1998), *Anuarul statistic al României 1997—Romanian statistical yearbook.* Bucharest: Comisia Națională pentru Statistică.

Coe, David and Elhanan Helpman (1993), "International R&D spillovers." Cambridge, MA: NBER Working Paper No. 4444.

Collier, Paul, Patrick Guillaumont, Sylviane Guillaumont-Jeanneney, and Jan-Willem Gunning (1997), "L'avenir de Lomé: que peut l'Europe pour la croissance de l'Afrique?" *Problémes Économiques*, No. 2540, 23-30.

Corado, Cristina (1994), "Textiles and clothing trade with central and eastern Europe: impact on members of the EC." London: CEPR, Discussion Paper No. 1004, August.

Coricelli, Fabrizio (1996), "Fiscal constraints—reforms, strategies, and the speed of transition: the case of central and eastern Europe." London: CEPR Discussion Paper, No. 1339, May.

Csaba, László (1997), "On the EU-maturity of central Europe: perceived and real problems." Frankfurt a.O.: Frankfurter Institut für Transformationstudien Discussion Papers, No. 11.

ČSÚ (1997), *Statistická Ročenka České Republiky.* Prague: Český Statistický Úřad.

Daviddi, Renzo and Fabienne Ilzkovitz (1997), "The eastern enlargement of the European Union: major challenges for macro-economic policies and institutions of central and east European countries," *European Economic Review*, Vol. 41, No. 3-5, 671-80. Expanded version in *EU-CEECs integration: policies and markets at work*, edited by Salvatore Baldone and Fabio Sdogati. Milan: FrancoAngeli, pp. 15-40.

Desai, Padma (1998), "Macroeconomic fragility and exchange rate vulnerability: a cautionary record of transition economies." New York: Columbia University Economics

Department, mimeo.

Devuyst, Youri (1992), "The EC's common commercial policy and the Treaty on European Union—an overview of the negotiations," *World Competition: Law and Economics Review*, Vol. 5, No. 2, 67-80.

Dinan, Desmond (1994), "The European Community, 1978-93," *The Annals of the American Academy of Political and Social Science*, Vol. 531, No. 1, 10-24.

Döhrn, Roland (1996), "EU enlargement and transformation in eastern Europe: consequences for foreign direct investment in Europe," *Konjunkturpolitik*, Vol. 42, No. 1, 113-32.

Dominick, Mary Frances (1993), "The European Economic Area agreement: its compatibility with the Community legal order," *Hastings International and Comparative Law Review*, Vol. 17, No. 4, 467-87.

Drumetz, Françoise, Hélène Erkel-Rousse, and Pierre Jaillard (1993), "La convergence régionale et l'UÉM," *Économie et Statistique*, No. 262-3, 135-47.

Dutheil de la Rochère, Jacqueline (1995), "Au-delà de Maastricht—le financement de la future Europe," *Revue des Affaires Européennes*, No. 1, 101-4.

Eatwell, John, Michael Ellman, Mats Karlsson, D. Mario Nuti, and Judith Shapiro (1997), *Not 'just another accession'—the political economy of EU enlargement to the east*. London: Institute for Public Policy Research.

EBRD (1995), *Transition report 1995—investment and enterprise development*. London: European Bank for Reconstruction and Development.

EBRD (1996), *Transition Report, 1996—infrastructure and savings*. London: European Bank for Reconstruction and Development.

EBRD (1997), *Transition report 1997—enterprise performance and growth*. London: European Bank for Reconstruction and Development.

Ehlermann, C. D. (1996), "Différenciation accrue ou uniformité renforcée," in *La conférence intergouvernementale sur l'Union européenne: répondre aux défis du XXIe siècle*, edited by Clément Mattera. Paris: Clément.

Eichengreen, Barry, Andrew Rose, and Charles Wyplosz (1996), "Contagious currency crises: first tests," *The Scandinavian Journal of Economics*, Vol. 98, No. 4, 463-84.

Ellman, Michael (1997), "EU accession should be a partnership, not a dictate," *Transition*, Vol. 8, No. 4, 1-2.

EPC (1997), European Policy Center, "Making sense of the Amsterdam Treaty." Brussels: European Commission, Internet Posting, 16 October.

ESA (1998), *Väliskaubandus—foreign trade*. Tallinn: Eesti Statistikaamet.

European Commission (1992), *Treaty on European Union*. Brussels: European Communities.

European Commission (1993), *Traité sur l'Union européenne—Traité instituant la Communauté européenne*. Brussels and Luxemburg: Office des Publications Officielles des Communautés Européennes.

European Commission (1995a), *Intergovernmental Conference 1996—Commission report for the Reflection Group*. Brussels and Luxembourg: Office for Official Publications.

European Commission (1995b), "Preparation of the associated countries of central and eastern Europe for integration into the internal market of the Union." Brussels: European Commission, document COM (95) 163 final, 2 vols., 3 May.

European Commission (1996a), "Représentants personnels des Ministres des Affaires Étrangères pour la Conférence intergouvernementale 1996." Brussels: European

Commission, 26 March.

European Commission (1996b), "Turin European Council, 29 March 1996, presidency conclusions." Brussels: European Commission, undated communication, probably 30 March.

European Commission (1996c), "Calendar: (EU) main European activities—96: April-May." Brussels: European Commission, communication of 15 April.

European Commission (1996d), "Calendar: (EU) main European activities—96: May-June. Brussels: European Commission, communication of 15 May.

European Commission (1996e), "Together in Europe—European Union Newsletter for Central Europe Number 86 (April 1st, 1996)." Brussels: European Commission, communication of 1 April.

European Commission (1996f), "Together in Europe—European Union Newsletter for Central Europe Number 89 (May 15, 1996)." Brussels: European Commission, communication of 15 May.

European Commission (1996g), "Together in Europe—European Union Newsletter for Central Europe Number 90 (June 1st, 1996)." Brussels: European Commission, communication of 1 June.

European Commission (1996h), "Together in Europe—European Union Newsletter for Central Europe Number 92 (July 1st)." Brussels: European Commission, communication of 1 July.

European Commission (1996i), "Together in Europe—European Union Newsletter for Central Europe Number 91 (June 15, 1996)." Brussels: European Commission, communication of 15 June.

European Commission (1997a), "WTO aspects of EU preferential trade agreements with third countries." Brussels: European Commission, communication of 10 January.

European Commission (1997b), "Note d'analyse sur le traité d'Amsterdam." Brussels: European Commission, Internet Posting, 18 July.

European Commission (1997c), *XXVI. Bericht über die Wettbewerbspolitik*. Brussels: European Commission.

European Commission (1997d), "Amsterdam European Council—presidency conclusions." Brussels: European Commission, SI(97)500, Internet Posting, 18 June.

European Commission (1997e), "Luxembourg European Council—presidency conclusions." Brussels: European Commission, SI(97)500, Internet Posting, 16 December.

European Commission (1997f), *Treaty of Amsterdam amending the Treaty on European Union, the treaties establishing the European Communities, and certain related acts*. Brussels: European Commission, Internet Posting, 10 December.

European Commission (1997g), "Declaration of Belgium, France and Italy on the protocol on the institutions with the prospect of enlargement of the European Union." Brussels: European Commission, document AF/TA/en 82, part of the Amsterdam Treaty, Internet Posting, 10 December.

European Commission (1997h), "Agenda 2000." Brussels: European Communities, two vols., Internet Posting, 25 July.

European Commission (1997i), *Green paper on relations between the European Union and the ACP countries on the eve of the 21st century*. Brussels and Luxemburg: European Commission.

European Commission (1997j), *Guidelines for the negotiation of the new co-operation agreement with the African, Caribbean and Pacific countries*. Brussels and Luxemburg,

European Commission, COM(97)537 final.

European Commission (1997k), *5. Bericht über staatliche Beihilfen in der Europäischen Union im verarbeitenden Gewerbe und in einigen weiteren Sektoren.* Brussels: European Commission.

European Commission (1998a), "Explanatory memorandum—the future of European agriculture." Brussels: European Commission, Internet Posting, 19 March.

European Commission (1998b), "Explanatory memorandum—reform of the structural funds." Brussels: European Commission, Internet Posting, 19 March.

European Commission (1998c), "EU restructures its relations with African, the Caribbean and Pacific," *European Dialogue*, Vol. 2, No. 3, Internet Posting.

European Commission (1998d), "Institutions of the European Union." Brussels: European Commission, communication of 13 March.

European Commission (1998e), "Commission communication to the Council and to the European Parliament on the establishment of a new financial perspective for the period 2000-2006." Brussels: European Commission, Internet Posting, 19 March.

European Commission (1998f), "Cardiff European Council—15 and 16 June 1998—presidency conclusions." Brussels: European Commission, Internet Posting, 22 June.

European Commission (1998g), "Financing the European Union—Commission report on the operation of the own resources system." Brussels: European Commission, 7 October.

European Commission (1998h) "The euro: explanatory notes," *Euro Papers*, No. 17.

European Commission (1998i), "Enlarging the European Union—reports on progress towards accession by each of the candidate countries." Brussels: European Commission, 4 November.

European Commission (1998j) "Countdown to membership," *European Dialogue*, Vol. 2, No. 4, Internet Posting.

European Commission (1999a) "Task force for accession negotiations." Brussels: European Commission, Internet Posting, 10 February.

European Commission (1999b) "Prospects for the negotiations under the German Presidency in the first half of 1999." Brussels: European Commission, Internet Posting, 27 January.

European Commission (1999c) "Screening process," *European Dialogue*, Vol. 3, No. 1, Internet Posting.

European Commission (1999d) "Report updating the Commission's opinion on Malta's application for membership." Brussels; European Commission, COM(1999)69 final, Internet Posting, 17 February.

EUROSTAT (1997), *Internal and external trade of the EU.* Luxemburg: Eurostat, CD-ROM.

Falvey, Richard E. (1981), "Commercial policy and intra-industry trade," *Journal of International Economics,* Vol. 11, No. 4, 495-511.

Favret, Jean-Marc (1997), "Le Traité d'Amsterdam: une revision *a minima* de la 'charte constitutionelle' de l'Union européenne—de l'intégration à l'incantation?" *Cahiers de Droit Européen*, Vol. 33, No. 5/6, 555-605.

Fayolle, Jacky (1996a), "Rattrapage, convergence, intégration: quelques enseignements à partir du cas espagnol," in *Europe, la nouvelle vague—perspectives économiques de l'élargissement,* edited by Jacques Le Cacheux. Paris: Presses de la Fondation Nationale des Sciences Politiques, pp. 77-104.

Fayolle, Jacky (1996b), "L'intégration des pays d'Europe centrale et orientale à l'Union européenne: un processus à construire," in *L'élargissement de l'Union européenne aux pays d'Europe centrale et orientale: une analyse prospective des conséquences économiques et budgétaires*. Paris: Les Rapports du Sénat, 1995-96, No. 228, annex, pp. 21-53.

Feldstein, Martin (1997), "EMU and international conflict," *Foreign Affairs*, Vol. 76, No. 6, 60-73.

Figaro (1998), "Les coulisses de l'Europe," *Figaro Économique*, 31 March 1998.

Fingleton, James, Eleanor Fox, Damien Neven, and Paul Seabright (1996), *Competition policy and the transformation of central Europe*. London: CEPR.

Fink, Gerhard, Peter R. Haiss, Lucjan T. Orlowski, and Dominick Salvatore (1998), "Capacity building and institutional development in central European transition economies: banks and stock exchanges," *The European Management Journal*, Vol. 16, No. 4, 431-46.

Fischer, Stanley, Ratna Sahay, and Carlos A. Végh (1998), "How far is eastern Europe from Brussels?" Washington, DC: International Monetary Fund, Working Paper No. WP/98/53.

Flam, Harry and Elhanan Helpman (1987), "Vertical product differentiation and north-south trade," *American Economic Review*, Vol. 77, No. 5, 810-22.

Fontagné, Lionel et al. (1996), "Trade patterns inside the single market," cited in *The CEPII-Newsletter*, No. 6.

Forstner, Helmut and Robert Ballance (1990), *Competing in a global economy*. London: Unwin Hyman.

France (1997), "Conseil européen conférence de presse conjointe du président de la république, M. Jacques Chirac, du premier ministre, M. Lionel Jospin, et du ministre des affaires étrangères, M. Hubert Védrine," *Bulletin d'information du 15 décembre 1997 (241/97)*, 19-24.

France (1998), "Conférence européenne—conférence de presse conjointe du président de la république, M. Jacques Chirac, du premier ministre, M. Lionel Jospin, et du ministre des affairs étrangères, M. Hubert Védrine," *Bulletin d'information du 13 mars 1998 (51/98)*, 1-8.

Franzmeyer, Fritz (1993), "Der Binnenmarkt 1993 und die Europäische Wirtschafts- und Währungsunion," in *Gesamteuropa—Analysen, Probleme und Entwicklungsperspektiven*, edited by Cord Jakobeit and Alparslan Yenal. Bonn: Bundeszentrale für politische Bildung, pp. 342-61.

Frieden, Jeffrey (1998), "The euro: who wins? who loses?" *Foreign Policy*, No. 112, 25-40.

Fritsch-Bournazel, Renata (1992), *Europe and German unification*. New York and Oxford: Berg.

Frohberg, Klaus and Monika Hartmann (1998), "Adjusting the common agricultural policy for an EU-east enlargement—alternatives and impacts on the central European associates," in *Macroeconomic effects of EU-enlargement on new member states*, edited by Hubert Gabrisch. Basingstoke: Macmillan. Forthcoming.

Froot, Kenneth A. and Jerome C. Stein (1991), "Exchange rates and foreign direct investment: an imperfect capital markets approach," *Quarterly Journal of Economics*, Vol. 106, No. 4, 1191-217.

Fukasaku, Kiichiro (1992), *Economic regionalisation and intra-industry trade: Pacific-Asian perspectives*. Paris: Organisation for Economic Co-operation and Development, Technical Papers No. 53.

Gabrisch, Hubert and Klaus Werner (1998), "Advantages and drawbacks of EU membership—the structural dimension," *Comparative Economic Studies*, Vol. 40, No.

3, 79-103.

Gács, János (1994), *Trade policy in the Czech and Slovak Republics, Hungary and Poland in 1989-1993—a comparison.* Warsaw: Center for Social and Economic Research, Studies and Analyses No. 11.

Galal, Ahmed and Bernard Hoekman, eds. (1997), *Regional partners in global markets: limits and possibilities in the Euro-Med agreements.* London: CEPR/ JECES.

Garrett, Geoffrey and George Tsebelis (1996), "An institutional critique of intergovernmentalism," *International Organization*, Vol. 50, No. 2, 269-99.

Garton Ash, Timothy (1998), "Europe's endangered liberal order," *Foreign Affairs*, Vol. 77, No. 2, 51-65.

Gasiorek, Michael, Alasdair Smith, and Anthony J. Venables (1994), "Modelling the effect of central and east European trade on the European Community," *European Economy*, Vol. 24, No. 6, 521-38.

Gautron, Jean-Claude (1996), "La politique et l'Union européenne (vetera et nova)," *Revue des Affaires Européennes*, No. 4, 315-23.

Gevrisse, Fernand (1998), "À propos de quelques institutions," *Revue du Marché Commun et de l'Union Européenne*, No. 422, 569-76.

Ghesquiere, Henri (1998), "Impact of European Union association agreements on Mediterranean countries." Washington, DC: International Monetary Fund Working Paper No. WP/98/116, August.

Giscard d'Estaing, Valéry (1995), "Manifeste pour une nouvelle Europe fédérative," *Revue des Affaires Européennes*, No. 1, 19-25.

Grauwe, Paul de (1996), "Reforming the transition to EMU," in *Making EMU happen—problems and proposals: a symposium*, edited by Peter B. Kenen. Princeton, NJ: Princeton University Economics Department, pp. 16-29.

Gray, Cheryl W. et al. (1996), "Hungary's bankruptcy experience, 1992-93," *The World Bank Economic Review*, Vol. 10, No. 3, 425-50.

Greenaway, David and Chris Milner (1987), "Intra-industry trade: current perspectives and unresolved issues," *Weltwirtschaftliches Archiv*, Vol. 123, No. 1, 39-57.

Greenaway, David, Robert Hine, and Chris Milner (1994), "Country-specific factors and the pattern of horizontal and vertical intra-industry trade in the UK," *Weltwirtschaftliches Archiv*, Vol. 130, No. 1, 77-100.

Griller, Stefan, Dimitri P. Droutsas, Gerda Falkner, Katrin Forgó, Michael Nentwich (1997a), *Regierungskonferenz 1996—der Vertragsentwurf der irischen Präsidentschaft.* Vienna: Forschungsinstitut für Europafragen, IEF Working Papers No. 25, January.

Griller, Stefan, Dimitri P. Droutsas, Gerda Falkner, Katrin Forgó, Michael Nentwich (1997b), *Regierungskonferenz 1996—der Vertrag von Amsterdam in der Fassung des Gipfels vom Juni 1997.* Vienna: Forschungsinstitut für Europafragen, IEF Working Papers No. 27, July.

Gros, Daniel and Niels Thygesen (1992), *European monetary integration.* London: Longman.

Grossman, Gene M. and Elhanan Helpman (1991), *Innovation and growth in the global economy.* Cambridge, MA: MIT Press.

Guigou, Élisabeth (1995), "Les enjeux de la Conférence de 1996," *Revue des Affaires Européennes*, No. 1, 35-42.

GUS (1997a), *Rocznik statystyczny 1997.* Warsaw: Główny Urząd Statystyczny.

GUS (1997b), *Biuletyn statystyczny*, no 7. Warsaw: Główny Urząd Statystyczny.

Hagen, Jürgen von (1996), "The political economy of eastern enlargement of the EU," in *Coming to terms with accession*, edited by Lorand Ambrus-Lakatos and Mark E. Schaffer. London: CEPR, pp. 1-41.

Haguenau-Moizard, Catherine (1998), "Le traité d'Amsterdam: une négociation inachevée," *Revue du Marché Commun et de l'Union Européenne*, No. 417, 240-52.

Halpern, László and Charles Wyplosz (1996), "Equilibrium exchange rates in transition economies." Washington, DC: International Monetary Fund, Working Paper No. 125.

Ham, Peter van (1993), *The EC, eastern Europe and European Unity—discord, collaboration and integration since 1947*. London and New York: Pinter.

Harrison, Glenn W., Thomas F. Rutherford, and David G. Tarr (1997), "Economic implications for Turkey of a customs union with the European Union," *European Economic Review*, Vol. 41, No. 3-5, 861-70.

Hart, Michael (1997), "The WTO and the political economy of globalization," *Journal of World Trade*, Vol. 31, No. 5, 75-93.

Havel, Václav (1996), "The hope for Europe," *The New York Review of Books*, Vol. 43, No. 11, 38-41.

Heilemann, Ulrich and Konrad Löbbe (1996), "The structural renewal of eastern Germany: some initial observations," in *Economic aspects of German unification*, edited by Paul J. J. Welfens. New York: Springer, 2nd edition, pp. 9-38.

Helpman, Elhanan and Paul Krugman (1985), *Market structure and foreign trade*. Cambridge, MA: MIT Press.

Herman, F. (1996), "Pour une constitution européenne," in *La conférence intergouvernementale sur l'Union européenne: répondre aux défis du XXIe siècle*, edited by Clément Mattera. Paris: Clément Juglar, pp. 41-50.

Hobsbawm, Eric J. (1992), *Nations and nationalism since 1780—programme, myth, reality*. Cambridge and New York: Cambridge University Press, 2nd ed.

Hoekman, Bernard and Simeon Djankov (1995), "Catching up with eastern Europe? The European Union's Mediterranean free trade initiative." London: CEPR Discussion Paper No. 1300, November.

Holzmann, Robert and Żukowska-Gagelmann, Katarzyna (1997), "Trade adjustment in eastern Europe during transition: tale of the determined, sophisticated and proximate?" Saarbrücken: Universität des Saarlands, Europa Institut.

Hosli, Martin O. (1993), "Admission of European Free Trade Association States to the European Community: effects of voting power in the European Community Council of Ministers," *International Organization*, Vol. 47, No. 4, 629-43.

Howell, John (1994), *Understanding eastern Europe*. London: Kogan Page.

Hrnčíř, Miroslav (1997), "The global and regional outlook in eastern Europe," in *Regionalism and the global economy—the case of central and eastern Europe*, edited by Jan Joost Teunissen. The Hague: FONDAD, pp. 93-126.

IMF (1996), "Tunisia concludes association agreement with EU," *IMF Survey*, 4 March, 77-79.

IMF (1997a), *World Economic Outlook*. Washington, DC: International Monetary Fund, May.

IMF (1997b), *International financial statistics*. Washington, DC: International Monetary Fund, December.

Inman, Robert P. and Daniel L. Rubinfeld (1998), "Subsidiarity and the European Union." Cambridge, MA; National Bureau of Economic Research, Working Paper Series No.

6556, May.

Inotai, András (1994), *The system of criteria for Hungary's accession to the European Union*. Budapest: Institute for World Economics.

Inotai, András (1996), "Sur le chemin de l'intégration: un point de vue hongrois," *Revue d'Études Comparatives Est-Ouest*, Vol. 27, No. 4, 79-107.

Inotai, András (1997a), "Interrelations between subregional co-operation and EU enlargement," in *Lessons from economic transition—central and eastern Europe in the 1990s*, edited by Salvatore Zecchini. Dordrecht, Boston, MA, and London: Kluwer Academic Publishers, pp. 527-54.

Inotai, András (1997b), "Correlations between European integration and sub-regional cooperation—theoretical background, experience and policy impacts." Budapest: Institute for World Economics, Working Paper 84, September.

Inotai, András (1997c), "Prospects for joining the European Union," in *Regionalism and the global economy—the case of central and eastern Europe*, edited by Jan Joost Teunissen. The Hague: FONDAD, pp. 200-35.

Inotai, András (1998a), "Prospects and priorities of regional integration in Europe with special regard to eastern enlargement," in *Regional integration and multilateral cooperation in the global economy*, edited by Jan Joost Teunissen. The Hague: FONDAD, pp. 41-54.

Inotai, András (1998b), "Floor discussion of the 'new Europe'," in *Regional integration and multilateral cooperation in the global economy*, edited by Jan Joost Teunissen. The Hague: FONDAD, pp. 65-73.

Interview (1996), "La CIG 96—réponses à quelques questions," *Revue du Marché Commun et de l'Union Européenne*, No. 394, 8-14.

Islam, Shada (1995), "EU and ACP agree on revised Lomé pact," *AfricaRecovery*, No. 4, 13.

James, Barry (1999). "France seeks changes in EU's plan to add members," *International Herald Tribune*, 4 February, 5.

Jasinski, Andrzej H. (1994). "R&D and innovation in Poland in the transition period," *Economic Systems*, Vol. 18, No. 2, 117-41.

Jasinski, Piotr and Paul J. J. Welfens (1994), *Privatization and foreign direct investment in transforming economies*. Aldershot and Dartmouth, NH: Edward Elgar.

Judt, Tony (1996), *A grand illusion—an essay on Europe*. New York: Hill and Wang.

Jungmittag, Andre and Paul J. J. Welfens (1998), "Telecommunication, innovation and the long-term production function: the Case of Germany." Potsdam: Europäisches Institut für Internationale Wirtschaftsbeziehungen, Discussion Paper No. 52.

Kämpfe, Martina (1996), *Ausländische Direktinvestitionen in der Automobilindustrie Ostmitteleuropas*. Halle a.d. Saale: Institut für Wirtschaftsforschung, Research Report No. 1.

Kantzenbach, Erhard (1997), "Globalisierung und Verteilung," in *Globalisierung —Ende nationaler Wirtschaftspolitik*. Bonn: Friedrich-Ebert Stiftung, pp. 1-13.

Karczmar, Mieczyslaw (1998), "How Americans view the euro," *The International Economy*, Vol. 12, No. 5, 50-53 and 61-63.

Kenen, Peter B. (1998), "EMU and transatlantic economic relations." Paper presented at the fifth HWWA conference on "Transatlantic Relations in a Global Economy," held in Hamburg, Germany, 6-8 May, HWWA Discussion Paper No. 60.

Keuschnigg, Christian and Wilhelm Kohler (1998), "Eastern enlargement of the EU: how much is it worth for Austria?" Paper presented at conference on "Using Dynamic

Computable General Equilibrium Models for Policy Analysis," organized by the Danish Ministry of Business and Industry, Statistics Denmark, and the Netherlands Bureau for Economic Policy Analysis, held at Assens, Denmark, 22 April.

Kiss, Judit (1997), "The political economy of Hungary's accession to the European Union." Budapest: Institute for World Economics, Working Paper 77, March.

Klein, Martin (1997), "Transition economies and the European monetary union: convergence criteria in the next millennium," in *Meeting the convergence criteria of EMU: problems of countries in transition.* Warsaw: Polish Economic Society, 15-16 September conference report, pp. 65-88.

Kleppe, Per (1992), "The single market and commercial relations for non-member countries: views from EFTA countries," *Journal of Development Planning,* No. 21, 147-62.

Kołodko, Grzegorz (1994), *Strategy for Poland.* Warsaw: Poltex.

Kołodko, Grzegorz (1996), *Poland 2000: the new economic strategy.* Warsaw: Poltex.

Kornai, János (1994), "Transformational recession: the main causes," *Journal of Comparative Economics,* Vol. 19, No. 1, 39-63.

Kosterna, Urszula (1998), "On the road to the European Union—some remarks on the budget: the performance in transition economies." Warsaw: CASE-CEU Working Papers Series, No. 1.

Kravis, Irvin B. and Richard E. Lipsey (1983), *Towards an explanation of national price levels.* Princeton, NJ: International Finance Institute, Princeton Studies in International Finance, No. 52.

Krzak, Maciej and Aurel Schubert (1997), "The present state of monetary governance in central and eastern Europe," *Focus on Transition,* No. 1, 28-56.

Lamers, Karl and Wolfgang Schäuble (1995), "Réflexions sur une politique européenne," *Revue des Affaires Européennes,* No. 1, 9-17.

Landesmann, Michael (1993), *Industrial policy and the transition in east-central Europe.* Vienna: Wiener Institut für Internationale Wirtschaftsvergleiche, Research Reports, No. 196.

Landesmann, Michael and Johann Burgstaller (1997), *Vertical product differentiation in EU markets: the relative position of east European producers.* Vienna: Wiener Institut für Internationale Wirtschaftsvergleiche, Research Reports, No. 234a.

Lannon, Erwan (1996), "La déclaration interministérielle de Barcelone, acte fondateur du partenariat euro-méditerranéen," *Revue du Marché Commun et de l'Union Européenne,* No. 398, 358-68.

Larre, Bénédictine and Raymond Torres (1991), "La convergence est-elle spontanée?—expérience comparée de l'Espagne, du Portugal et de la Grèce," *Revue Économique de l'OCDE,* No. 16, 193-223.

Laski, Kazimierz and Amit Bhaduri (1997), "Lessons to be drawn from main mistakes in the transition strategy," in *Lessons from the economic transition,* edited by Salvatore Zecchini. Dordrecht, Boston, MA, and London: Kluwer Academic Publishers, pp. 103-23.

Laursen, Finn and Søren Riishøj, eds. (1996), *The EU and central Europe: status and prospects.* Esbjerg: South Jutland University Press.

Lavigne, Marie (1998), "Conditions for accession to the EU," *Comparative Economic Studies,* Vol. 40, No. 3, 38-57.

Lee, Young Sun (1989), "A study of the determinants of intra-industry trade among the Pacific Basin countries," *Weltwirtschaftliches Archiv,* Vol.125, No. 2, 346-58.

Lenz, Carl Otto, ed. (1994), *Kommentar zu dem Vertrag zur Gründung der Europäischen Gemeinschaften*. Cologne: Bundesanzeiger, Basel: Helbing & Lichtenhahn, and Vienna: Ueberreuter.

Linder, S. Burenstam (1961), *An essay on trade and transformation*. Stockholm: Almqvist & Wiksell.

Lopandic, Dusko (1998), "L'Union européenne et le sud-est de l'Europe—'l'approche globale' pour une région particulière," *Revue du Marché Commun et de l'Union Européenne*, No. 418, 322-29.

Loufir, Rahim and Lucrezia Reichlin (1993), "Convergences nominale et réelle parmi les pays de la CE et de l'AELÉ," *Observations et diagnostics économiques*, No. 43, 69-92.

Lucas, Robert E. (1988), "On the mechanics of economic development," *Journal of Monetary Economics*, Vol. 22, No. 1, 3-42.

Ludlow, Peter and Niels Ersbøll (1996), "Towards 1996: the agenda of the Intergovernmental Conference," in *Preparing for 1996 and a larger European Union: principles and priorities*. Brussels: Centre for European Policy Studies, pp. 1-61.

Marglin, Stephen A. and Juliet B. Schor, eds. (1990), *The golden age of capitalism: reinterpreting the postwar experience*. Oxford: Clarendon Press.

Matejka, Harriet (1998), "L'élargissement de l'UE à la République tchèque—quelle conséquences pour la Slovaquie?" *Le Courrier des Pays de l'Est*, No. 430, 30-37.

Mayer, Hartmut (1997), "Early at the beach and claiming territory?—the evolution of German ideas on a new European order," *International Affairs*, Vol. 73, No. 4, 721-37.

Mayhew, Alan (1998), *Recreating Europe—the European Union's policy towards central and eastern Europe*. Cambridge: Cambridge University Press.

McQueen, Matthew (1998), "Lomé versus free trade agreements: the dilemma facing the ACP countries," *The World Economy*, Vol. 21, No. 4, 421-43.

Mercenier, Jean and Erinç Yeldan (1997), "On Turkey's trade policy: is a customs union with Europe enough?" *European Economic Review*, Vol. 41, No. 3-5, 871-80.

Messerlin, Patrick (1996), "The MFN and preferential trade policies of the CECs: Singapore and Geneva are on the shortest road to Brussels." Paris: Institut d'Études Politiques, mimeo, August.

Meyer, Klaus (1995), "Direct foreign investment in eastern Europe: the role of labor costs," *Comparative Economic Studies*, Vol. 37, No 4, 69-88.

Milward, Alan S. (1992), *The European rescue of the nation-state*. London: Routledge.

Mink, Georges and Gérard Wild (1996), "Introduction," *Revue d'Études Comparatives Est-Ouest*, Vol. 27, No. 4, 5-14.

Mishkin, Frederic S. (1997), "The causes and propagation of financial instability: lessons for policy makers," in *Maintaining financial stability in a global economy*. Kansas, MO: The Federal Reserve Bank of Kansas, pp. 55-96.

Moravcsik, Andrew (1993), "Preferences and power in the European Community," *Journal of Common Market Studies*, Vol. 31, No. 4, 473-524.

Müller, Friedemann and Susanne Ott, eds. (1998), *Bridging divides—transformation in eastern Europe: connecting energy and the environment*. Baden-Baden: Nomos.

Nentwich, Michael and Gerda Falkner (1997), *The Treaty of Amsterdam: towards a new institutional balance*. Vienna: Forschungsinstitut für Europafragen, IEF Working Papers No. 28, September.

Neven, Damien and Claudine Gouyette (1994), "European integration and regional growth," *Revue Économique*, Vol. 45, No. 3, 703-13.

Newhouse, John (1997), *Europe adrift*. New York: Pantheon.

Nguyen. Kim (1996), "La convergence réelle en Europe," *Lettre de conjoncture de la BNP*, February.

Nicolaides, Phedon. (1998), "Negotiating effectively for accession to the European Union: realistic expectations, feasible targets, credible arguments," *Eipascope*, No.1, pp. 8-13.

Norberg, Sven (1992), "The agreement on a European economic area," *Common Market Law Review*, Vol. 30, No. 6, 1171-98.

Nsouli, Saleh M., Amer Bisat, and Oussama Kanaan (1996), "The European Union's new Mediterranean strategy," *Finance & Development*, Vol. 33, No. 3, 14-17.

Nyssen, Lars (1996), "L'Ostpolitik de l'Union européenne à la lueur de l'accord d'association avec la République tchèque," *Revue d'Études Comparatives Est-Ouest*, Vol. 27, No. 4, 15-44.

OA (1998), "EASTERN EUROPE/EU: accession obstacles," *Oxford Analytica Daily Brief*. Oxford: Oxford Analytica, 30 October.

OECD (1992), *Industrial policy in OECD countries annual review, 1992*. Paris: Organisation for Economic Co-operation and Development.

OECD (1995), *Review of industry and industrial policy in Hungary*. Paris: Organisation for Economic Co-operation and Development.

OFCE (1996), *L'élargissement de l'Union européenne aux pays d'Europe centrale et orientale: une analyse prospective des conséquences économiques et budgétaires*. Paris: Les Rapports du Sénat, 1995-96, No. 228, annex.

Olson, Mancur (1965), *The logic of collective action: public goods and the theory of groups*. Cambridge, MA: Harvard University Press.

Olson, Mancur (1982), *The rise and decline of nations*. New Haven, CT: Yale University Press.

Orlowski, Lucjan T. (1995), "Preparations of the Visegrad group countries for admission to the European Union: monetary policy aspects," *Economics of Transition*, Vol. 3, No. 3, 333-53.

Orlowski, Lucjan T. (1997a), "Exchange rate policies in transforming economies of central Europe," in *Trade and payments in central and eastern Europe's transforming economies*, edited by Lucjan T. Orlowski and Dominick Salvatore. Westport, CT: Greenwood Press, pp. 123-44.

Orlowski, Lucjan T. (1997b), "Economic conditions for accession of central European countries to the European Union: a policy proposal," *Repères—Bulletin Économique et Financier*, Vol. 49, No. 2, 28-41.

Orlowski, Lucjan T. (1997c), "Euroscenariusz," *Gazeta Bankowa*, 30 November.

Orlowski, Lucjan T. (1998a), "Monetary policy targeting in central Europe's transition economies: the case for direct inflation targeting." Warsaw: Center for Economic and Social Research, June and Budapest: Central European University, Working Paper No. 11.

Orlowski, Lucjan T. (1998b), "Exchange-rate policies in central Europe and monetary union," *Comparative Economic Studies*, Vol. 40, No. 3, 58-78.

Orlowski, Lucjan T. and Thomas D. Corrigan (1997), "The link between real exchange rates and capital accounts in central European transforming economies," *Journal of Emerging Markets*, Vol. 2, No. 3, 5-19.

O'Rourke, Breffni (1999a), "EU: eastern candidates prepare for more complex negotiations." Prague: Radio Free Europe/Radio Liberty, Internet Posting, 11 January.

O'Rourke, Breffni (1999b), "EU: five countries set to intensify pre-accession process." Prague: Radio Free Europe/Radio Liberty, Internet Posting, 26 February.

Paasi, Marianne (1998), "Inherited and emerging absorptive capacities of the firms and growth prospects in Estonia." Halle a.d. Saale: Institut für Wirtschaftsforschung, Research Report No. 3.

Pangeti, Evelyn (1997), "The role and place of intra-regional cooperation in the framework of future ACP-EU relations." Paper presented to the "Summit of ACP Heads of State and Government," Libreville, Gabon, 6-7 November.

Panić, Mića (1992), "The single market and official development assistance: the potential for multilateralizing and raising EC assistance," *Journal of Development Planning*, No. 22, 3-18.

Parfitt, Trevor (1997), "Europe's Mediterranean designs: an analysis of the Euromed relationship with special reference to Egypt," *Third World Quarterly*, Vol. 18, No. 5, 865-81.

Pelkmans, Jacques (1997), *European integration—methods and economic analysis*. London: Addison Wesley Longman for Netherlands Open University.

Pelkmans, Jacques and Christian Egenhofer (1993), "Defizite in Politikfeldern der EG-Integration," in *Gesamteuropa—Analysen, Probleme und Entwicklungsperspektiven*, edited by Cord Jakobeit and Alparslan Yenal. Bonn: Bundeszentrale für politische Bildung, pp. 313-41.

Pisani-Ferry, Jean (1995), "L'Europe à géométrie variable: une analyse économique," *Politique Étrangère*, No. 2, 447-65.

Podkaminer, Leon (1997), "Slower growth in central and eastern Europe, delayed stabilization in Russia and Ukraine." Vienna: Wiener Institut für Internationale Wirtschaftsvergleiche, Working Paper No. 228.

Pöhl, Karl-Otto (1995), "International monetary policy: a personal view," in Yegor Gaidar and Karl-Otto Pöhl, *Russian Reform/ International Money*. Cambridge, MA: The MIT Press, pp. 55-140.

Pouliquen, Alain (1998), "Agricultural enlargement of the EU under Agenda 2000: surplus of farm labour versus surplus of farm products," *Economics of Transition*, Vol. 6, No. 2. Forthcoming.

Preston, Christopher (1997), *Enlargement and integration in the European Union*. London and New York: Routledge.

Radosevic, Slavo (1997), "Strategic policies for growth in post-socialism: theory and evidence based on the case of Baltic States," *Economic Systems*, Vol. 21, No. 2, 165-97.

Reflection Group (1995), *Reflection Group's report*. Brussels: European Commission, 5 December 1995, SN 520/95, Reflex 21.

Reinicke, Wolfgang H. (1992), *Building a new Europe—the challenge of system transformation and systemic reform*. Washington, DC: The Brookings Institution.

RFE (1998a), "Turkey: foreign policy program announced." Prague: Radio Free Europe/Radio Liberty, Internet Posting in two parts of 13 August.

RFE (1998b), "Germany: stance changes on EU expansion to east." Prague: Radio Free Europe/Radio Liberty, Internet Posting of 29 October.

Richards, Anthony J. and Gordon H. Tersman (1996), "Growth, nontradables, and price convergence in the Baltics," *Journal of Comparative Economics*, Vol. 23, No. 1, 121-45.

Richez-Battesti, Nadine (1994), "Convergence nominale versus convergence réelle dans l'UÉM: conséquences pour la cohésion économique et sociale," *Document de travail du*

CEFI, No 17, May.

Richter, Sándor (1997), "European integration: the EFTA and the Europe Agreements." Vienna: Wiener Institut für Internationale Wirtschaftsvergleiche, Forschungsberichte, No. 237, May.

Richter, Sándor (1998), "EU eastern enlargement: challenge and opportunity." Vienna: Wiener Institut für Internationale Wirtschaftsvergleiche, Research Report No. 249, July.

Rodrik, Dani (1997), *Has globalization gone too far?* Washington, DC: Institute for International Economics.

Rollet, Philippe (1993), "Convergence réelle, convergence structurelle et UÉM," in *Trois défis de Maastricht: convergence, cohésion, subsidiarité,* edited by Pierre Maillet. Paris: L'Harmattan, pp. 17-38.

Romer, Paul M. (1986), "Increasing returns and long-run growth," *Journal of Political Economy,* Vol. 94, No. 6, 1002-37.

Rosati, Dariusz (1996), "Exchange rate policies during transition from plan to market," *Economics of Transition,* Vol. 4, No. 1, 159-84.

Rosati, Dariusz et al. (1998), "Transition countries in the first quarter 1998: widening gap between fast and alow reformers." Vienna: Wiener Institut für Internationale Wirtschaftsvergleiche, Forschungsberichte, No. 248, June.

Rydelski, Michael S. and G. A. V. R. Zonnekeyn (1997), "The EC trade barriers regulation—the EC's move towards a more aggressive market access strategy,"*Journal of World Trade,* Vol. 31, No. 5, 147-66.

Sachs, Jeffrey D. (1996), "Economic transition and the exchange rate regime," *The American Economic Review,* Vol. 86, No. 2, 147-52.

Sapir, André (1998), "The political economy of EC regionalism," *European Economic Review,* Vol. 42, Nos. 3-5, 717-32.

Scott, Andrew, John Peterson, and David Millar (1994), "Sudsidiarity: a 'Europe of the regions' v. the British constitution?" *Journal of Common Market Studies,* Vol. 32, No. 1, 47-67.

Siebert, Horst and Michael Rauscher (1991), "Neuere Entwicklung der Außenhandelstheorie." Kiel: Institut für Weltwirtschaft, Discussion Papers, No. 478.

Silva, Joaquim Ramos and Maria Antonina Lima (1997), "L'expérience européenne des 'pays de la cohésion': rattrapage ou paupérisation accrue?" Orleans: Institut Orléanais de Finance, Document de recherche, 1997/1/EI.

Slay, Ben (1995), "Industrial demonopolization and competition policy in Poland and Hungary," *Economics of Transition,* Vol. 3, No. 4, 479-504.

Smith, Anthony (1997), "The labour market effects of international trade: a computable general equilibrium model." Florence: European University Institute, mimeo.

Stern, Nicholas (1997), "The transition in eastern Europe and the former Soviet Union: some strategic lessons from the experience of 25 countries over six years." London: EBRD, Working Paper No. 18.

Stevens, Christopher (1992), "The single market, all-European integration and the developing countries: the potential for aid diversion," *Journal of Development Planning,* No. 22, 19-35.

Story, Jonathan and Ingo Walter (1997), *Political economy of financial integration in Europe—the battle of the systems.* Cambridge, MA: The MIT Press.

Swann, Dennis (1972), *The economics of the common market.* Harmondsworth: Penguin Books.

Tangermann, Stephan (1997), "Reforming the CAP: a prerequisite for eastern enlargement," in *Quo vadis Europe?*, edited by Horst Siebert. Tübingen: Mohr, pp. 151-79.

Temprano-Arroyo, Heliodoro and Robert A. Feldman (1998), "Selected transition and Mediterranean countries: an institutional primer on EMU and EU relations." Washington, DC: International Monetary Fund Working Paper No. WP/98/82, June.

Thomas, Ingo P. (1994), "Finanzausgleich und Kohäsion in der Europäischen Union," *Die Weltwirtschaft*, No. 4, 472-91.

Tosi, Dario (1997a), "La Conférence intergouvernementale 1996-97: résultats et perspectives pour l'élargissement de l'Union européenne," *Est-Ovest*, Vol. 28, No. 4, 5-21.

Tosi, Dario (1997b), "L'élargissement de l'Union européenne—de la fin de la préparation à l'ouverture des négociations d'adhésion," *Est-Ovest*, Vol. 28, No. 6, 49-89.

Toth, A. G. (1992), "The principle of subsidiarity in the Maastricht Treaty," *Common Market Law Review*, Vol. 30, No. 6, 1079-1105.

UNCTAD (1997), *World investment report 1997—transnational corporations, market structure and competition policy*. New York and Geneva: United Nations Publication, sales No. E.97.II.D.10.

UNCTAD (1998), "Press release: future EU-ACP convention will be different from LOME IV." Geneva: UNCTAD, TAD/INF/2739 of 28 January.

UNECE (1992), *Economic survey of Europe in 1991-1992*. New York: United Nations Publication, sales No. E.92.II.E.1.

UNECE (1995), *Economic bulletin for Europe,* Vol. 47. New York and Geneva: United Nations Publication, sales No. E.95.II.E.24.

UNECE (1996), *Economic bulletin for Europe*, Vol. 48. New York: United Nations Publication, sales no E.96.II.E.29.

UNECE (1997a), *Economic survey of Europe in 1996-1997*. New York: United Nations Publication, sales no. E.97.II.E.1.

UNECE (1997b), *International migration in central and eastern Europe and the Commonwealth of Independent States*. New York: United Nations Publication, sales no E.97.II.E.29.

UNECE (1997c), *Economic bulletin for Europe*, Vol 49. New York: United Nations Publication, sales No. E.97.II.E.23.

UNECE (1998), *Economic survey of Europe 1998 No 1*. New York: United Nations Publication, sales no. E.98.II.E.1.

United Kingdom (1996), *A partnership of nations*. London: Foreign and Commonwealth Office, 12 March.

Valbonesi, Paola (1995), "Large-scale privatisation and management incentives in central eastern Europe," *Economic Systems*, Vol. 19, No. 1, 125-46.

Velo, Dario (1996), "Europe's policy between variable geometry and single market," *Revue des Affaires Européennes*, No. 4, 336-40.

Vernon, Raymond (1966), "International investment and international trade in the product cycle," *Quarterly Journal of Economics*, Vol. 80, No. 2, 190-207.

Vona, Stefano (1991), "On the measurement of intra-industry trade: some further thoughts," *Weltwirtschaftliches Archiv*, Vol. 127, No. 4, 678-700.

Wallace, Helen (1994), "The Council and the Commission on the brink of Maastricht," *The Annals of the American Academy of Political and Social Science*, Vol. 531, No. 1, 56-68.

Welfens, Paul J. J. (1992), *Market-oriented systemic transformation in eastern Europe*. New York: Springer.

Welfens, Paul J. J. (1994), "The EU facing economic opening-up in eastern Europe: problems, issues and policy options," in *European integration as a challenge to industry and government*, edited by Richard Tilly and Paul J. J. Welfens. New York: Springer, pp. 103-71.

Welfens, Paul J. J. (1997), "Privatization, structural change, and productivity: toward convergence in Europe," in *Europe's economy looks east: implications for Germany and the European Union*," edited by Stanley W. Black. Cambridge and New York: Cambridge University Press, pp. 212-57.

Welfens, Paul J. J. and Holger Wolf, eds. (1997), *Banking, international capital markets and growth in Europe*. New York: Springer.

Winters, L. Alan (1992), "The Europe agreements: with a little help from our friends," in *The association process: making it work—central Europe and the European Community*. London: CEPR, Occasional Paper No. 11, pp. 17-33.

Winters, L. Allan and Zhen-Kun Wang (1994), *Eastern Europe's international trade*. Manchester: Manchester University Press.

Wolf, Susanna (1997), "The future of cooperation between the EU and ACP countries," *Intereconomics*, Vol. 32, No. 3, 126-33.

World Bank (1997), *World development report—the state in a transforming world*. Washington, DC: The World Bank.

Woyke, Wichard (1993), "Die Politische Union der Europäischen Gemeinschaft," in *Gesamteuropa—Analysen, Probleme und Entwicklungsperspektiven*, edited by Cord Jakobeit and Alparslan Yenal. Bonn: Bundeszentrale für politische Bildung, pp. 362-77.

Wyplosz, Charles (1997), "Monetary policy options for the 'outs'," in *Monetary policy in transition in east and west: strategies, instruments and transmission mechanisms*. Vienna: Oesterreichische Nationalbank, pp. 104-13.

Yakemtchouk, Romain (1997), "L'Union européenne face aux nouveaux états indépendants issus de l'ancienne URSS," *Revue du Marché Commun et de l'Union Européenne*, No. 410, 444-52.

Yvars, Bernard (1997), *Économie européenne*. Paris: Dalloz.

Index

Abd-el-Rahman, Kamal, 147

accession claims by transition economies (TEs), xviii, 2, 4; and European Union (EU) attitudes, xviii, 2, 4;

accession criteria, 3, 6, 7, 10, 18, 42, 43-46, 48, 49, 51, 60-61, 112, 136-37, 163; ability to comply with the *acquis*, 43, 44, 169-70; acceptance of overall ambitions of European integration, 65; affordability, 65; budgetary impact, 16, 165-66, 169, 170, 177; coping with competitive pressures, 43, 44, 45, 51; coping with enlargement, 65, 180-81; democratic maturity and political stability, 43, 65, 170; discrimination, 65-66; domestic political pluralism, 65; economic concerns, xviii, 65; and economic union, 43; environmental standards, 44, 52; European identity or vocation, 2, 4, 65, 189, 190, 206, 219; functioning market economy, 17, 43, 44, 45, 65; health protection, 44, 53; and infrastructure, 45; institution building, 51; labor standards, 44; and monetary union, 43, 45, 47, 48; and political conditionality, 43, 45; and political union, 43; political concerns, xviii, 6, 7, 42, 65; respect for human rights, 43, 65; role of state, xviii, 45; rule of law, 43, 65, 170; safety standards, 44, 52; and social chapter, 45; verifying compliance, 50-52, 112. *See also* accession difficulties for transition economies (TEs), accession negotiations, convergence criteria, desirable profile of European Union (EU) candidate, enlargement of the European Union (EU), membership in the European Union (EU)

accession difficulties for transition economies (TEs), xvii-xix, 5, 53-62, 165. *See also acquis*, membership in the European Union (EU), transformation of transition economies (TEs)

accession negotiations, xviii, 5, 7, 10, 11, 12, 18, 41, 42, 51, 52, 60-61, 83, 86-87, 112, 123, 125, 132, 133, 135-36, 137, 163-65, 180, 181, 198, 205-6, 211-20; and audiovisual policy, 52, 215, 217; in Baltic Free Trade Agreement (BFTA), 50, 218; in Central European Free Trade Agreement (CEFTA), 49, 218; and Commission selection and strategy, 45, 46, 52, 199, 200, 210-14; and common agricultural policy (CAP), 58, 112, 217; and competition, 6, 58-60, 190, 201, 215, 217; and customs union, 49, 218; and derogations, 10, 52, 53, 135, 156-59,

241

forint, 96, 98, 115, 135
forward-looking monetary policy, 100, 101. *See also* transformation policies in transition economies (TEs)
four freedoms of the European Union (EU), 12, 32, 34, 51, 56-57, 58, 166, 196. *See also* pillar 1, pillar 3, Treaty of Rome, Treaty on European Union (TEU)
France, 17, 26, 29-30, 31, 34, 35, 61, 72, 83, 87, 88, 91, 115, 116, 147, 180, 185, 186, 190, 206, 207, 210, 219, 220
free riding with monetary union, 47, 68
free-trade agreement (FTA), 141, 146-47, 156, 181, 186-87, 190, 197, 198. *See also* Euro-Mediterranean Partnership, Europe Agreement (EA), Mediterranean agreements, preferential arrangements of the European Union (EU)
free-trading area, 49, 67, 68, 188
free-trading arrangement, 67, 186. *See also* free-trade agreement (FTA), free-trading area, preferential arrangements of the European Union (EU)
Froot, Kenneth A., 177
Fund, *see* International Monetary Fund (IMF)
Fund for Social Cohesion, 124. *See also* budget policy in the European Union (EU), pillar 1, pillar 3, pillar 4, Social Charter, Social Protocol

Gabrisch, Hubert, 11, 139-62
game theory, 179
Garton Ash, Timothy, 15, 16-19, 38
Gaulle, Charles de, 21, 91
General Agreement on Tariffs and Trade (GATT), 49, 88, 155, 184. *See also* global economic organization, trade liberalization, Uruguay Round, World Trade Organization (WTO)
Generalized System of Preferences (GSP), 185
General Secretariat of the Council, 78-79, 215, 216
Georgia, 8, 127, 130, 199
German Democratic Republic (GDR), 8, 167. *See also* Germany, new German Länder

German mark, 96, 103
German question, 30-31
German unification, 9, 17, 22, 23, 29, 30, 35, 36, 70, 151
Germany, 17, 26, 29-30, 31, 35, 54, 61, 72, 83, 88, 115, 116, 150, 151, 158, 163, 165, 176, 178, 180, 189, 190, 199, 207, 210, 219, 220. *See also* German question, German unification, new German Länder
Giscard d'Estaing, Valéry, 24
global economic organization, 15-16, 17, 20, 21
globalization, 164, 183, 196
golden age of capitalism, 20, 29
governance of the European Union (EU), 4, 5, 12, 14, 18, 19, 21, 22, 23, 27, 32, 33-34, 36, 64-65, 81, 124, 136, 159, 164, 178-79, 180, 181, 182, 205, 208, 211, 219, 220; criteria of, 21, 33-34; decision making in the European Union (EU), 170, 178-79; and enlargement, 66, 178-79, 180, 181, 182, 205; institutional challenges of, 21, 22, 23-28, 33-34, 42, 169-71, 211, 219; and Intergovernmental Conference (IGC) of 1996, 63-91, 219; and Intergovernmental Conferences (IGCs) of 1990, 22, 63, 64; internal clubs, 179; and large members, 26, 82, 90, 178; and poor members, 178-79; and rich members, 178-79; and small members, 26, 54, 82, 90, 178-79, 182. *See also* constitution of the European Union (EU), Council of Ministers, European Commission, European Council, European Court of Justice, European Parliament, federalism, intergovernmentalism, subsidiarity, supranationalism
gradualism in the European Union (EU), 6, 28, 66
gradualism in transition economies (TEs), 132, 133, 134, 135
Great Britain, *see* United Kingdom
Greece, 43, 45, 47, 54, 55, 56, 87, 88, 90, 106, 108, 111, 114, 115, 116, 117, 124, 141, 142, 158, 163, 170, 171, 189, 206,

219
Greenaway, David, 147
Green Paper, 61. *See also* White Paper
gross domestic product (GDP), 53, 55, 56,
   97, 98, 100, 120, 121, 123-24, 126-27,
   131, 133, 171, 176, 182
gross national product (GNP), 34, 55, 88,
   165, 171, 176
Group of Seven (G-7), 190
Group of Twenty-four (G-24), 190
Grubel-Lloyd index, 141, 142, 143, 147,
   160. *See also* intra-industry trade (IIT)
Gulf Cooperation Council, 192

Halpern, László, 97
health policies in the European Union
   (EU), 32, 211
hegemony of the European Union (EU),
   184, 188
Helpman, Elhanan, 174
Hine, Robert, 174
hubs-and-spokes currency system, 104. *See
   also* exchange-rate mechanism (ERM) II,
   transformation policies in transition
   economies (TEs)
human capital, 56, 57-58, 152, 153, 154,
   169, 175, 196
human rights and transition economies
   (TEs), 45, 77, 191
Hungary, 8, 37, 41, 42, 45, 49, 50, 55, 57,
   59, 60, 90, 96, 97, 98, 102, 103, 115,
   116, 117, 119, 125, 129, 133, 134, 135,
   141, 142, 143, 146, 147, 148, 153, 154,
   155, 161, 165, 166, 167, 168, 169, 171,
   173, 174, 180, 190, 203, 209

Iceland, 187
Ilzkovitz, Fabienne, 45
IMF, *see* International Monetary Fund
   (IMF)
immigration policies in the European Union (EU), 33, 35, 85. *See also* four freedoms, migration, pillar 3, Treaty on
   European Union (EU)
imperfect competition, 172
industrial policy, 140-41, 149-60, 170; and
   developmental institutions in east and

southeast Asia, 150; and European Union (EU) regulations, 141, 155-59, 162;
and role of state, 152-59; and trade policy, 155
industry in the European Union (EU), 55
industry in transition economies (TEs), 55,
   59-60, 154
infant industry, 149
inflation, 98, 99, 100, 101, 102, 103, 107.
   See also transformation policies in transition economies (TEs)
Inman, Robert P., 12
Inotai, András, 65, 90
institutional convergence, 11, 26
institutional reform of the European Union
   (EU), *see* governance of the European
   Union (EU),
integration theory's relevance to transition
   economy (TE) accession, 164, 171-78
interest-rate targeting, 99-100, 101, 105.
   See also euro, exchange-rate mechanism
   (ERM) II, monetary policy in transition
   economies (TEs), transformation policies
   in transition economies (TEs)
Intergovernmental Conference (IGC), 9, 10,
   14, 86, 206; critical importance of earlier
   ones, 27-28, 75-76; role in governance of
   the European Union (EU), 23, 26-28, 75-
   76
Intergovernmental Conference (IGC) of
   1996, 14, 26, 35, 36-37, 42, 63, 63-91,
   206, 219, 220; agenda backdrop, 35, 36-
   37, 42, 63, 69-74, 76; citizen-friendly
   European Union (EU), 76-77; expectations on eve of, 74-76; external dimension, 76-77; institutional reform, 76-77;
   interim report, 81; negotiations at, 64,
   79-82; periods of negotiations, 80-82
Intergovernmental Conference (IGC) of
   1996, precepts, 73-75, 179; of the
   European Commission, 73, 74, 75; of the
   European Council, 73, 74, 75; of the
   European Parliament, 73, 74, 75; of
   member states, 73, 74; of the Reflection
   Group, 73, 74, 75-76, 77. *See also* Review Conference
Intergovernmental Conference (IGC) of

About the Editor and Contributors

Wladimir Andreff is currently professor of economics at the Université de Paris I (Panthéon-Sorbonne), France, and director of ROSES, a large French research network devoted to the economics of transition under the auspices of the French national research foundation. Having been vice-president in 1995-1996, he became president of the European Association for Comparative Economic Studies during 1997-1998. He previously taught for many years at the university of Grenoble before moving to Paris, as well as lectured for shorter periods in Algiers, Beijing (Beida), Istanbul (Marmara), Laval (Québec Ville), Lomonosov (Moscow), Rio de Janeiro, and San Marino. His research interests encompass many topics, but chiefly items revolving around the comparative economics of central planning and the transformation process. He is the author of eight books (most recently: *La crise des économies socialistes—la rupture d'un système* [Grenoble: Presses Universitaires de Grenoble, 1993]) and editor or co-editor of seven (most recently: *Convergence and System Change—The Convergence Hypothesis in the Light of Transition in Eastern Europe*, with Horst Brezinski and Bruno Dallago [Dartmouth: Aldershot, 1992]). He has also written over 200 journal and book-contribution publications, mostly in French. He is on the editorial board of several English and French journals.

Jozef M. van Brabant was educated in business, economics, philosophy, mathematics, and teaching at the Katholieke Universiteit van Leuven (Belgium) and in Russian and East European Studies and economics at Yale University, where he took his Ph.D. in economics. After an academic career in Belgium and Germany, he joined the United Nations Secretariat in New York in 1975, where he is presently principal economic affairs officer in the Department of Economic and Social Affairs and chief of the Economic Assessment and Outlook Branch. He has pursued in parallel a quasi-academic career, involving frequent lecturing and participation in conferences, chiefly in Europe and North America, but occasionally in southeast Asia. He has published widely on the economic problems of the eastern part of Europe, recently on the economics of transformation and integration with the EU. He is the author of seventeen books (most recently: *The Political Economy of Transition—Coming to Grips with History and Methodology* [London and New York: Routledge, 1998]), two pamphlets, editor of eight (most recently: *Governance and Institutional Changes in the EU and Eastern Accession* as a special issue of *Comparative Economic Studies* [Vol. 40, No. 3]), and author of some 200 articles in American and European academic journals and collected volumes. He is on the editorial board of several European and American journals.

Hubert Gabrisch is presently division head at the Institut für Wirtschaftsforschung in Halle a.d. Saale, Germany. Prior to assuming this function in September 1993, he was research fellow and deputy director of the Wiener Institut für Internationale Wirtschaftsvergleiche (Vienna, Austria). Prior to that he conducted a wide range of economic-research projects on central and eastern European countries, including while executing a research grant for Poland and while he was research fellow at the HWWA-Institut für Wirtschaftsforschung (Hamburg, Germany). His special interests have been macroeconomic analyses, mainly stabilization policies, theory of effective demand, and international trade relations, with a particular concentration on Poland. He is the author of some sixty publications on central and eastern Europe, including several edited volumes and articles in refereed English and German journals. His most recent edited volume includes *Macroeconomic Effects of EU Enlargement to the East* (London: Macmillan, 1998). His own book-length studies include: *Polen im RGW* (Hamburg: HWWA, 1986). He has contributed to many edited volumes in English and German.

Marie Lavigne is currently emeritus professor of economics at the Université de Pau et des Pays de l'Adour, Pau, France, and a Senior Research Fellow at the Institut des Sciences Mathématiques et d'Économie Appliquées (ISMEA) in Paris. She previously taught at the Université de Paris I (Panthéon-Sorbonne), where she chaired for many years (1973-1990) the largest research unit in France on the centrally planned economies, the Centre d'Économie Internationale des Pays Socialistes. She has visited many institutions as a visiting professor or guest researcher, including Barnard College, Columbia University, the Institute for East-West Security Studies, the Kennan Institute, and Stanford University. Her research has focused on the political economy of socialism, international economic relations of the (former) Soviet Union and eastern Europe, integration of eastern Europe into the world economy, and transition to the market in Russia and eastern Europe.

Recently she has expanded her research agenda to include the transitions to market and patterns of growth in Cambodia, Laos, and Vietnam. Among her numerous books in French and English the most recent is *The Economics of Transition—From Socialist Economy to Market Economy* (London: Macmillan and New York: St. Martin's Press; 1995, 2nd ed. forthcoming in mid-1999). She has published many articles in American and European scholarly journals.

Lucjan T. Orlowski is professor of economics and international finance at Sacred Heart University (Fairfield, CT). His academic career began at the Academy of Economics in Katowice, Poland. He has held visiting appointments at New York University, University of Notre Dame, and the Kiel Institute of World Economics (Germany). His research has focused on stabilization policies in TEs and on emerging international financial issues. He is currently investigating economic aspects of accession of central European countries to the EU. He has published numerous articles in American and European journals and contributed chapters to several books. He recently co-edited (with Dominick Salvatore) *Trade and Payments in Central and Eastern Europe's Transforming Economies* (Westport, CT: Greenwood Press, 1997, Handbook of Comparative Economic Policies, Vol. 6).

Paul J. Welfens is presently president of the Europäisches Institut für Internationale Wirtschaftsbeziehungen (EIIW) and professor of economic policy and international economic relations, both at the University of Potsdam (Germany). He studied economics in Duisburg, Paris, and Wuppertal, and obtained his Ph.D. and habilitation in economics. He previously taught at various academic institutions in Germany and the United States and has obtained several academic awards. His recent research includes a project on infrastructure policies in Russia for the European Commission in cooperation with academic institutions in Russia and the United Kingdom. He has published widely as author, editor, and coauthor. Among his recent books is *EU Eastern Enlargement and Transformation Crisis in Russia* (New York: Springer Verlag, 1999). He has edited several volumes singly or with others. He is also the author of many articles primarily in European academic journals.

Klaus Werner is currently researcher at Institut für Wirtschaftsforschung in Halle a.d. Saale (Germany). Before assuming this post, he was research fellow and head of division at the Ökonomisches Forschungsinstitut Berlin. In 1989, he joined the Institut für Angewandte Wirtschaftsforschung Berlin, where he headed the Central East European division until 1992. His prime interest concentrates on the analysis of economic growth and development in central Europe (including the former GDR), as well as the assessment of emerging patterns of the international division of labor and shifts in the structure of their foreign trade, following their integration into the world market. His publications comprise more than seventy titles.